Spiritual Disciplines for the Christian Life

REVISED
AND
UPDATED

SPIRITUAL
DISCIPLINES
FOR THE
CHRISTIAN
LIFE

DONALD S. WHITNEY

NAVPRESS

A NavPress resource published in alliance
with Tyndale House Publishers, Inc.

NavPress is the publishing ministry of The Navigators, an international Christian organization and leader in personal spiritual development. NavPress is committed to helping people grow spiritually and enjoy lives of meaning and hope through personal and group resources that are biblically rooted, culturally relevant, and highly practical.

For more information, visit www.NavPress.com.

Library of Congress Cataloging-in-Publication Data

Whitney, Donald S.
   Spiritual disciplines for the Christian life / Donald S. Whitney. — Revised and Updated.
     pages cm
   Includes bibliographical references.
   ISBN 978-1-61521-617-8
1. Spiritual life—Christianity. 2. Discipline—Religious aspects—Christianity. I. Title.
   BV4501.3.W4695 2014
   248.4'861—dc23   2013050852

Printed in the United States of America

21	20	19	18	17	16	15
9	8	7	6	5	4	3

CONTENTS

ACKNOWLEDGMENTS

Thanks to all the pastors, teachers, Bible study leaders, the ministers to singles, college students, and youth, and all the other disciple-makers in all the local churches who used the first edition of this book.

Thanks to all the students who have taken a Personal Spiritual Disciplines class with me in seminary and read *Spiritual Disciplines for the Christian Life* as a part of the course study.

Thanks to all the students in colleges, universities, seminaries, and other educational institutions who have studied it as a textbook.

Thanks to those around the world who have read the book in one of the non-English versions.

Thanks to all those who have read a digital copy of the original edition.

Thanks to those who have listened to the audio version of the book.

And thanks to everyone who is reading or listening to this revised and updated edition.

Thanks to the many friends inside and outside of NavPress who helped with the original publication and revision of this book. You know who you are. Most important, so does the Lord (Hebrews 6:10).

Thanks to Caffy, who patiently endured so much that this book might be written, and to both Caffy and Laurelen (who wasn't born when the book was first written), who patiently endured so much that it might be revised.

I am humbled and honored by you all.

In all cases, may the Lord bring much lasting fruit in your life from this book.

FOREWORD

I was asked to write a foreword for this book before I saw it. Having now gone through it, I would in any case have volunteered for the job, so that I can go on record as urging all Christians to read what Don Whitney has written; indeed, to read it three times over, with a month's interval (certainly not less, and ideally, I think, not more) between each reading. This will not only make the book sink in, but will also give you a realistic picture of your seriousness, or lack of it, as Jesus' disciple. Your first reading will show you several particular things that you should start doing. In your second and third readings (for each of which you should choose a date on the day you complete the previous reading) you shall find yourself reviewing what you have done and how you have fared in doing it. That will be very good for you, even if the discovery comes as a bit of a shock at first.

Ever since Richard Foster rang the bell with his *Celebration of Discipline* (1978), discussing the various spiritual disciplines has become a staple element of conservative Christian in-talk in North America. This is a happy thing. The doctrine of the disciplines (Latin *disciplinae*, meaning "courses of learning and training") is really a restatement and extension of classical Protestant teaching on the means of grace (the Word of God, prayer, fellowship, the Lord's Supper). Don Whitney's spiritual feet are blessedly cemented in the wisdom of the Bible, as spelled out by the Puritan and older evangelical masters, and he plots the path of discipline with a sure touch. The foundations he lays are evangelical, not legalistic. In other words, he calls us to pursue godliness through practicing the disciplines out of gratitude for the grace that has saved us, not as self-justifying or self-advancing effort. What he builds on these foundations is as beneficial as it is solid. He is in truth showing us the path of life.

If, then, as a Christian you want to be really real with your God, moving beyond the stage of playing games with yourself and Him, this book provides practical help. A century and a half ago the Scottish professor "Rabbi" Duncan sent his students off to read John Owen, the Puritan, on indwelling sin with the admonition, "But, gentlemen, *prepare for the knife.*" As I pass you over to Don Whitney, I would say to you, "Now, friend, *prepare for the workout.*" And you will find health for your soul.

—*J. I. Packer*

CHAPTER 1

THE SPIRITUAL DISCIPLINES . . . FOR THE PURPOSE OF GODLINESS

Ours is an undisciplined age. The old disciplines are breaking down. . . . Above all, the discipline of divine grace is derided as legalism or is entirely unknown to a generation that is largely illiterate in the Scriptures. We need the rugged strength of Christian character that can come only from discipline.

V. RAYMOND EDMAN

Discipline without direction is drudgery.

Imagine six-year-old Kevin, whose parents have enrolled him in music lessons. After school every afternoon, prompted by his mother, he slouches into the living room and strums songs he must practice but doesn't like while watching his buddies play baseball in the park across the street. That's discipline without direction. It's drudgery.

Now suppose Kevin is visited by an angel one afternoon during guitar practice. In a vision, he's transported to Carnegie Hall. He's shown a guitar virtuoso giving a concert. Usually bored by classical music, Kevin is astonished by what he sees and hears. The musician's fingers dance on the strings with fluidity and grace. Kevin thinks of how stupid and clunky his own hands feel when they halt and falter over the chords. The virtuoso blends clean, soaring notes into a musical aroma that wafts from his guitar. Kevin remembers the toneless, irritating discord that comes stumbling out of his.

But Kevin is enchanted. His head tilts to one side as he listens. He drinks in everything. He never imagined that anyone could play the guitar like this.

"What do you think, Kevin?" asks the angel.

The answer is a soft, slow, six-year-old's "W-o-w!"

The vision vanishes, and the angel is again standing in front of Kevin in his living room. "Kevin," says the angel, "the wonderful musician you saw is you in a few years." Then pointing at the guitar, the angel declares, "But you must practice!"

Suddenly the angel disappears and Kevin finds himself alone with his guitar. Do you think his attitude toward practice will be different now? As long as he remembers what he's going to become, Kevin's discipline will have a direction, a goal that will pull him into the future. Yes, effort will be involved, but you could hardly call it drudgery.

When it comes to discipline in the Christian life, many believers feel as Kevin did toward guitar practice—it's discipline without direction. Prayer threatens to be drudgery. The practical value of meditation on Scripture seems uncertain. The real purpose of a discipline such as fasting is often a mystery.

First, we must understand what we shall become. The Bible says of God's elect, "For those whom he foreknew he also predestined to be conformed to the image of his Son" (Romans 8:29). God's eternal plan ensures that every Christian will ultimately conform to Christlikeness. We will be changed "when he appears" so that "we shall be like him" (1 John 3:2). If you are born again (see John 3:3-8), this is no vision; this is you, Christian, as soon as "he appears."

So why talk about discipline? If God has predestined our conformity to Christlikeness, where does discipline fit in? Why not just coast into the promised Christlikeness and forget about discipline?

Although God will grant Christlikeness to us when Jesus returns, until then He intends for us to grow toward it. We aren't merely to wait for holiness; we're to pursue it. "Strive for peace with everyone," we're commanded in Hebrews 12:14, "and for the

holiness without which no one will see the Lord." Notice carefully what that says: Without holiness—that is, Christlikeness or
godliness—no one will see the Lord, regardless of how many times
they have been to church or how often they have engaged in religious activities or how spiritual they believe themselves to be.

It's crucial—*crucial*—to understand that it's not our pursuit of
holiness that qualifies us to see the Lord. Rather, we are qualified
to see the Lord *by the Lord*, not by good things we do. We cannot
produce enough righteousness to impress God and gain admit-
tance into heaven. Instead we can stand before God only in the
righteousness that's been earned by another, Jesus Christ. Only
Jesus lived a life good enough to be accepted by God and worthy
of entrance into heaven. And He was able to do so because He was
God in the flesh. Living a perfect life qualified Him to be a sacrifice
that the Father accepts on behalf of others who by sin disqualify
themselves from heaven and a relationship with God. As proof of
God's acceptance of Jesus' life and sacrifice, God raised Him from
the dead. In other words, Jesus lived a perfectly righteous life in
complete obedience to the commands of God, and He did so in
order to give the credit for all that obedience and righteousness to
those who had not kept all of God's Law, and He died for them on
a Roman cross in order to receive the punishment they deserved
for all their sins against God's Law.

As a result, all who come to God trusting in the person and work
of Jesus to make them right with God are given the Holy Spirit (see
Ephesians 1:13-14). The presence of the *Holy* Spirit causes all those in
whom He resides to have new *holy* hungers they didn't have before.
They hunger, for example, for the Holy Word of God—the Bible—
that they used to find boring or irrelevant. They have new holy longings, such as the longing to live in a body without sin and to have
a mind no longer tempted by sin. They yearn to live in a holy and
perfect world with holy and perfect people, and to see at last the One
the angels perpetually praise as "holy, holy, holy" (Revelation 4:8).
These are some of the holy heartbeats in all those in whom the Holy

4 || SPIRITUAL DISCIPLINES FOR THE CHRISTIAN LIFE

Spirit resides. Consequently, when the Holy Spirit indwells someone, that person begins to prize and pursue holiness. Thus, as we have seen in Hebrews 12:14, anyone who is not striving for holiness will not see the Lord. And the reason he or she will not see the Lord in eternity is because he or she does not know the Lord now, for those who know Him are given His Holy Spirit, and all those indwelled by the Holy Spirit are compelled to pursue holiness.

And so, the urgent question every Christian should ask is, "How then shall I pursue holiness, the holiness without which I will not see the Lord? How can I become more like Jesus Christ?"

We find a clear answer in 1 Timothy 4:7: "Discipline yourself for the purpose of godliness" (NASB). In other words, if your purpose is godliness—and godliness *is* your purpose if you are indwelled by the Holy Spirit, for He makes godliness your purpose—then how do you pursue that purpose? According to this verse, you "discipline yourself for the purpose of godliness."

This verse is the theme for the entire book. In this chapter, I will attempt to unpack its meaning; the rest of the book is an effort to apply it in practical ways. I will refer to the scriptural ways Christians discipline themselves in obedience to this verse as the Spiritual Disciplines. I will maintain that the only road to Christian maturity and godliness (a biblical term synonymous with Christlikeness and holiness) passes through the practice of the Spiritual Disciplines. I will emphasize that godliness is the goal of the Disciplines, and when we remember this, the Spiritual Disciplines become a delight instead of drudgery.

THE SPIRITUAL DISCIPLINES—
WHAT ARE THEY?

The Spiritual Disciplines[1] are those practices found in Scripture that promote spiritual growth among believers in the gospel of Jesus Christ. They are the habits of devotion and experiential Christianity that have been practiced by the people of God since biblical times. The Disciplines could be described in several ways.

First, the Bible prescribes *both personal and interpersonal* Spiritual Disciplines. This book is about personal Spiritual Disciplines, but they are not more important than the interpersonal Spiritual Disciplines, even if they are emphasized more frequently in most of the literature about spiritual growth.[2] So while some Disciplines are practiced alone, some are to be practiced with others. The former are personal Spiritual Disciplines and the latter are interpersonal Spiritual Disciplines. For example, Christians should read and study the Word of God on their own (personal Spiritual Disciplines), but they should also hear the Bible read and study it with the church (interpersonal Spiritual Disciplines). Christians should worship God privately, but they should also worship Him publicly with His people. Some Spiritual Disciplines are by nature practiced alone, such as journaling, solitude, and fasting (though individuals sometimes fast in conjunction with a congregational fast). Other Disciplines are by nature congregational, such as fellowship, hearing God's Word preached, and participation in the Lord's Supper—all of which require the presence of people.

Both the personal and interpersonal Disciplines are means of blessings for followers of Jesus and a part of growth in godliness, for the Bible teaches both. Moreover, Jesus practiced both, and becoming like Jesus is the purpose of practicing the Disciplines. So, for instance, the Bible tells us that on at least four occasions Jesus got alone to pray (Matthew 4:1; 14:3; Mark 1:35; Luke 4:42), thereby practicing *personal* Spiritual Disciplines. Conversely, we're told in Luke 4:16, "as was his custom, [Jesus] went to the synagogue on the Sabbath Day," thus engaging in *interpersonal* Spiritual Disciplines.

Each of us is perhaps inclined a little more toward Disciplines that are practiced individually or toward those that are practiced corporately. Some, for instance, might think they could be all that God wants them to be, even without the local church, just by practicing the personal Spiritual Disciplines faithfully. Others may be equally deceived into thinking that they'll make sufficient spiritual progress if they are deeply involved in the life of their church, believing that somehow their participation in meaningful church activities will compensate for the lack of a personal devotional life. To lean too far toward our own personal inclination, however, will get us out of balance and deform our pursuit of holiness. Christians are individuals, but we are also part of the body of Christ. We experience God and we grow in His grace through both personal and interpersonal Spiritual Disciplines. So even though this book is about personal Spiritual Disciplines, understand that Christlikeness also requires the pursuit of God through the interpersonal Spiritual Disciplines.

Second, Spiritual Disciplines are *activities, not attitudes.* Disciplines are practices, not character qualities, graces, or "fruit of the Spirit" (Galatians 5:22-23). Disciplines are things you do— such as read, meditate, pray, fast, worship, serve, learn, and so on. The goal of practicing a given Discipline, of course, is not about *doing* as much as it is about *being,* that is, *being* like Jesus. But the biblical way to grow in *being* more like Jesus is through the rightly motivated *doing* of the biblical Spiritual Disciplines. Note it again—"Discipline yourself for the purpose of godliness." Godliness—being like Jesus—is the purpose, but the God-given path to that purpose is through certain activities found in Scripture known as the Spiritual Disciplines. To put it another way, there are specific practices we are to do sometimes that cultivate generally being like Jesus all the time. So fasting is a Spiritual Discipline, because that's something you do. Joy, strictly speaking, is not a Spiritual Discipline, because joy is something you experience, not something you do. Fasting itself is not the goal; rather joy is part of the goal of fasting, because joy is a Christlike quality. Joy does not come to you if you are spiritually passive; rather, joy is cultivated, but joy is cultivated by things you do. And the "things you do" that cultivate Christlike joy are the Spiritual Disciplines.

Third, I want to limit the subject matter of this book to those Spiritual Disciplines that are *biblical,* that is, to practices taught or modeled in the Bible. Without this limitation, we leave ourselves open to calling anything we fancy a Spiritual Discipline. Thus some might declare, "Gardening is a Spiritual Discipline for me," or "Exercise is one of my Spiritual Disciplines," or claim that some other hobby or pleasurable habit is a valid Spiritual Discipline. One of the problems with this approach is that it can tempt people to assert something like, "Maybe meditation on Scripture works for you, but gardening does just as much for my soul as the Bible does for yours." And the result is that virtually anything can be designated a Spiritual Discipline, and worse, it means that we determine for ourselves what practices are best for our spiritual health and maturity rather than accepting those God has revealed in Scripture. I believe a case can be made—to a greater or lesser extent for each—that the following personal Spiritual Disciplines are commended in Scripture: Bible intake, prayer, worship, evangelism, service, stewardship, fasting, silence and solitude, journaling, and learning. Is this an exhaustive list? No, I wouldn't presume to maintain that. A survey of other literature on the subject would reveal additional candidates for consideration as biblical Spiritual Disciplines to be practiced by individual Christians. But I do believe it can be argued that the ones discussed in these pages are the more prominent ones in Scripture.

Fourth, this book takes the position that the Spiritual Disciplines found in Scripture are *sufficient* for knowing and experiencing God, and for growing in Christlikeness. This is based upon the fact that "all Scripture is breathed out by God and profitable for teaching, for reproof, for correction, and for training in righteousness, that the man of God may be complete, equipped for every good work" (2 Timothy 3:16-17). These verses tell us that Scripture, because it is divinely inspired, provides the guidance Christians need to "be complete, equipped for every good work," including the good work of pursuing "the purpose of godliness." So whatever else a person might claim regarding the spiritual benefits he or she receives from a practice not found in the Bible, at the very least we can say this about that activity—it is not necessary. If it were necessary for spiritual maturity and progress in holiness it would have been recorded and promoted in Scripture.

Fifth, the Spiritual Disciplines are practices *derived from the gospel, not divorced from the gospel*. When the Disciplines are rightly practiced, they take us deeper into the gospel of Jesus and its glories, not away from it as though we've moved on to more advanced levels of Christianity. New Testament scholar D. A. Carson makes this point eloquently:

> The gospel is not a minor theme that deals with the point of entry into the Christian way, to be followed by a lot of material that actually brings about the life transformation. Very large swaths of evangelicalism simply presuppose that this is the case. Preaching the gospel, it is argued, is announcing how to be saved from God's condemnation; believing the gospel guarantees you won't go to hell. But for actual transformation to take place, you need to take a lot of discipleship courses, spiritual enrichment courses, "Go deep" spiritual disciplines courses, and the like. You need to learn journaling, or asceticism, or the simple lifestyle, or Scripture memorization; you need to join a small group, an accountability group, or . . . Bible study. Not for a moment would I speak against the potential for good of all of these steps; rather, I am speaking against the tendency to treat these as postgospel disciplines, disciplines divorced from what God has done in Christ Jesus in the gospel of the crucified and resurrected Lord. . . .
>
> Failure to see this point has huge and deleterious consequences. . . . First, if the gospel becomes that by which we slip into the kingdom, but all the business of transformation turns on postgospel disciplines and strategies, then we shall constantly be directing the attention of people *away* from the gospel, *away* from the cross and resurrection. Soon the gospel will be something that we quietly assume is necessary for salvation, but not what we are excited about, not what we are preaching, not the power of God. What is really

important are the spiritual disciplines. Of course, when we point this out to someone for whom techniques and disciplines are of paramount importance, there is likely to be instant indignation. *Of course* I believe in the cross and resurrection of Jesus, they say. And doubtless they do. Yet the question remains: What are they excited about? Where do they rest their confidence? On what does their hope of transformation depend? When I read, say, Julian of Norwich, I find an example of just how far an alleged spirituality may be pursued, in medieval form, directly attempting to connect with God *apart* from self-conscious dependence on the substitutionary death and resurrection of Jesus—the very matters the apostle labels "of first importance." Wherever contemporary pursuit of spirituality becomes similarly distanced from the gospel, it is taking a dangerous turn.[3]

Sixth, the Spiritual Disciplines are *means, not ends.* The end— that is, the purpose of practicing the Disciplines—is godliness. I define *godliness* as both closeness to Christ and conformity to Christ, a conformity that's both inward and outward, a growing conformity to both the heart of Christ and the life of Christ. This Christlikeness is the goal, the reason we should practice the Disciplines. Without this purpose in our practice, the performance of Spiritual Disciplines—no matter how consistent or vigorous—is vain and nothing more than an empty husk of godliness. So while we cannot be godly without the practice of the Disciplines, we can practice the Disciplines without being godly if we see them as ends and not means. The next section of the chapter is devoted to developing this crucial aspect of the theology behind the practice of the Spiritual Disciplines.

So the Spiritual Disciplines are those personal and interpersonal activities given by God in the Bible as the sufficient means believers in Jesus Christ are to use in the Spirit-filled, gospel-driven pursuit of godliness, that is, closeness to Christ and conformity to Christ.

THE SPIRITUAL DISCIPLINES—
THE MEANS TO GODLINESS

The most important feature of any Spiritual Discipline is its purpose. Just as there is little value in practicing the scales on a guitar or piano apart from the purpose of playing music, so there is little value in practicing Spiritual Disciplines apart from the single purpose that unites them (see Colossians 2:20-23; 1 Timothy 4:8). That purpose is godliness. Thus we are told in 1 Timothy 4:7 to discipline ourselves "for the purpose of *godliness*" (NASB).[4]

That's what the godly heroes of Christian history have done. From biblical times to our time, godly people have always been spiritually disciplined people. Call to mind some heroes of church history, people such as Augustine, Martin Luther, John Calvin, John Bunyan, George Whitefield, Lady Huntingdon, Jonathan and Sarah Edwards, Charles Spurgeon, Lottie Moon, George Müller, Dawson Trotman, Jim and Elisabeth Elliot, and Martyn Lloyd-Jones. How did they develop such a reputation for godliness? It wasn't as though God somehow anointed them with holiness in ways He hasn't bestowed on the rest of us. It may be true that He blessed these believers in terms of ministry fruitfulness in ways that He hasn't conferred upon many others, but in terms of conformity to Christ, they made progress the same way that all Christians do—through the Spiritual Disciplines. And in my own pastoral and personal Christian experience, I can say that I've never known a man or woman who came to spiritual maturity except through discipline. Godliness comes through discipline.

Actually, God uses three primary catalysts for changing us and conforming us to Christlikeness, but only one is largely under our control. One catalyst the Lord uses to change us is people. "Iron sharpens iron," says Proverbs 27:17, "and one man sharpens another." Sometimes God uses our friends to sharpen us into more Christlike living, and sometimes He uses our enemies to file away our rough, ungodly edges. Parents, children, spouses, coworkers, customers, teachers, neighbors, pastors—God changes us through these people.

Another change agent God uses in our lives is circumstances. The classic text for this is Romans 8:28: "And we know that for those who love God all things work together for good, for those who are called according to his purpose." Financial pressures, physical conditions, even the weather are used in the hands of Divine Providence to stimulate His elect toward holiness.

Then there is the catalyst of the Spiritual Disciplines. This catalyst differs from the first two in that when He uses the Disciplines, God works primarily from the inside out. When He changes us through people and circumstances, the process works mainly from the outside in. The Spiritual Disciplines also differ from the other two methods of change in that God grants us a greater measure of choice regarding involvement with the Disciplines. We often have little choice regarding the people and circumstances God brings into our lives, but we can decide, for example, whether we will read the Bible or fast today.

So on the one hand, we recognize that even the most iron-willed self-discipline by itself will not make us more holy; instead, it may make us more like the Pharisees. Growth in holiness is a gift from God (see John 17:17; 1 Thessalonians 5:23; Hebrews 2:11). On the other hand, that doesn't mean that we're to do nothing to pursue godliness, just living the life we want until and unless God decides to make us holy. What we are to do is discipline ourselves for the purpose of godliness, practicing the God-given Spiritual Disciplines as a means of receiving His grace and growing in Christlikeness.

In Colossians 1:29 the apostle Paul illustrated how these two— the efforts of a Christian and the work of God—can occur simultaneously in a person indwelled by the Holy Spirit. In this text Paul spoke of his labors to help believers become "mature in Christ," declaring, "For this I toil, struggling with all his energy that he powerfully works within me" (Colossians 1:29). Notice that Paul said that he himself was toiling, but he then affirmed that the energy for this struggle came from Christ. That Paul had the desire and the power for ministry was entirely of the grace of God (see Philippians 2:13). And if any lasting fruit resulted from his labors, Paul gave all the glory to God. But sometimes it surely felt as though all the toil was of Paul, and at the end of each day, Paul was the one who was work-weary.

That's the way it is with the Spiritual Disciplines. The desire and the power for them are produced by the grace of God. But Christians themselves must practice the Disciplines. For example, a deep, insatiable hunger for the Bible is a gift from God, but we are the ones who must turn the pages and read the words. God doesn't pull our passive bodies over to the desk and cause our hands to open the Bible and draw our eyes back and forth over the pages without any effort on our part.

The New Testament was originally written in the Greek language. The word rendered "discipline" in the New American Standard translation is the Greek word *gumnasia* from which our English words *gymnasium* and *gymnastics* derive. This word means "to exercise or discipline," which is why the King James Version renders 1 Timothy 4:7 as "exercise thyself rather unto godliness," the English Standard Version as "train yourself for godliness," and the New International Version as "train yourself to be godly." It's a sweaty word with the smell of the gym to it. So think of the Spiritual Disciplines as spiritual exercises. To go to your favorite spot for prayer or journaling, for example, is the spiritual equivalent of going to a gym and using a weight machine. As physical disciplines like this promote bodily strength, so the Spiritual Disciplines promote godliness.

A Bible story that illustrates another way of thinking of the role of the Spiritual Disciplines is in Luke 19:1-10. It's the famous account of the conversion of the tax collector, Zacchaeus. Because he was so short, Zacchaeus was unable to see Jesus in the crowd. So he ran ahead and climbed a sycamore tree in order to see Jesus when He passed by. When Jesus came to the place, He looked up, called

Zacchaeus by name, and told him to come down. The two went to the tax collector's house, where he believed in Christ for salvation and resolved to give half his possessions to the poor and return with interest all tax money he had wrongfully taken.

Think of the Spiritual Disciplines as ways by which we can spiritually place ourselves in the path of God's grace and seek Him, much like Zacchaeus placed himself physically in Jesus' path and sought Him. The Lord, by His Spirit, still travels down certain paths, paths that He Himself has ordained and revealed in Scripture. We call these paths the Spiritual Disciplines, and if we will place ourselves on these paths and look for Him there by faith, we can expect to encounter Him. For instance, when we come to the Bible, or when we engage in any of the biblical Disciplines—looking by faith to God through them—we can anticipate experiencing God. As with this tax collector, we will find Him willing to have mercy on us and to have communion with us. And in the course of time we, too, will be transformed by Him from one level of Christlikeness to another (see 2 Corinthians 3:18). So again, by means of these Bible-based practices we consciously place ourselves before God in anticipation of enjoying His presence and receiving His transforming grace.

Tom Landry, coach of the Dallas Cowboys football team for most of three decades, said, "The job of a football coach is to make men do what they don't want to do in order to achieve what they've always wanted to be."[5] In much the same way, Christians are called to make themselves, by the Spirit's power, do what they would not naturally do—practice the Spiritual Disciplines—in order to experience what the Spirit gives them a desire to be, that is, to be with Christ and like Christ. "Discipline yourself," says the Scripture, "for the purpose of godliness" (NASB).

THE SPIRITUAL DISCIPLINES— GOD'S WILL FOR CHRISTIANS

The original language of the words "discipline yourself for the purpose of godliness" (NASB) makes it plain that this is a command of God, not merely a suggestion. Holiness is not an option for those who claim to be children of the Holy One (see 1 Peter 1:15-16), so neither are the means of holiness—that is, the Spiritual Disciplines—an option.

The expectation of disciplined spirituality is implied in Jesus' offer of Matthew 11:29: "Take my yoke upon you, and learn from me." The same is true in this offer of discipleship: "And he said to all, 'If anyone would come after me, let him deny himself and take up his cross daily and follow me'" (Luke 9:23). These verses tell us that to be a disciple of Jesus means, at the very least, to learn from and follow Him. That's what the twelve apostles of Jesus did—they followed Him around, and as they did, they learned from Him. But for them to follow Jesus required discipline; they had to go where He went and when. Following Jesus today and learning from Him still involves discipline, for you don't follow someone accidentally—at least not for very long—nor do you learn as much accidentally as you do by discipline. Are you a disciplined follower of Jesus?

That discipline is at the heart of discipleship is validated by 2 Timothy 1:7, which says, "God gave us a spirit not of fear but of power and love and self-control." A key component of this self-control in a follower of Jesus is spiritual self-discipline.[6] Further, Galatians 5:22-23 declares that one evidence of the influence of this God-given spirit of self-control is greater self-control in our own lives, especially as followers of and learners from Jesus.

The Lord Jesus not only expects these biblical Spiritual Disciplines of those who follow Him, He is the model of discipline for the purpose of godliness. And if we are going to be Christlike, we must live as Christ lived—insofar as sinful humans can. We cannot do what Jesus did as God, but *Christ*ian living means we should seek to follow His human example of how a person lives in fellowship with the Father. Although Jesus is much more than our example of spirituality—for He is also our Lord, our King, our Savior, our Substitute, our Righteousness, our Judge, and many other things to us—He is not less than our example of spirituality. And when we look to Jesus we see an example of disciplined personal piety, of how to live in consistent communion with God.

Despite the example of Jesus and the teaching of the New Testament about Christianity as a life of disciplined spirituality, many professing Christians are spiritually undisciplined and seem to have little Christlike fruit and power in their lives. However, many of them are remarkably disciplined in other areas of their lives. I've seen men and women who discipline themselves with zeal for the purpose of excelling in their career, but who discipline themselves very little "for the purpose of godliness." I'm sure you've seen people who will devote time to learning to play an instrument, knowing that it takes countless hours to acquire the skills; who will practice hard to improve their sports performance, knowing it takes work to become proficient; who will commit to a long curriculum of intense study to complete a degree, knowing it takes sacrifice to succeed. Then many of these same people will give up quickly if they find that the Spiritual Disciplines don't come easily, as though becoming like Jesus would not take much effort.

I've seen Christians who are faithful to the church of God, who frequently demonstrate genuine enthusiasm for the things of God, and who are committed to the preaching of the Word of God, yet who trivialize their effectiveness for the kingdom of God through lack of discipline. A woman in her sixties once came to my wife and me for counsel, a woman who had spent a lifetime in conservative Bible-believing churches. Over the decades this faithful worker had served in just about every volunteer ministry position open to her. But through tears she admitted, "I know how to do everything in the church, but I don't know how to read the Bible and pray." Spiritually such people are a mile wide and an inch deep. There are no deep, time-worn channels of communing discipline between them and God. They have dabbled in everything but disciplined themselves in nothing.

MORE APPLICATION

There is danger in neglecting the Spiritual Disciplines. The greatest danger of neglecting the Spiritual Disciplines is the danger of missing God—forever; not because personal piety earns anyone a place in heaven, but because it characterizes those who are on their way there. In other words, some who fail to practice the Disciplines disregard them because they simply have no appetite for them, and they have no appetite for them because they have no hunger for God. They do not know God, so the God-given means of personally experiencing and enjoying God have little appeal. To them, the Spiritual Disciplines are tedious religious duties to be endured as little as conscience or reputation will allow, not a banquet of God on which their famished souls long to feed as much as possible.

For those who do know God through the gospel of Christ, there's another danger in neglecting the Disciplines. A selection from the pen of a writer many years ago timelessly illustrates the danger. Commenting on the difference between the disciplined and the undisciplined way, he wrote,

> Nothing was ever achieved without discipline; and many an athlete and many a man has been ruined because he abandoned discipline and let himself grow slack. Coleridge[7] is the supreme tragedy of indiscipline. Never did so great a mind produce so little. He left Cambridge University to join the army; but he left the army because, in spite of all his erudition, he could not rub down a horse; he returned to Oxford and left without a degree. He began a paper called *The Watchman* which lived for ten numbers and then died. It has been said of him: "He lost himself in visions of work to be done, that always remained to be done. Coleridge had every poetic gift but one—the gift of sustained and concentrated effort." In his head and in his mind he had all kinds of books, as he said himself, "completed save for transcription." "I am on the eve," he says,

"of sending to the press two octavo volumes." But the books were never composed outside Coleridge's mind, because he would not face the discipline of sitting down to write them out. No one ever reached any eminence, and no one having reached it ever maintained it, without discipline.[8]

Likely from your own observations you could name athletes, musicians, or students who displayed enormous potential, but who failed to live up to that God-given potential simply because they could not discipline themselves to practice. Something similar can happen in the spiritual realm to Christians. While few of us will have Coleridge's intellectual or poetic gifts, all believers have been given spiritual gifts (see 1 Corinthians 12:4-7). The mere presence of spiritual gifts, however, guarantees no more spiritual fruitfulness than Coleridge's mental gifts assured the production of books and poetry. Just as with athletic, musical, or intellectual gifts, so also spiritual gifts must be developed by discipline in order to bear spiritual fruit. Thus, the danger of neglecting the Spiritual Disciplines is the danger of bearing little spiritual fruit—your life counting little for the sake of the kingdom.

There is freedom in embracing the Spiritual Disciplines. Many hear the term *Spiritual Disciplines* and think of bondage and burdens—things they have to do, not freedom. Nevertheless, there is a freedom in the Christian life that comes not through indolence, but discipline.

We can illustrate this principle by observing the freedom that comes through mastery of any discipline. For instance, watching a consummate guitar player pluck and strum those six strings almost gives the impression that he was born with the instrument attached to his body. He has an intimacy and a freedom with the guitar that make playing the thing look easy. Anyone who's ever tried to play realizes that such musical liberty and flair with a guitar comes only from decades of disciplined practice. Likewise, freedom through discipline is seen not only in proficient musicians, but also in all-star shortstops, expert carpenters, successful executives, skilled craftsmen, excellent students, and moms who daily manage home and family well.

Freedom through discipline is the idea behind what has become known as "the ten-thousand-hour rule."[9] This is an observation based upon research indicating that to become an expert in anything, for anything to become second nature, you must perform that activity—such as playing the guitar—for at least ten thousand hours. And it's not just a matter of repeating an identical task—such as playing the same song—for something like four hours per day, five days per week, fifty weeks per year for ten years; rather there must also be a deliberate, ongoing effort (usually under the guidance of another) to improve overall performance. Thus in the case of a musician, a wide variety of songs, styles, and drills would be rehearsed so consistently and with such increasing complexity that an ever-developing freedom with the instrument would result.

In one sense we might call discipline "the price" we must pay for freedom. But Elisabeth Elliot is more precise when she explains that "freedom and discipline have come to be regarded as mutually exclusive, when in fact freedom is not at all the opposite, but the final *reward*, of discipline."[10] So while stressing that freedom requires discipline, let us not forget to emphasize that discipline rewards us with freedom.

What is this freedom of godliness? Think again of our illustrations. For instance, a guitar virtuoso is "free" to play a difficult arrangement by Segovia while I am not. Why? Because of his years of disciplined practice. Similarly, those who are "free" to quote Scripture are those who have disciplined themselves to memorize God's Word. We may experience a measure of freedom from spiritual lethargy through the Discipline of fasting. Or we may sense some liberation from self-centeredness while engaged in Disciplines such as worship, service, and evangelism. The freedom of godliness is the freedom to do what God calls us through Scripture to do and the freedom to express the character qualities of Christ through our own personality. This kind of freedom is the "reward" or result of the blessing of God upon our engagement in the Spiritual Disciplines.

But we must remember that the mature freedoms of discipline-nurtured godliness do not develop in a single reading through the Bible or in a few forays through some of the other Disciplines. Scripture reminds us that self-control, such as that expressed through the Spiritual Disciplines, must persevere before it ripens into the mature fruit of godliness. Observe closely the sequence of development in 2 Peter 1:6—"to self-control, perseverance; and to perseverance, godliness" (NIV). The bridge between Spirit-empowered self-control and godliness is perseverance. Occasional self-control results in occasional godliness. But self-control with perseverance results in more consistent Christlikeness. True godliness requires not merely a ten-thousand-hour pursuit, but a lifetime of perseverance.

There is an invitation to all Christians to enjoy God and the things of God through the Spiritual Disciplines. All in whom the Spirit of God dwells are invited to taste the joy of a Christ-centered, gospel-based, Spiritual Disciplines lifestyle.

Remember Kevin and his guitar? The drudgery of his daily practice would take on an entirely new spirit once he realized that someday he would be playing for a packed house in Carnegie Hall. The discipline of practice would gradually become the means to one of the greatest enjoyments of his life.

Any discipline—from guitar practice to Scripture memory—without direction is drudgery. But the Spiritual Disciplines are never drudgery as long as we practice them with the goal of godliness (that is, closeness to and conformity to Christ) in mind. If your picture of a disciplined Christian is one of a grim, tight-lipped, joyless half-robot, then you've missed the point. Jesus was the most disciplined Man who ever lived and yet the most joyful and truly alive. Though more than our example, nevertheless He is our example of discipline. Let us follow Him to joy through the

Spiritual Disciplines. Focus on the person and work of Jesus in each of the Disciplines. Through them, learn from, gaze upon, and enjoy who Jesus is and what He has done. By means of the Disciplines, let the truths of the gospel restore your soul. Engage in the Spiritual Disciplines given by God in Scripture so that you are continually shown your need for Christ and the infinite supply of grace and mercy to be found by faith in Jesus Christ.

CHAPTER 2

BIBLE INTAKE (PART 1) ...
FOR THE PURPOSE OF GODLINESS

The alternative to discipline is disaster.

VANCE HAVNER

Several years ago, I had the privilege of participating in a mission trip to the bush country of East Africa. Four of us from the church I pastored lived in tents in front of a tiny, unfinished, mud-and-sticks church building six miles from the nearest settlement.

I've been overseas enough to know that many customs I have come to identify with Christianity will clash at some points with the culture of our hosts. My experiences have taught me to anticipate swallowing with difficulty some of my American expectations (not to mention a few other things!) about how Christians should live. But I was unprepared for some of my encounters with many of the professing Christians in this equatorial setting. Lying, stealing, and immorality were common and generally accepted, even among the leadership of the church. Theological understanding was as scarce as water, the disease of doctrinal error as common as malaria.

Soon I discovered one of the main reasons this church looked as though it had been started by Corinthian missionaries. No one had a Bible—not the pastor, not a deacon, no one. The pastor had only half-a-dozen sermons, all half-baked over the coals of a few Bible-story recollections. Every sixth week came the same sermon. The only real contact with Scripture happened with the occasional visit of a missionary (the nearest one was one hundred miles away) or when an area denominational worker preached. For almost everyone in the church, these infrequent, vicarious brushes with the Bible were all they'd ever known. Only one man had any measure of spiritual maturity, and that was because he had lived most of his life elsewhere and had attended a Bible-teaching church.

The four of us pooled our resources and bought inexpensive Bibles for many of the church members. After evangelistic visitation each day we led Bible studies for the church in the afternoon and again at night by flashlight. We left with prayers that the Holy Spirit would cause the Word of God to take deep root in this dry, bush-country assembly.

Most of us shake our heads in pity at such sad conditions. Fact is, however, that many of us have more Bibles in our homes than entire churches have in some impoverished or isolated parts of the world. But it's one thing to be unfamiliar with Scripture when you don't own a Bible; it's another when you have a bookshelf full.

No Spiritual Discipline is more important than the intake of God's Word. Nothing can substitute for it. There simply is no healthy Christian life apart from a diet of the milk and meat of Scripture. The reasons for this are obvious. In the Bible God tells us about Himself, and especially about Jesus Christ, the incarnation of God. The Bible unfolds the Law of God to us and shows us how we've all broken it. There we learn how Christ died as a sinless, willing Substitute for breakers of God's Law and how we must repent and believe in Him to be right with God. In the Bible we learn the ways and will of the Lord. We find in Scripture how God wants us to live, and what brings the most joy and satisfaction in life. None of this eternally essential information can be found anywhere else except the Bible. Therefore if we would know God and be godly, we must know the Word of God—intimately.

However, many who yawn with familiarity and nod in agreement to these statements spend no more time with God's Word in an average day than do those with no Bible at all. My pastoral experience bears witness to the validity of surveys that reveal that great numbers of professing Christians know little more about the Bible than poor Christians in remote parts of the world who possess not even a shred of Scripture. Some wag remarked that the worst dust storm in history would happen if all church members who were neglecting their Bibles dusted them off simultaneously.

So even though we honor God's Word with our lips, we must confess that our hearts—as well as our hands, ears, eyes, and minds—are often far from it. Regardless of how busy we become with all things Christian, we must remember that the most transforming practice available to us is the disciplined intake of Scripture.

Bible intake is not only the most important Spiritual Discipline, it is also the most broad. It actually consists of several subdisciplines. It's much like a university comprised of many colleges, each specializing in a different discipline, yet all united under the general name of the university.

Let's examine the "colleges," or subdisciplines, of Bible intake, proceeding from the least to the most difficult.

HEARING GOD'S WORD

The easiest of the Disciplines related to the intake of God's Word is simply hearing it. Why consider this a Discipline? Because if we don't discipline ourselves to hear God's Word regularly, we may hear it only accidentally, just when we feel like it, or never hear it at all. For most of us, disciplining ourselves to hear God's Word means primarily developing the practice of steadfastly attending a Bible-believing church where the Word of God is faithfully preached.

Jesus once said, "Blessed rather are those who hear the word of God and keep it!" (Luke 11:28). Merely listening to God-inspired words is not the point. The purpose of all methods of Bible intake is to "keep it," that is, to do what God says and thereby develop in Christlikeness. But the method of intake Jesus encourages in this verse is hearing God's Word.

Another passage emphasizing the importance of hearing is Romans 10:17: "So faith comes from hearing, and hearing through the word of Christ." This doesn't mean that a person can come to faith in Christ through no other means except by hearing Scripture, for multitudes have become believers as Jonathan Edwards did— and many hearing-impaired people have—through reading the Bible. Still, this verse concerns itself with the power of hearing. We may add, however, that most who, like Edwards, were converted while reading Scripture are also like him in that they often heard the proclamation of God's Word prior to conversion. Furthermore, whereas this passage teaches that initial faith in Christ comes from hearing the inspired Word about Jesus Christ, it's also true for Christians that much of the faith we need for day-to-day living after conversion comes from hearing the Bible's message. From a scriptural word about God's provision may come the faith that a family with financial struggles needs. Hearing a biblically based sermon on the love of Christ may be God's means of granting assurance of faith to a downcast believer. I recently heard a recorded message that the Lord used to give me the faith to persevere in a difficult matter. Gifts of faith are often given to those who discipline themselves to hear the Word of God.

There are other ways we may discipline ourselves to hear God's Word in addition to the most important way, namely, hearing it preached as part of a local church ministry. The most obvious of these is by some form of recording of Bible-based content. These can be used in creative ways and times such as while dressing, cooking, commuting, and so on. If you do not have access to the Internet or portable devices with biblical content taken from the Internet, consider radio, including shortwave radio.[1]

One other text worthy of note on this subject is 1 Timothy 4:13.

There the apostle Paul instructed his young friend in the ministry: "Until I come, devote yourself to the public reading of Scripture, to exhortation, to teaching." Though a lot more explanation could be given, it's enough to say that it was important in the ministry of Paul and important to the Lord, who inspired these words, for God's people to hear God's Word. Since this is so, it should become a disciplined priority for us to hear it. If someone says, "I don't need to go to church to worship God; I can worship Him on the golf course or at the lake just as well, if not better, than in church," we may agree that our omnipresent God can be worshiped there. But the ongoing worship of God cannot be separated from the Word of God, which you don't expect to be read aloud or preached on the golf course or at the lake. We are to discipline ourselves to go and hear the Word of God.

Incidentally, if you have the privilege of reading God's Word to God's people—whether to an entire congregation or to a small group—learn to read it well. You may not be gifted with a remarkable voice, but you can learn to read the Scriptures expressively. This is an acquired skill, for no one naturally reads well aloud. Far too many read the Bible publicly in such a flat, unenthusiastic way that it sounds like a book no one would want to read on his or her own. Read it for what it is: the living Word of the living God. Practice reading the passage aloud. Listen to it in your favorite recording of the Bible. Use the Scripture reading time in family worship as ongoing training in reading well to others. I just did an Internet search on how to read aloud well. There are plenty of tips and resources available. Resolve to glorify God by being an excellent public reader of His Word. So few do, but what a difference it makes.

A brief word is in order here about preparing ourselves to hear the Word of God. If you enter the typical evangelical church two minutes before the start of the worship service, it sounds almost like you've walked into a gymnasium two minutes before a basketball game. Part of my pastoral heart appreciates the good things represented by people who are glad to see and talk with each other.

There is a spirit of family reunion in the air when the family of God gathers together. But I think a larger part of my heart longs for reverence and a spirit of seeking God among those who come to hear His Word.

For a while a congregation of Korean Christians used our church building for their midweek service. I was impressed by the way they entered the worship center. Whether they were first to arrive or came in after the service had already started, as soon as each was seated he or she immediately bowed in prayer for several moments before arranging belongings, unbuttoning a coat, or acknowledging the presence of anyone else. This served as an effective reminder to his or her own heart and to everyone else of his or her main purpose for that time. Most churches I'm familiar with could stand more of this. One way to do so is to celebrate the "family reunion" until shortly before the beginning of worship, then call for a time of quiet reflection and focus a couple of minutes prior to the start of the service.

Similarly, one of the English Puritans, Jeremiah Burroughs, wrote before his death in 1646 the following words of counsel regarding preparation for the Discipline of hearing God's Word:

> First, when you come to hear the Word, if you would sanctify God's name, you must possess your souls with what it is you are going to hear, that what you are going to hear is the Word of God. . . . Therefore you find that the Apostle, writing to the Thessalonians, gives them the reason why the Word did them so much good as it did. It was because they heard it as the Word of God, 1 Thess. 2:13, "For this cause also thank we God without ceasing, because when ye received the Word of God, which ye heard of us, ye received it not as the word of men, but (as it is in truth) the Word of God, which effectually worketh also in you that believe."[2]

So hearing the Word of God is not merely passive listening; it is a Discipline to be cultivated.

READING GOD'S WORD

If you still doubt that Christians need to be exhorted to discipline themselves to read the Bible, consider this: *USA Today* reported a poll that showed only 11 percent of Americans read the Bible every day. More than half read it less than once a month or never at all.[3]

Of course, we attempt to comfort ourselves by noting that the poll included all Americans, not just professing Christians. Lamentably, little comfort may be found. A survey taken less than a year earlier by the Barna Research Group among those claiming to be "born-again Christians" disclosed these disheartening numbers: Only 18 percent—less than two of every ten—read the Bible every day. Worst of all, 23 percent—almost one in four professing Christians—say they never read the Word of God.[4] Polls and surveys come and go, but there's little reason to believe that these numbers fluctuate dramatically over time. Consider these statistics in light of 1 Timothy 4:7, "Discipline yourself for the purpose of godliness" (NASB).

Jesus often asked questions about people's understanding of the Scriptures, sometimes beginning with the words, "Have you not read . . . ?" (Matthew 19:4; Mark 12:10). He assumed that those claiming to be the people of God would have read the Word of God. And a case can be made that this question implies a familiarity with the *entire* Word of God.

When Jesus said, "Man shall not live by bread alone, but by every word that comes from the mouth of God" (Matthew 4:4), surely He intended at the very least for us to read "every word," for how can we "live . . . by every word that comes from the mouth of God" if we've never even *read* "every word that comes from the mouth of God"?

Since "all Scripture is breathed out by God and profitable for teaching, for reproof, for correction, and for training in righteousness" (2 Timothy 3:16), shouldn't we read it?

Revelation 1:3 tells us, "Blessed is the one who reads aloud the words of this prophecy, and blessed are those who hear, and who keep what is written in it, for the time is near." God promises that those who read and heed His Word will be blessed. But only those who discipline themselves to do so will receive those blessings.

The main reason, remember, for disciplining ourselves is godliness. We have learned that the Spiritual Disciplines are scriptural paths where we may expect to encounter the transforming grace of God. The most critical Discipline is the intake of God's Word. No factor is more influential in making us more like the Son of God than the Spirit of God working through the Word of God. If you want to be changed, if you want to become more like Jesus Christ, discipline yourself to read the Bible.

How often should we read it? British preacher John Blanchard, in his book *How to Enjoy Your Bible*, answers,

> Surely we only have to be realistic and honest with ourselves to know how regularly we need to turn to the Bible. How often do we face problems, temptation and pressure? *Every day!* Then how often do we need instruction, guidance and greater encouragement? *Every day!* To catch all these felt needs up into an even greater issue, how often do we need to see God's face, hear his voice, feel his touch, know his power? The answer to all these questions is the same: *every day!* As the American evangelist D. L. Moody put it, "A man can no more take in a supply of grace for the future than he can eat enough for the next six months, or take sufficient air into his lungs at one time to sustain life for a week. We must draw upon God's boundless store of grace from day to day as we need it."[5]

Here are the three most practical suggestions for consistent success in Bible reading. First, find the *time*. Perhaps one of the main reasons Christians never read through the entire Bible is discouragement. Many people have never read a thousand-page book before and get discouraged at the sheer length of the Bible. Do you realize that recorded readings of the Bible have proven that you can read through the entire Book in seventy-one hours? That's less time than the average American spends in front of the television every month.[6] In other words, if most people would exchange their TV time for Scripture reading, they'd finish reading the entire Bible in four weeks or less. If that sounds unworkable, consider this: In no more than fifteen minutes a day you can read through the Bible in less than a year's time. Only five minutes a day takes you through the Bible in less than three years. And yet the majority of Christians never read God's Word all the way through in a lifetime of decades. So we're back to the idea that it's primarily a matter of discipline and motivation.

Discipline yourself to find the *time*. Try to make it the same time every day. If possible, read the Bible at a time other than just before you go to sleep. There's value in reading the Bible just before you drop off, but if this is the only part of your day when you read Scripture then you should try to find another time. There are at least two reasons for this. First, you will retain very little of what you read when you're so tired and sleepy. And second, you probably do very little evil in your sleep. You need to encounter Christ in the Scriptures when it will still have an impact on your day.

The second practical suggestion is to find a Bible-reading *plan*. It's no wonder that those who simply open the Bible at random each day soon drop the discipline. Bible-reading plans abound on the Internet. Many study Bibles contain a reading schedule somewhere within the pages. Most local churches can provide you with a daily reading guide also.

Apart from a specific plan, reading three chapters every day and five on Sundays will take you through the Bible in a year's time. Read three in the Old Testament and three in the New Testament every day, and you will finish the Old Testament once and the New Testament four times in a twelve-month span.

My favorite plan involves reading in five places in the Bible each day. I begin in Genesis, Joshua, Job, Isaiah, and Matthew and read an equal number of chapters in each section. A variation of this plan is to read in three places daily, starting in Genesis, Job, and Matthew, respectively. The three sections are roughly the same in length, so you will finish them all about the same time. The great advantage of such a design is its variety. Many who intend to read straight through the Bible become confused in Leviticus, discouraged in Numbers, and give up completely by Deuteronomy. But when you are reading in more than one place each day, the variety makes it easier to keep up the momentum.

Even if you don't read through the Bible in a year's time, keep a record of which books you have read. Put a mark beside a chapter when you read it or by the title of a book in the table of contents when you've completed it. That way, regardless of how long it takes, or in what order they're read, you'll know when you've read every book in the Bible.

The third suggestion is to find at least one word, phrase, or verse to *meditate* on each time you read. We'll look at meditation more closely in the next chapter, but you should recognize now that without meditation you may close your Bible and not be able to remember a single thing you've read. And if that happens, your Bible reading is not likely to change you. Even with a good plan, it can become a mundane chore instead of a Discipline of joy. Take at least one thing you've read and think deeply about it for a few moments. Your insight into Scripture will deepen, and you'll better understand how it applies to your life. And the more you apply the truth of Scripture, the more you'll become like Jesus.

We should all have the following man's passion for reading God's Word. Robert L. Sumner, in *The Wonder of the Word of God*, tells of a man in Kansas City who was severely injured in an explosion. His face was badly disfigured, and he lost his eyesight as well as both hands. He had only recently become a Christian when the accident happened, and one of his greatest disappointments was that he could no longer read the Bible. Then he heard about a lady in England who read Braille with her lips. Hoping to do the same, he sent for some books of the Bible in Braille. But he discovered that the nerve endings in his lips had been too badly damaged to distinguish the characters. One day, as he brought one of the Braille pages to his lips, his tongue happened to touch a few of the raised characters and he could feel them. Like a flash he realized, *I can read the Bible using my tongue.* At the time Sumner wrote his book, the man had read through the entire Bible four times.[7] If he can do that, can you discipline yourself to read the Bible?

STUDYING GOD'S WORD

If reading the Bible can be compared to cruising the width of a clear, sparkling lake in a motorboat, studying the Bible is like slowly crossing that same lake in a glass-bottomed boat. The motorboat crossing provides an overview of the lake and a swift, passing view of its depths. The glass-bottomed boat of study, however, takes you beneath the surface of Scripture for an unhurried look of clarity and detail that's normally missed by those who simply read the text. As author Jerry Bridges put it, "Reading gives us breadth, but study gives us depth."[8]

Let's look at three examples of a heart to study the Word of God. The first is the Old Testament figure Ezra: "For Ezra had set his heart to study the Law of the LORD, and to do it and to teach his statutes and rules in Israel" (Ezra 7:10). There's an instructive significance to the sequence in this verse. Ezra (1) "set his heart," (2) "to study the Law of the LORD," (3) "and to do it," (4) "and to teach his statutes and rules in Israel." Before he taught the Word of God to the people of God, he practiced what he learned. But Ezra's learning came from a study of the Scriptures. Before he studied, however, he first "set his heart" to study. In other words, Ezra disciplined himself to study God's Word.

A second example is from Acts 17:11. Missionaries Paul and Silas had barely escaped with their lives from Thessalonica after their successful evangelistic work had provoked the Jews there to jealousy. When they repeated the same course of action in Berea, the Jews there responded differently: "Now these Jews were more noble than those in Thessalonica; they received the word with all eagerness, examining the Scriptures daily to see if these things were so." According to the next verse, the result was that "many of them therefore believed" (verse 12). The willingness to examine the Scriptures is commended here as noble character.

My favorite example of a heart to study the truth of God is in 2 Timothy 4:13. The apostle Paul was in prison and writing the last chapter of his final New Testament letter. Anticipating the arrival of his younger friend Timothy, he wrote, "When you come, bring the cloak that I left with Carpus at Troas, also the books, and above all the parchments." The scrolls and parchments Paul requested almost certainly included copies of the Scriptures. In his cold and miserable confinement, the godly apostle asked for two things: a cloak to wear so his body could be warmed and God's Word to study so his mind and heart could be warmed. Paul had seen heaven (see 2 Corinthians 12:1-6) and the resurrected Christ (see Acts 9:5), he had experienced the Holy Spirit's power for miracles (see Acts 14:10) and even for writing Holy Scripture (see 2 Peter 3:16); nevertheless, he continued to study God's Word until he died. So if Paul, with all his firsthand knowledge of heaven, Jesus, miracles, and more needed to study God's Word, surely you and I need to study it and should discipline ourselves to do it.

Then why don't we? Why do so many Christians neglect the study of God's Word? R. C. Sproul said it painfully well: "Here then, is the real problem of our negligence. We fail in our duty to study God's Word not so much because it is difficult to understand, not so much because it is dull and boring, but because it is work. Our problem is not a lack of intelligence or a lack of passion. Our problem is that we are lazy."[9]

Besides laziness, part of the problem for some may be an insecurity about how to study the Bible or even where to begin. Actually, starting is not so difficult. The basic difference between Bible reading and Bible study is simply a pen and paper (or some other means of preserving your thoughts). Write down observations about the text as you read, and record questions that come to your mind. If your Bible has cross-references,[10] look up the ones that relate to the verses that prompt your questions, then record your insights. Find a key word in your reading and use the concordance found in the back of most Bibles to review the other references that use the word, and again note your findings. Another way to begin is to outline a chapter, one paragraph at a time. When you finish that chapter, move on to the next until you've outlined the entire book. Before long you'll have a far stronger grasp on a section of Scripture than you had by just reading it.

As you advance in the study of the Book of God, you will learn the value of in-depth word studies, character studies, topical studies, and book studies. You'll discover a new richness in the Scripture as your understanding grows of how the grammar, history, culture, and geography surrounding a text factor into its interpretation.

Don't let a feeling of inadequacy keep you from the delight of learning the Bible on your own. Books, thick and thin, abound on how to study the Bible. They can provide more guidance regarding methods and tools than I can in this chapter. Don't settle only for spiritual food that's been "predigested" by others. Experience the joy of discovering biblical insights firsthand through your own Bible study.

MORE APPLICATION

If your growth in godliness were measured by the quality of your Bible intake, what would be the result? This is an important question, for the truth is, your growth in godliness is greatly affected by the quality of your Bible intake. In His magnificent High Priestly prayer of John 17, Jesus asked this of the Father for us: "Sanctify them in the truth; your word is truth" (verse 17). God's plan for sanctifying us, that is, for making us holy and godly, is accomplished by means of "the truth"—His Word. If we settle for a poor quality intake of hearing, reading, and studying God's Word, we severely restrict the main flow of God's sanctifying grace toward us.

As I say this, I realize that it would be easy to cause guilt feelings in us all (myself included) over past failures regarding the intake of God's Word. Above all, remember that heaven's door is opened to us not by the works we do (such as our intake of God's Word), but by the work of God in Jesus Christ. Beyond that, let's apply the message of Philippians 3:13 to any previous inconsistency with our Bible intake and start "forgetting what lies behind and straining forward to what lies ahead" in this area.

This leads us to a final application question.

What is one thing you can do to improve your intake of God's Word? Unless providentially hindered, joining a group of like-minded believers to hear God's Word preached each week should be a minimum. Many Bible-believing churches provide more than one opportunity each week to hear God's Word. You may want to consider recordings of the Bible, as well as Bible teaching on the Internet or radio, as options to increasingly hear God's Word. Set goals of earnestly attempting to read the Bible every day and regularly completing the entire Book. Also, inexpensive workbooks and study guides on every book in the Bible and a multitude of topics are available about anywhere Christian books are sold. Besides launching out individually, join a Bible study group in your church or community, or even start a group study.

Whatever way you choose, discipline yourself for the purpose of godliness by committing to at least one way of improving your intake of the Holy Word of God. For those who use their Bibles little are really not much better off than those who have no Bible at all.

Let's finish this chapter with a substantial word of encouragement. It's from a helpful booklet, *Reading the Bible*, by a Welsh pastor named Geoffrey Thomas. Whenever he writes of reading the Bible, we should also apply his words to hearing and studying it.

Do not expect to master the Bible in a day, or a month, or a year. Rather expect often to be puzzled by its contents.

It is not all equally clear. Great men of God often feel like absolute novices when they read the Word. The Apostle Peter said that there were some things hard to understand in the epistles of Paul (2 Peter 3:16). I am glad he wrote those words because I have felt that often. So do not expect always to get an emotional charge or a feeling of quiet peace when you read the Bible. By the grace of God you may expect that to be a frequent experience, but often you will get no emotional response at all.

Let the Word break over your heart and mind again and again as the years go by, and imperceptibly there will come great changes in your attitude and outlook and conduct. You will probably be the last to recognize these. Often you will feel very, very small, because increasingly the God of the Bible will become to you wonderfully great. So go on reading it until you can read no longer, and then you will not need the Bible any more, because when your eyes close for the last time in death, and never again read the Word of God in Scripture you will open them to the Word of God in the flesh, that same Jesus of the Bible whom you have known for so long, standing before you to take you for ever to His eternal home.[11]

CHAPTER 3

Bible Intake (Part 2) . . . for the Purpose of Godliness

There is discipline involved in Christian growth.
The rapidity with which a man grows spiritually and
the extent to which he grows, depends upon this discipline.
It is the discipline of the means.

RICHARD HALVERSON

Because you are reading this book, it's likely that you are a person who, at least to some degree, already engages in hearing, reading, and studying the Word of God as advocated in the previous chapter. Despite this, there is also a strong possibility that you do not perceive a great deal of fruit being produced in your life from these Disciplines. Your experience does not measure up to your expectation, so perhaps you conclude that you are the problem, that maybe you are a second-rate Christian.

The reality is that *you* may not be the problem at all. The problem may simply be your *method*. I know, for example, many people who read the Bible every day. They may even read multiple chapters of God's Word each morning. But as soon as they close the Bible, on most days they would have to admit that they can't remember a thing they've read.

"I just don't have a good memory," they conclude with a sigh. Or they may believe that they can't remember what they've read because they don't have a high IQ, or didn't have a good education, or they are just too old. Well, I've had some twenty-two-year-old geniuses in my seminary classes who have the same problem. So I would contend that in most cases the reason people can't remember what they read in the Bible is not their age, mental ability, or training, but their method.

Moreover, does anyone want to argue that ordinary people—people with no more than an average intellect or education—are unable to profit satisfyingly from the Bible on a regular basis? Surely not, especially since observation confirms that what the apostle Paul said of the Christians in Corinth is true of Christians everywhere: "For consider your calling, brothers: not many of you were wise according to worldly standards, not many were powerful, not many were of noble birth" (1 Corinthians 1:26). In other words, since the majority of those God calls are not "wise according to worldly standards," does that mean most Christians can't benefit much from Scripture on an individual basis? No, for doubtless God wants all His children to grow in grace and in their knowledge of Him through His Word.

So what's the problem? Why is it that the words of Scripture can go through our ears or eyes and then out of our minds so quickly and commonly, despite the depth of our devotion to the Bible? The problem is that hearing and reading the Bible, by themselves, usually aren't sufficient for remembering what we've received. They are invaluable and irreplaceable Disciplines, but they are incomplete without other Disciplines of the Word. While hearing and reading plant the seed of Scripture into the soil of our souls, other Disciplines are the water and sun God uses to bring the growth and fruit of Christlikeness in our lives. As the previous pages have indicated, studying the Bible is one way to water and warm the seed planted by hearing or reading. In this chapter are three more important Disciplines for the intake of God's Word that, when rightly practiced, promote the increased knowledge of God and closer conformity to Christ.

MEMORIZING GOD'S WORD— BENEFITS AND METHODS

Many Christians consider the Spiritual Discipline of memorizing God's Word as something tantamount to modern-day martyrdom. Ask them to memorize Bible verses and they react with about as much eagerness as a request for volunteers to face Nero's lions. How come? Perhaps because many associate all memorization with the memory efforts required of them in school. It was work, and most of it was uninteresting and of limited value. Frequently heard, also, is the excuse of having a bad memory. But what if I offered you one thousand dollars for every verse you could memorize in the next seven days? Do you think your attitude toward Scripture memory and your ability to memorize would improve? Any financial reward would be minimal when compared to the accumulating value of the treasure of God's Word deposited within your mind.

Memorization Supplies Spiritual Power

When Scripture is stored in your mind, it is available for the Holy Spirit to bring to your attention when you need it most. That's why the author of Psalm 119 wrote, "I have stored up your word in my heart, that I might not sin against you" (verse 11). It's one thing, for instance, to be watching or thinking about something when you know you shouldn't, but there's added power against the temptation when a specific verse can be brought to your mind, like Colossians 3:2: "Set your minds on things that are above, not on things that are on earth."

When the Holy Spirit brings a definite verse to mind like that, it's an illustration of what Ephesians 6:17 can mean when it refers to "the sword of the Spirit, which is the word of God." A pertinent scriptural truth, brought to your awareness by the Holy Spirit at just the right moment, can be the weapon that makes the difference in a spiritual battle.

There is no better illustration of this than Jesus' confrontation with Satan in the lonely Judean wilderness (see Matthew 4:1-11). Each time the Enemy thrust a temptation at Jesus, He parried it with the Sword of the Spirit. It was the Spirit-prompted recollection of specific texts of Scripture that helped Jesus experience victory. One of the ways we can experience more spiritual victories is to do as Jesus did—memorize Scripture so that it's available within us for the Holy Spirit to bring to our remembrance when it's needed.

Memorization Strengthens Your Faith

What Christian doesn't want his or her faith strengthened? One thing you can do to strengthen it is to discipline yourself to memorize Scripture. Let's walk through Proverbs 22:17-19, which says, "Incline your ear, and hear the words of the wise, and apply your heart to my knowledge, for it will be pleasant if you keep them within you, if all of them are ready on your lips. That your trust may be in the LORD, I have made them known to you today, even to you." To "apply your heart" to the "words of the wise" spoken of here and to "keep them within you" certainly pertains to Scripture memory. Notice the reason given here for keeping the wise words of Scripture within you and "ready on your lips." It's so "that your trust may be in the LORD." Memorizing Scripture strengthens your faith because it repeatedly reinforces the truth, often just when you need to hear it again.

A church I pastored sought to build a new worship center. We believed that in our situation we would most honor God if we built the building without going into debt. There were times when my faith in the Lord's provision began to sink. More often than not, what renewed my faith was the reminder of God's promise in 1 Samuel 2:30: "Those who honor me I will honor." Scripture memory is like reinforcing steel to a sagging faith.

Memorization Prepares Us for Witnessing and Counseling

On the Day of Pentecost (the Jewish holiday being celebrated when the Holy Spirit came in great power upon Jesus' followers), the apostle Peter was suddenly inspired by God to stand and preach to the crowd about Jesus. Much of what he said consisted of quotations from the Old Testament (see Acts 2:14-40). Although there's a qualitative difference between Peter's uniquely inspired sermon and our Spirit-led conversations, his experience illustrates how Scripture memory can prepare us for unexpected witnessing or counseling opportunities that come our way.

Recently, while I was talking to a man about Jesus, he said something that brought to mind a verse I had memorized. I quoted that verse, and it was the turning point in a conversation that resulted in him professing faith in Christ. I often experience something similar in counseling conversations. But until the verses are hidden in the heart, they aren't available to use with the mouth.

Memorization Provides a Means of God's Guidance

The psalmist wrote, "Your testimonies are my delight; they are my counselors" (Psalm 119:24). Just as the Holy Spirit retrieves scriptural truth from our memory banks for use in counseling others, so also will He bring it to our own minds in providing timely guidance for ourselves.

Many times when I have been trying to decide whether to say what I think in a given situation, the Lord brings Ephesians 4:29 to my mind: "Let no corrupting talk come out of your mouths, but only such as is good for building up, as fits the occasion, that it may give grace to those who hear." I'm sure that sometimes I misunderstand the leading of the Holy Spirit, but His guidance could hardly be more clear than when He brings to mind a verse like that! When it happens, it's the fruit of disciplined Scripture memory.

Memorization Stimulates Meditation

One of the most underrated benefits of memorizing Scripture is that it provides fuel for meditation. When you have memorized a verse of Scripture, you can meditate on it anywhere at any time during the day or night. If you love God's Word enough to memorize it, you can become like the writer of Psalm 119:97, who exclaimed,

"Oh how I love your law! It is my meditation all the day." Whether you're standing in line, taking a walk, driving the car, riding the train, waiting at the airport, cleaning the house, mowing the yard, rocking a baby, or eating a meal, you can benefit from the Spiritual Discipline of meditation if you have made the deposits of memorization.

The Word of God is the "sword of the Spirit," but if there is no Bible physically accessible to you, then the weapon of the Word must be present in the armory of your mind in order for the Spirit to wield it. Imagine yourself in the midst of a decision and needing guidance, or struggling with a difficult temptation and needing victory. The Holy Spirit enters your mental arsenal and looks around for available weapons, but all He finds is a John 3:16, a Genesis 1:1, and a Great Commission. Those are great swords, but they're not made for every battle. How do we go about filling our personal spiritual arsenal with a supply of swords for the Holy Spirit to use?

You Can Memorize Scripture

Most people think they have a bad memory, but it's not true. As we've already discovered, most of the time memorizing is mainly a problem of motivation. If you know your birthday, phone number, and address, and can remember the names of your friends and family, then you have a functioning memory and can memorize Scripture. The question becomes whether you are willing to discipline yourself to do it.

When Dawson Trotman, founder of the Christian organization called The Navigators, was converted to faith in Christ in 1926, he began memorizing one Bible verse every day. He was driving a truck for a lumberyard in Los Angeles at the time. While driving around town he would work on his verse for that day. During the first three years of his Christian life he memorized his first thousand verses. If he could memorize over three hundred verses a year while driving, surely we can find ways to memorize a few.

Have a Plan

There are many good prepackaged Scripture memory resources available in print and digital formats. But you might prefer selecting verses yourself on a particular topic where the Lord is working in your life right now. If your faith is weak, memorize verses on faith. If you're struggling with a habit, find verses that will help you experience victory over it. One man told Dawson Trotman that he was afraid that following his example of Scripture memory would make him prideful. Trotman's reply: "Then make your first ten verses on humility!" Another option is to memorize a section of Scripture, such as a psalm, rather than isolated verses.

If you are using a digital resource to help you with Scripture memory, it probably provides you with plenty of guidance on how to utilize it. But if not, or to supplement your use of that digital guide, the following tips will be helpful.

Write Out the Verses

Make a list of the verses on-screen or on a sheet of paper, leaving an inch or so of space between each one, or write each verse on a separate index card.

Draw Picture Reminders

Nothing elaborate is needed here, just a few lines or stick figures beside each verse, or some sort of picture or clip art if done on-screen. This makes the verse "visual" and puts the picture-is-worth-a-thousand-words principle to work for you. One simple image can remind you of a couple dozen words. This is especially true if the drawing illustrates some action described in the verse. For instance, with Psalm 119:11, you might make a crude drawing of a heart with a Bible inside to remind you of treasuring God's Word in the heart. For Ephesians 6:17, a sketch of a sword is an obvious reminder. You'll find this method particularly helpful when memorizing a section of consecutive verses. I realize that you are probably no more of an artist than I am, but no one else has to see the pictures and they can certainly make Scripture memory easier.

Memorize the Verses Word-Perfectly

There's a great temptation, especially when first learning a verse, to lower this standard. Don't settle for just getting close, or getting the "main idea." Memorize it word for word. Learn the reference, too. Without an objective standard of measurement, the goal is unclear and you may tend to continue lowering the standard until you quit altogether. Moreover, if you don't have the verse memorized exactly, you lose confidence in using it in conversation and witnessing. So even though memorizing "every jot and tittle" is harder in the beginning, it's easier and more productive in the long run. Incidentally, verses you know word-perfectly are easier to review than those you don't know so accurately.

Find a Method of Accountability

Because of our tendency toward sloth, most of us need more accountability on Scripture memory than on other Disciplines. And the busier we are, the more we tend to excuse ourselves from this commitment. Some, as Dawson Trotman did, develop personalized means of accountability to this Discipline that keep them faithful. Most Christians, however, are more consistent when they meet or talk regularly with someone else—not always another Christian— with whom they review their verses.

Review and Meditate Every Day

No principle of Scripture memory is more important than the principle of review. Without adequate review you will eventually lose most of what you memorize. But once you really learn a verse, you can mentally review it in a fraction of the time it would take to speak it. And when you know a verse this well, you don't have to review but once a week, once a month, or even once every six months to keep a sharp edge on it. It's not unusual, however, to reach a point where you spend 80 percent of your Scripture memory time in review. Don't begrudge devoting so much time to polishing your swords. Rejoice instead at having so many!

Integrating Scripture memory review into one or more of your life routines leverages the regularity of your habits to strengthen your grip on Scripture. Thus you might want to incorporate a few minutes of review into your daily devotional time. Or you might find that you can review your verses while you are brushing your teeth, working out, or making your daily commute. A great time to review your better-known verses is while going to sleep. Since you don't need a written copy of the verses before you, you can repeat them and meditate on them while dozing off or even when you have trouble sleeping. And if you can't stay awake, that's okay, since you're supposed to be sleeping anyway. If you can't go to sleep, you're putting the most profitable and peaceful information possible into your mind, as well as making good use of the time.

As we finish this section on the Discipline of Scripture memory, remember that memorizing verses is not an end in itself. The goal is not to see how many verses we can memorize; the goal is godliness. The goal is to memorize the Word of God so that it can transform our minds and our lives.

Jerry Bridges said in this regard,

> I am very much aware that Scripture memorization has largely fallen by the wayside in our day. . . . But let me say as graciously but firmly as I can: We cannot effectively pursue holiness without the Word of God stored up in our minds where it can be used by the Holy Spirit to transform us. . . . I know it requires work and is sometimes discouraging when we can't recall accurately a verse we have worked hard to memorize. The truth is, however, all forms of discipline require work and are often discouraging. But the person who perseveres in any discipline, despite the hard work and discouraging times, reaps the reward the discipline is intended to produce.[1]

MEDITATING ON GOD'S WORD— BENEFITS AND METHODS

One sad feature of our contemporary culture is that meditation has become identified more with non-Christian systems of thought than with biblical Christianity. Even among believers, the practice of meditation is often more closely associated with yoga, transcendental meditation, relaxation therapy, or some New Age practice than with Christian spirituality. Because meditation is so prominent in many spiritually counterfeit groups and movements, some Christians are uncomfortable with the whole subject and suspicious of those who engage in it. But we must remember that meditation is both commanded by God and modeled by the godly in Scripture. Just because a cult adopts the cross as a symbol doesn't mean the church should cease to use it. In the same way, we shouldn't discard or be afraid of scriptural meditation simply because the world engages in something it calls meditation.

The kind of meditation encouraged in the Bible differs from other kinds of meditation in several ways. While some advocate a kind of meditation in which you do your best to empty your mind, Christian meditation involves filling your mind with God and His truth. For some, meditation is an attempt to achieve complete mental passivity, but biblical meditation requires constructive mental activity. Worldly meditation employs visualization techniques intended to "create your own reality." And while Christian history has always had a place for the sanctified use of our God-given imagination in meditation, imagination is our servant to help us meditate on things that are true (see Philippians 4:8). Furthermore, instead of "creating our own reality" through visualization, we link meditation with prayer to God and responsible, Spirit-filled human action to effect changes.

In addition to these distinctives, let's define *meditation* as deep thinking on the truths and spiritual realities revealed in Scripture, or upon life from a scriptural perspective, for the purposes of understanding, application, and prayer. Meditation goes beyond hearing, reading, studying, and even memorizing as a means of taking in God's Word. A simple analogy would be a cup of tea. In this analogy your mind is the cup of hot water and the tea bag represents your intake of Scripture. Hearing God's Word is like one dip of the tea bag into the cup. Some of the tea's flavor is absorbed by the water, but not as much as would occur with a more thorough soaking of the bag. Reading, studying, and memorizing God's Word are like additional plunges of the tea bag into the cup. The more frequently the tea enters the water, the more permeating its effect. Meditation, however, is like immersing the bag completely and letting it steep until all the rich tea flavor has been extracted and the hot water is thoroughly tinctured reddish brown. Meditation on Scripture is letting the Bible brew in the brain. Thus we might say that as the tea colors the water, meditation likewise "colors" our thinking. When we meditate on Scripture it colors our thinking about God, about God's ways and His world, and about ourselves. Similarly, as the tea bag flavors the water, so through meditation we consistently "taste" or experience the reality taught in the text. The information on the page becomes experience in our hearts and minds and lives. Reading the Bible tells the believer, for example, of God's love. Meditation is more likely to convince him or her of it personally and, in biblically appropriate ways, to cause a person to feel loved by God.

Joshua 1:8 and the Promise of Success

A specific scriptural connection between success and the practice of meditation on God's Word is found in Joshua 1:8. As the Lord was commissioning Joshua to succeed Moses as the leader of His people, He told him, "This Book of the Law shall not depart from your mouth, but you shall meditate on it day and night, so that you may be careful to do according to all that is written in it. For then you will make your way prosperous, and then you will have good success."

We must remember that the prosperity and success the Lord spoke of here is prosperity and success in His eyes and not necessarily in the world's. From a New Testament perspective we know that the main application of this promise would be eternal riches and Christ-centered success—the prosperity of the soul and spiritual success (though some measure of success in our human endeavors would ordinarily occur as well when we live according to God's wisdom). Having made that qualification, however, let's not lose sight of the relationship between meditation on God's Word and true success.

True success is promised to those who meditate on God's Word, who think deeply on Scripture, not just at one time each day, but at moments throughout the day and night. They meditate so much that Scripture saturates their conversation. The fruit of their meditation is action. They do what they find written in God's Word, and as a result God prospers their way and grants success to them. Why? For striving "to do according to all that is written in" God's Word is just one of the biblical ways of describing what the New Testament would characterize as the pursuit of Christlikeness, and God loves to bless conformity to His Son. From eternity past, God predestined that all those who are in Christ will be made like Christ (see Romans 8:29). For all eternity future, all those in Christ will be glorified (see Romans 8:30), that is, "we shall be like him" (1 John 3:2)—sinless, perfect people reflecting the glory of God forever. So during our earthly pilgrimage, the more we obey God's Word—the more we become like Jesus—the more we are fulfilling God's eternal plan to make us like His Son. That's why God loves to bless obedience. And so as meditation leads to obedience, obedience results in God's blessing. We are not told how much of that blessing is material or spiritual, or how much of that blessing is in this world or the next, but we know that God does bless obedience.

How does the Discipline of meditation change us and place us in the path of God's blessing? David said in Psalm 39:3, "As I mused, the fire burned." The Hebrew word translated "mused" here is closely related to the one rendered "meditate" in Joshua 1:8. Analogous to David's musing that caused the fire of his anger to burn higher, whenever we hear, read, study, or memorize the fire of God's Word (see Jeremiah 23:29), the addition of meditation becomes like a bellows upon the fire of what we've encountered, causing it to burn more intensely in our experience at that moment. And just as when a fire blazes with more intensity it radiates both more light and more heat, so when we apply the bellows of meditation to the fire of God's Word, we see more light (insight and understanding) and feel more heat (passion for obedient action). And as a result of this growth in Christlike obedience, "then," says the Lord, "you will make your way prosperous, and then you will have good success."

Besides a bellows on a fire, meditation can also be compared to lingering by a fire. Imagine that you've been outside on an icy day and then come inside where there's a hot, crackling fire in the fireplace. As you walk toward it, you are very cold. You stretch out your hands to the fire and rub them together briskly during the two seconds it takes to walk past the glow and the warmth. When you reach the other side of the room, you realize, *I'm still cold.* Is there something wrong with you? Are you just a second-class "warmer-upper"? No, the problem isn't you; it's your method. You didn't stay by the fire. If you want to get warm, you have to linger by the fire until it warms your skin, then your muscles, then your bones until you are fully warm.

The failure to linger is the reason why many fail to remember or find their hearts warmed by the fire of God's Word. It takes their eyes about two seconds to go past the fire of verse one in the chapter they are reading for the day. Then it takes their eyes two seconds or so to read over verse two. And then another two seconds as their eyes go past verse three, and so on until they've finished reading. It doesn't matter how many of those two-second episodes you have; you will rarely remember or be moved by something you look at for two seconds. Thus the problem is probably not your memory or the coldness of your heart, but your method. So why don't you remember what you read in the Bible? Could it be that you simply do not let your mind linger over something you've read? And why does the intake of God's Word often leave us so cold and seem to produce so little success in our spiritual lives? Puritan pastor Thomas Watson has the answer: "The reason we come away so cold from reading the word is because we do not warm ourselves at the fire of meditation."[2]

Psalm 1:1-3—the Promises

God's promises in Psalm 1:1-3 regarding meditation are every bit as generous as those in Joshua 1:8:

> Blessed is the man
>   who walks not in the counsel of the wicked,
> nor stands in the way of sinners,
>   nor sits in the seat of scoffers;
> but his delight is in the law of the LORD,
>   and on his law he meditates day and night.
>
> He is like a tree
>   planted by streams of water
>
> that yields its fruit in its season,
>   and its leaf does not wither.
>
> In all that he does, he prospers.

We think about what we delight in. A man and woman who have found romantic delight think about each other at all hours. When we delight in God's Word (because it is the revelation of God) we think about it; that is, we meditate on it, at times all throughout the day and night. According to Psalm 1, the result of such meditation is stability, fruitfulness, perseverance, and prosperity. One writer said it crisply: "They usually thrive best who meditate most."[3]

The tree of your spiritual life thrives best with meditation because it helps you absorb the water of God's Word (see Ephesians 5:26). Merely hearing or reading the Bible, for example, can be like a short rainfall on hard ground. Regardless of the amount or intensity of the rain, most runs off and little sinks in. Conversely, meditation opens the soil of the soul and lets the water of God's Word percolate deeply. The result is an extraordinary fruitfulness and spiritual prosperity.

Consider that again. Many who read this book are folk who hear much of the Bible at church and perhaps again in a midweek Bible study. You may often listen to recorded Bible teaching and Christian music as well. You may read the Scriptures almost every day, and possibly other Christian books like this one. As a result you encounter a torrential amount of God's truth (not to mention the river of all the other information that rushes through your eyes and ears) each week. But without absorbing some of the water of the Word of God you encounter, you will be little better for the contact. Hearing and reading the Bible is the exposure to Scripture—that's needful, but it's only the starting place. After the exposure to Scripture we need to absorb it. Meditation is the absorption of Scripture. And it's the absorption of Scripture that leads to the experience with God and the transformation of life we long for when we come to the Bible. Yes, we want to hear and read the Bible—often and much—but without the addition of meditation, warned the great man of prayer and faith George Müller, "the simple reading of the Word of God" can become information that "only passes through our minds, just as water runs through a pipe."[4]

The author of Psalm 119 was confident that he was wiser than all his enemies (see verse 98). Moreover, he said, "I have more understanding than all my teachers" (verse 99). Is it because he heard or read or studied or memorized God's Word more than every one of his enemies and his teachers? Probably not. The psalmist was wiser, not necessarily because of more input, but because of more insight. But how did he acquire more wisdom and insight than anyone else? His explanation, expressed in a prayer, was,

Your commandment makes me wiser than my enemies,
    for it is ever with me.
I have more understanding than all my teachers,
    for your testimonies are my meditation.
    (PSALM 119:98-99)

I believe meditation is even more important for spiritual fruitfulness and prosperity in our day than it was in ancient Israel. Even if the total input of God's Word were the same for us as for those in the psalmist's day, combined with our intake of Scripture we also experience a flash flood of information that the writer of Psalm 119 could never have imagined. Join this with some of our additional modern responsibilities and the result is a mental distraction and dissipation that overwhelms our capacity to absorb Scripture. Due to today's deluge of data, more new information becomes available to us every few minutes than Jonathan Edwards would have encountered in his entire eighteenth-century lifetime. Granted, he had many time-consuming responsibilities (such as care for his horse) no longer required of most people now. On the other hand, he never once had to answer a telephone in his entire life! Despite his inconveniences, his mind, like the psalmist's, was not as distracted as ours by instant, ubiquitous information and entertainment. Because of these things, it's more difficult for us today to concentrate our thoughts, especially on God and Scripture, than it ever has been.

So what do we do? We can't return to the days of Edwards, unless we move to the jungles of Papua New Guinea. And even then we have already lived too long in the information age to escape its influence. We can, however, restore an order to our thinking and recapture some of the ability to concentrate—especially on spiritual truth—through biblical meditation. But it will require discipline.

In fact, this is exactly the way men like Edwards disciplined themselves. In her winsome biography of Edwards' wife, Sarah, Elisabeth Dodds said this about Jonathan's resolve regarding meditation:

When he was younger, Edwards had pondered how to make use of the time he had to spend on journeys. After the move to Northampton he worked out a plan for pinning a small piece of paper to a given spot on his coat, assigning the paper a number and charging his mind to associate a subject with that piece of paper. After a ride as long as the three-day return from Boston he would be bristling with papers. Back in his study, he would take off the papers methodically, and write down the train of thought each slip recalled to him.[5]

We don't have to walk around bristling like a paper porcupine, but we can be transformed by the renewing of our minds (see Romans 12:2) through disciplined meditation upon Scripture. We may not be as fruitfully productive or as spiritually successful as a Jonathan Edwards, but we can be wiser than our enemies, have more insight than our teachers, experience all the promises of Joshua 1:8 and Psalm 1, and be more godly if we meditate biblically.

James 1:25—New Testament Promises

The expansive promises God gives to those who meditate on His Word continue from the Old Testament into the New. For instance, there's this assurance: "But one who looks intently at the perfect law, the law of liberty, and abides by it, not having become a forgetful hearer but an effectual doer, this man will be blessed in what he does" (James 1:25, NASB). Observe first that the promise is not just for someone who looks at "the perfect law" of God as a casual reader, but rather for the "one who looks intently" at it. That's meditation.

Notice that the opposite of a meditator is called "a forgetful hearer." There's not a lot of difference between "having become a forgetful hearer" of God's Word and being a forgetful reader of it, which is what many Bible readers must admit they have become. So, according to this verse, why do we forget what we read in the Bible? Is it just a poor memory? No, it's a failure to meditate.

Next, James 1:25 teaches that meditatively looking at Scripture turns you into "an effectual doer" of Scripture. This, let's remember, is the goal. Obedience to God, that is, Christlikeness, is the end; meditation is just one of the means. In other words, our primary purpose is not to become more proficient or disciplined with meditation; our purpose is godliness.

And then, the one who is an "effectual doer," who is becoming more like Jesus—who was perfectly obedient to "the perfect law" of God—"will be blessed in what he does." Sound familiar? It sounds a lot like the promise in Psalm 1:3 to those who meditate on God's Word: "In all that he does, he prospers." We have seen that as meditation leads to obedience, so obedience results in God's blessing. Do you want God's blessing on your life? Of course you do. According to the texts we've examined, the blessing of God is associated with our obedience to God. Our obedience doesn't earn God's blessing, for His blessings are always by grace. In fact, sometimes God blesses us even in and in spite of our disobedience. But we know that we cannot *expect* God's blessing apart from obedience. So the question is, what makes us more obedient tomorrow than today? Is it just reading the Bible? Well, as we've seen, people can read the Bible every day and basically remain unchanged by it. It's usually not the mere reading of the Bible that causes us to become "an effectual doer" of it, but meditation.

How then do we meditate Christianly?

Select an Appropriate Passage

The easiest way to decide what to meditate on is to choose the verse, phrase, or word that impresses you most from the passage of Scripture you've read. So, after your reading, return to that which attracted your attention and meditate on that. Obviously, this is a subjective approach, but any approach is going to be somewhat subjective. Besides, meditation is essentially a subjective activity, a fact that underscores the importance of basing it on Scripture, the perfectly objective resource.[6]

Verses that conspicuously relate to your concerns and personal needs are clearly targets for meditation. Although we don't want to approach the Bible simply as a digest of wise advice, a collection of promises, or an "answer book," it is God's will that we give our attention to those things He has written that directly pertain to our circumstances. If you have been struggling with your thought life and you read Philippians, then you probably need to meditate on 4:8: "Finally, brothers, whatever is true, whatever is honorable, whatever is just, whatever is pure, whatever is lovely, whatever is commendable, if there is any excellence, if there is anything worthy of praise, think about these things." Is the salvation of a friend or family member on your mind? Should you encounter John 4, you could profit from meditating on Jesus' manner of communication there and drawing parallels to your own situation. Sensing distance from God or a dryness in your spiritual condition? Looking for clues to the character of God and focusing on them is a good choice.

One of the most consistently profitable ways to select a passage for meditation is to discern the main message of the section of your encounter with the Scripture and meditate on its meaning and application. For instance, recently I read Luke 11. There are ten paragraphs to that chapter in the version I was using. I chose one section, verses 5-13. The main theme of that paragraph is persistence in prayer. I reflected on that idea, especially as it is set forth in verses 9-10, which talk about asking, seeking, and knocking.[7]

Or you can narrow the focus to determine the key verse or verses of the passage you've read. Choosing one of these as your subject of meditation enables you to spotlight the main themes— the big ideas—of Scripture. For no matter how familiar a key verse may be, we never fully plumb the depths of the great truths of the Bible. We can never reflect too much, for example, on subjects such as the person and work of Jesus, any aspect of the gospel, or the attributes of God.

The general rule, then, in your personal, daily intake of Scripture is to both read and meditate. Read at length—such as a chapter or more—then go back over what you've read and select something specific from that as the focus of your meditation. Read big; meditate small.

Select a Method of Meditation

Meditation is not folding your arms, leaning back in your chair, and staring at the ceiling. That's daydreaming, not meditation. Daydreaming isn't always a waste of time; it can be a much-needed, well-deserved respite for the mind as important as relaxation often is for the body. Our gracious Father is not always goading us to "produce," and, as I've written elsewhere, it is possible to daydream, to "Do Nothing—and Do It to the Glory of God."[8]

As opposed to daydreaming wherein you let your mind wander, with meditation you focus your thoughts. You give your attention to the verse, phrase, word, or teaching of Scripture you have chosen. Instead of mental aimlessness, in meditation your mind is on a track—it's going somewhere; it has direction. The direction your mind takes is determined by the method of meditation you choose.

Here are seventeen methods of meditating on Scripture. I use all of them some of the time and none of them all the time. Why do I present so many?[9] Because you'll likely resonate with some of these methods more than others, while the inclinations of someone else might be just the opposite of yours. And like me, you'll probably want some variety.

Meditation Method #1: Emphasize Different Words in the Text

This method takes the verse or phrase of Scripture and turns it like a diamond to examine every facet.

A meditation on Jesus' words at the beginning of John 11:25 would look like this:

> "*I* am the resurrection and the life."
> "I *am* the resurrection and the life."
> "I am *the* resurrection and the life."

"I am the *resurrection* and the life."

"I am the resurrection *and* the life."

"I am the resurrection and *the* life."

"I am the resurrection and the *life*."

Of course, the point is not simply to repeat vainly each word of the verse until they've all been emphasized. The purpose is to think deeply upon the light (truth) that flashes into your mind each time the diamond of Scripture is turned. It's simple, but effective. I've found it especially helpful when I have trouble concentrating on a passage.

Meditation Method #2: Rewrite the Text in Your Own Words

From his earliest homeschool days, Jonathan Edwards' father taught him to do his thinking with pen in hand, a habit he retained throughout his life. Meditating with pen in hand or fingers on the keyboard can help you to focus your attention on the matter at hand, while stimulating your flow of thinking. With this method, imagine that you are sending the verse you've chosen in a message to someone. How would you convey the content of the verse faithfully, yet without using the words of that verse?

Paraphrasing the verse you are considering is also a good way to make sure you understand the meaning. I have a friend who says that paraphrasing verses after the fashion of the Amplified Bible is the most productive method of opening a text for him. The very act of thinking of synonyms and other ways of restating the meaning of a part of God's Word is in itself a way of meditation.

Meditation Method #3: Formulate a Principle from the Text— What Does It Teach?

While this method can work when you are meditating on a section as short as one verse or as long as a chapter, it works especially well when your focus is on more than just a sentence or two. Think of it as a type of summary of the main message of the passage. This method might be compared to developing a thesis statement for the section of Scripture you've read. Thus a principle derived from Matthew 6:9-13 might be stated as, "Jesus teaches His followers how to pray," and a principle formulated from a long passage like Luke 8:19-56 might be, "Jesus has authority over creation, over demons, over illness, and over death."

The more memorably you can state the principle, the better. That's what Dr. R. G. Lee did in one of the best-known American sermons of the twentieth century. He condensed the Old Testament story of Naboth, Ahab, and Jezebel into the unforgettable line, "Pay-Day—Someday!" Once you've developed the principle, take the second step and think of a way to reformulate it into a phrase or line that will be easy to remember later when you ask yourself, "Now what was that verse I was meditating on this morning?"

Meditation Method #4: Think of an Illustration of the Text— What Picture Explains It?

An illustration is a word picture that explains, clarifies, or confirms the object of your meditation. It can be a personal anecdote, an event in the news or in history, a quotation, an analogy, a song— anything that throws light upon the text. An illustration is the completion of a sentence that begins with, "That's like . . ."

Jesus often used illustrations in His teaching. In Luke 13:18-21,

> He said therefore, "What is the kingdom of God like? And to what shall I compare it? It is like a grain of mustard seed that a man took and sowed in his garden, and it grew and became a tree, and the birds of the air made nests in its branches." And again he said, "To what shall I compare the kingdom of God? It is like leaven that a woman took and hid in three measures of flour, until it was all leavened."

Evidently at some time before this episode, in His humanity He had meditated upon the nature of the kingdom of God and arrived at these two analogies, or else He did the reverse and once while observing a tree with nests and once while seeing leaven put into flour He asked Himself what biblical truth each might illustrate. The apostle Paul used illustrations in 1 Thessalonians 5:2-3, as did James in James 1:6.

The first thing to do when you want to picture a passage is to consider whether there is a story in the Bible that illustrates the point of the verse upon which you are meditating, or, if you are meditating on a story, whether there is a single verse somewhere in Scripture that summarizes the point of that story. If the verse you are considering is not in the Gospels, ponder whether it illustrates something Jesus said or did.

Another way to use this method is to reverse it and ask what this particular text might illustrate. Is it, for example, an illustration of another passage of Scripture, or of something in the words or deeds of Jesus?

Meditation Method #5: Look for Applications of the Text

The outcome of meditation should be application. Like chewing without swallowing, so meditation is incomplete without some type of application. This is so important that the entire next section of this chapter is devoted to applying God's Word. So ask yourself, "How am I to respond to this text? What would God have me to do as a result of my encounter with this part of His Word? The Bible tells us to 'be doers of the word' (James 1:22); how then should I do this portion of it? Is there something to start, to stop, to confess, to pray about, to believe, to say to someone?"

If you'll say to yourself, "I will not close my Bible until I know at least one thing the Lord wants me to do with this verse," you'll meditate.

Meditation Method #6: Ask How the Text Points to the Law or the Gospel

One way of thinking of the Bible is that it presents us with God's Law and God's gospel. The Law (basically the Old Testament) consists of what our holy and just God requires of people for them to have the righteousness necessary to live with Him in heaven. The gospel (basically the New Testament) is the good news of how our loving and merciful God has provided through Jesus the righteousness He requires in His Law. With this meditation method, you look for how the text you are considering points to some aspect of the Law, the gospel, or both.

With a verse like Psalm 23:1, for example—"The LORD is my shepherd"—we might say it points to the gospel in that Jesus said of Himself, "I am the good shepherd. The good shepherd lays down his life for the sheep" (John 10:11). But why do we need a shepherd, and why did the Good Shepherd have to lay down His life for the sheep? Because—and here Psalm 23:1 can indirectly point also to the Law—we're all like sheep that have turned from God's Law. As Isaiah 53:6 puts it, "All we like sheep have gone astray; we have turned—every one—to his own way; and the LORD has laid on him the iniquity of us all."

It may not often be as easy to trace lines to other texts or to make connections to both the Law and the gospel as it is from Psalm 23. But with a little practice you'll find yourself becoming much more perceptive to these major themes of the Scripture even as you are considering a very small part of it.

Meditation Method #7: Ask How the Text Points to Something About Jesus

This is similar to the previous method, but it focuses entirely on the person and work of Jesus Christ. After His resurrection, as Jesus was walking on the road to Emmaus with two believers, we're told that "beginning with Moses and all the Prophets, he interpreted to them in all the Scriptures the things concerning himself" (Luke 24:27). Essentially this approach to meditation attempts to do the same thing; that is, it examines the text to see how it might point to something about who Jesus is or what He did.

So you might look for how Jesus fulfilled or epitomized the

text (as we saw in Psalm 23:1) or, conversely, how He is the perfectly pure opposite of it (if it speaks of sin). Look to see if what you are considering is like some aspect of what Jesus accomplished by His life or death, or someday will do upon His return. As Jesus taught us, let's train ourselves to think of the text before us Christocentrically.

Meditation Method #8: Ask What Question Is Answered or What Problem Is Solved by the Text

In this approach, you regard the text before you as the answer to a question or the solution to a problem. With that assumption, you ask, "What is the question?" or "What is the problem?" If you are meditating on "Jesus wept" (John 11:35), what question does that answer? How about, "Was Jesus fully human?" Well, "Jesus wept." That doesn't answer everything about the question, but it does tell you something important about His humanity. If you are meditating on John 3:16 and you consider that verse the solution to a problem, then what is the problem? One way the problem could be stated is, "What is God's plan for providing eternal life?"

Meditation Method #9: Pray Through the Text

This method especially can help you express the spirit of the psalmist in Psalm 119:18: "Open my eyes, that I may behold wondrous things out of your law." The Holy Spirit is the Great Guide into God's truth (see John 14:26). Moreover, Christian meditation is more than just riveted human concentration or creative mental energy. Praying your way through a verse of Scripture submits the mind to the Holy Spirit's illumination of the text and intensifies your spiritual perception. The Bible was written under the Holy Spirit's inspiration; pray for His illumination in your meditation.

I recently meditated on Psalm 119:50: "This is my comfort in my affliction, that Your word has revived me" (NASB). I prayed through the text along these lines:

Lord, You know the affliction I'm going through right now. Your Word promises to comfort me in my affliction. Your Word can revive me in my affliction. I really believe that is true. Your Word has revived me in affliction during the past, and I confess my faith to You that it will revive me in this experience. I pray that You will revive me now through the comfort of Your Word.

As I prayed through this text, the Holy Spirit began to bring to my mind truths from Scripture about the sovereignty of God over His church, His providence over the circumstances in my life, His power, His constant presence and love, and so on. In this extended time of meditation and prayer, my soul was revived and I felt comforted by the Comforter.

Biblical meditation must always involve two parties—the Christian and the Holy Spirit. Praying over a text[10] is the Christian's invitation for the Holy Spirit to hold His divine light over the words of Scripture to show what you cannot see without Him.

Meditation Method #10: Memorize the Text

As mentioned earlier in this chapter, "memorization stimulates meditation." Simply put, when you are memorizing a verse, you think about it. The mental repetition of the text required by memorization simultaneously fosters reflection on it. And after you memorize a verse of Scripture, you can meditate on it during your commute, while on a walk, as you are preparing a meal, when you are falling asleep, or any other time you choose.

The most consistent and diligent memorizer of Scripture that I have personally known is Dr. Andrew Davis, who wrote, "There is no more useful discipline to this careful process of verse-by-verse meditation than memorization. Memorization is not the same as meditation, but it is almost impossible for someone to memorize a passage of Scripture without somewhat deepening his/her understanding of those verses. Plus, once the passage is memorized, a lifetime of reflection is now available."[11]

Meditation Method #11: Create an Artistic Expression of the Text

This approach to the text consists of giving tangible expression to your meditations with a sketch or some other material manifestation of your thoughts. You could compose a song or poem based on the text. As Psalm 96:1 urges us, "Oh sing to the LORD a new song." It doesn't have to be laborious or lengthy, or even more than one note and thus chant-like. Most often it might be entirely spontaneous. Jonathan Edwards wrote that this was often his practice: "walking alone in the woods, and solitary places, for meditation, soliloquy, and prayer, and converse with God; . . . it was always my manner, at such times, to sing forth my contemplations."[12] You can do that. On the spur of the moment, improvise a tune and sing the text and/or your thoughts about it as "a new song" to the Lord as you reflect on His Word.

Meditation Method #12: Ask the Philippians 4:8 Questions of the Text

Recently I was meditating on Philippians 4:8: "Finally, brothers, whatever is true, whatever is honorable, whatever is just, whatever is pure, whatever is lovely, whatever is commendable, if there is any excellence, if there is anything worthy of praise, think about these things." It occurred to me that the directions given here about meditating on "these things" could provide guidance for meditating on any verse of Scripture, as well as for meditating on "life." As a result (and after consulting several translations of Philippians 4:8), I developed a series of questions based upon "these things."

- What is *true* about this, or what truth does it exemplify?
- What is *honorable* about this?
- What is *just* or right about this?
- What is *pure* about this, or how does it exemplify purity?
- What is *lovely* about this?
- What is *commendable* about this?

- What is *excellent* about this (that is, excels others of this kind)?
- What is *praiseworthy* about this?

So whether meditating on a verse or story in the Bible, or on something in your life—circumstances, an event, an experience, an encounter with someone, a part of creation—in fact, when thinking about *anything*, the Philippians 4:8 questions can be a helpful guide.

Meditation Method #13: Ask the Joseph Hall Questions of the Text

Joseph Hall (1574–1656) was a devoted Anglican bishop in Norwich, England. His 1606 book, *The Art of Divine Meditation*, was one of the best-selling and most influential books of its day. In this Puritan devotional classic he discussed and illustrated the use of ten questions helpful in meditating on Scripture. I find Hall's questions extremely thought-provoking whenever I am preparing to preach or write or make any sort of presentation, but especially so during my devotional meditation on Scripture. I have modified and expanded them slightly to make them clearer to contemporary readers.

1. What is it (*define and/or describe* what it is) you are meditating upon?
2. What are its *divisions or parts*?
3. What *causes* it?
4. What does *it cause*; that is, what are its *fruits and effects*?
5. What is its *place, location, or use*?
6. What are its *qualities and attachments*?
7. What is *contrary, contradictory, or different* to it?
8. What *compares* to it?
9. What are its *titles or names*?
10. What are the *testimonies or examples of Scripture* about it?

The first question is the most difficult, but it is also the most important, for the answer becomes the "it" referred to in the following questions. So if the verse you were meditating upon were, say, Romans 8:28, your answer to the first question might be something like, "God's control of all things for the good of His people." Then "its divisions or parts" (from question two) would include "God's control," "all things," "the good," and "His people," for these are the "divisions or parts" of "it" as defined in answer to question one.

You might find it useful to keep a copy of these questions in your Bible and digitally in locations where they'll always be available to you.

Are ten questions too many for a single time of meditation? Then take one or two per day, perhaps using this method to meditate on a single verse for an entire week. Whether many or few, it's often much easier in meditation to answer specific questions about the text than to think about it without any guidance at all. For this reason, besides those provided above you might develop other lists of questions to use in meditation. When you are sleepy or tired or distracted, looking for the answers to particular questions will help you minimize the mind-wandering that happens when there is no particular method to help you focus on the text.

Meditation Method #14: Set and Discover a Minimum Number of Insights from the Text

With this method you determine at the outset that you will not stop meditating on your text until you discover at least a certain number of insights from it. The first time I did this I was meditating on Hebrews 12:29: "For our God is a consuming fire." I resolved to continue poring over the verse until I found a minimum of ten insights. In this case, I resolved to think of ten comparisons between God and fire. The first ones were rather easy: "God is light," the Bible says in 1 John 1:5, and fire gives off light. Next, God is the ultimate Judge, and in the Bible fire is sometimes the means of God's judgment. But after about four quick comparisons between God and fire, I had a more difficult time. But that's when I began to go beyond what was rather simple or obvious to that which required more thought. Only then did I sense that I was growing past what was already familiar. If I had not set the bar at ten, I would have stopped at about four on that occasion, because that's when the mental challenge came. But I often need that kind of mental challenge to go deeper in the Word of God.

I've had at least four friends confirm a legendary assignment each experienced in a seminary class on Bible study methods taught at Dallas Theological Seminary by professor Howard Hendricks. He would tell his students to come back to the next class with at least twenty-five observations on Acts 1:8. Having done so, they would be required in the next class to return with twenty-five more observations on that verse. Finally, they were given the assignment to make as many observations as they could beyond the original fifty. Most were thinking they had almost exhausted Acts 1:8 by that point, until Hendricks exhorted the class with, "Oh, by the way, the all-time record is over six hundred."

Not every verse in the Bible is as fertile as Acts 1:8. Nevertheless, this method is founded upon the belief that an infinite mind has inspired every text in Scripture, and for that reason there's always more to see there than you've yet seen, no matter how well you think you know a given verse. Perhaps it's an observation, an insight, or an application—but there's almost certainly something you've not previously noticed or articulated in that text.

Meditation Method #15: Find a Link or Common Thread Between All the Paragraphs or Chapters You Read

If you read one chapter and it has, say, three paragraphs, then search for a connection between all three. In Luke 15, for example, there is a lost sheep, a lost coin, and a lost son. All are found, and there is rejoicing. In Mark 5 we read of Jesus demonstrating His divinity by exercising authority over the spiritual realm, over illness, and over death.

If you read from more than one book of the Bible, look for a common thread in all that you read. Can you, for instance, see Jesus in the various chapters of your reading? Or how does each relate to the gospel? Or how would each speak to the "current crisis" in your life? You may eventually conclude from one or more of the chapters you've read that you can't see any application whatsoever to your current crisis. But even when that's so, there's profit in mentally scouring the Scriptures, examining and reflecting on them in a way that's far more thoughtful than mere reading.

Meditation Method #16: Ask How the Text Speaks to Your Current Issue or Question

Suppose the current issue in your life is financial. After you have completed your Bible reading, review what you've read and search for any texts that address or might apply to finances. Then consider what the text says, perhaps praying through the text or using one of the previous methods to meditate further. If the immediate concern in your life relates to your family, look for those verses that would have something to say about relationships. If you are wrestling with a persistent question, go back over all you've read in the past few minutes and scan it for something the Holy Spirit might illumine in relation to the answer. When you ask the Author of Scripture, "Open my eyes, that I may behold wondrous things out of your law" (Psalm 119:18), you may be surprised by the texts He uses to give you insight, understanding, or application regarding your issue or question.

Meditation Method #17: Use Meditation Mapping

Meditation mapping applies the principles of mind mapping to record one's meditation on a text of Scripture. If you are unfamiliar with mind mapping or similar methods, you might want to briefly explore the topic on the Internet. It's a quick study, especially if you find examples of basic mind maps.[13] Essentially a mind map is a diagram that outlines information in a more visually appealing and memorable way than words on lines. The idea you want to explore is placed in the center of a page. Then as ideas come, they are connected by lines to the central image, radiating out from it.

Subcategories are similarly connected by thinner branches to the main ideas, and so forth. The use of simple images, symbols, and color is highly recommended.

Suppose you were to use this method to meditate on Romans 8:28. You'd begin by putting the words of that verse in the middle of the page, perhaps drawing a circle, box, or "cloud" around it. The first major branch radiating from it might be about "And we know," and as you gave thought to how "we know," as well as to the connection this verse has with the immediate context, you would connect your insights with lines or thinner branches to that first branch. The next large branch might be about "those who love God." Minor branches on "who are they?" and "loving God" would grow out of this first-level branch. Next, you might have a major branch about "all things," another on "work together," and more. Each major branch would bear as much fruit as your meditations would produce.

Personally, this is one of my favorites. It's not a different way to think, just a different way to write down what you think. But as fresh insights often follow fresh approaches, I've found this method of meditation on Scripture helps me to stay focused on the biblical text while stimulating my mental processes about what I'm seeing.

Don't Rush—Take Time!

What value is there to reading one, three, or more chapters of Scripture only to find that after you've finished, you can't recall a thing you've read? It's better to read a small amount of Scripture and meditate on it than to read an extensive section without meditation.

Scotsman Maurice Roberts wrote,

> Our age has been sadly deficient in what may be termed spiritual greatness. At the root of this is the modern disease of shallowness. We are all too impatient to meditate on the faith we profess. . . . It is not the busy skimming over religious books or the careless hastening through religious duties which makes for a strong Christian faith. Rather, it

is unhurried meditation on gospel truths and the exposing of our minds to these truths that yields the fruit of sanctified character.[14]

Read less (if necessary) in order to meditate more. Although many Christians need to find the time to increase their Bible reading, there may be some who are spending all the time they can reading the Bible. If you could not possibly add more time to your devotional schedule for meditating on your Scripture reading, read less in order to have some unhurried time for meditation. Even though you may find moments throughout the day when you meditate on God's Word (see Psalm 119:97), the best meditation generally occurs when it's part of your main daily encounter with the Bible.

May our experience in scriptural meditation be as joyful and fruitful as that of Jonathan Edwards, who penned these lines in his journal soon after his conversion: "I seemed often to see so much light exhibited by every sentence, and such a refreshing food communicated, that I could not get along in reading; often dwelling long on one sentence to see the wonders contained in it, and yet almost every sentence seemed to be full of wonders."[15]

APPLYING GOD'S WORD— BENEFITS AND METHODS

God made all the essentials of the Bible—that is, those things that are essential for knowing Him—abundantly clear. Still, parts of the Bible are hard to understand. Even the apostle Peter said of the letters of Paul, "There are some things in them that are hard to understand" (2 Peter 3:16). Despite our occasional struggles to understand parts of Scripture, however, understanding the Bible isn't our chief problem. Much more often our difficulty lies in knowing how to apply the clearly understood parts of God's Word to everyday living. What does it say about raising my children? How should Scripture influence my decisions and relationships at work? What is the biblical perspective on the upcoming choice I must make? How can I know God better? These are the kinds of questions Bible readers ask frequently, thereby proving the urgency of learning the Discipline of applying God's Word.

The Value of Applying God's Word

The Bible promises the blessing of God on those who apply the Word of God to their lives. The classic New Covenant statement on the value of integrating the spiritual with the concrete is James 1:22-25:

> Be doers of the word, and not hearers only, deceiving yourselves. For if anyone is a hearer of the word and not a doer, he is like a man who looks intently at his natural face in a mirror. For he looks at himself and goes away and at once forgets what he was like. But the one who looks into the perfect law, the law of liberty, and perseveres, being no hearer who forgets but a doer who acts, he will be blessed in his doing.

Pithy and powerful is Jesus' similar statement, "If you know these things, blessed are you if you do them" (John 13:17).

These verses tell us there can be a dangerous delusion in hearing God's Word. Without minimizing either the sufficiency of Scripture or the power of the Holy Spirit to work through even the most casual brush with the Bible, we can frequently be deluded about the Scripture's impact on our lives. According to James 1:22-25, we can experience God's truth so powerfully that what the Lord wants us to do becomes as plain to us as our face in the morning mirror. But if we do not apply the truth as we meet it, regardless of how wonderful the experience of discovering the truth has been, we deceive ourselves if we think we will be blessed for giving attention to the Bible on those occasions. The one who "will be blessed in his doing" is the one who *does* what Scripture says.

For someone to "be blessed in his doing" is the equivalent of the promises of blessing, success, and prosperity given in Joshua 1:8 and Psalm 1:1-3 to those who meditate on God's Word. That's because meditation should ultimately lead to application, to Christlike obedience. When God instructed Joshua to meditate on His Word day and night, He told him the purpose for meditating was "so that you may be careful to do according to all that is written in it." The promise "then you will make your way prosperous, and then you will have good success" would be fulfilled, not as the result of meditation only, but as God's blessing upon meditation-forged application.

Expect to Discover an Application

Because God wills for you to be a doer of His Word, you may be confident that He wants you to find an application whenever you come to the Scriptures. For the same reason you may believe that the Holy Spirit is willing to help you discern how to flesh out your insights. Therefore, open the Book expectantly. Anticipate the discovery of a practical response to the truth of God. It makes a big difference to come to the Bible with the faith that you will find an application for it as opposed to believing that you won't.

The Puritan minister and writer Thomas Watson, whose influence was so great he was called by Charles Spurgeon "the nursing mother of gigantic evangelical divines,"[16] encouraged anticipation about application when he said,

> Take every word as spoken to yourselves. When the word thunders against sin, think thus: "God means my sins"; when it presseth any duty, "God intends me in this." Many put off Scripture from themselves, as if it only concerned those who lived in the time when it was written; but if you intend to profit by the word, bring it home to yourselves: a medicine will do no good, unless it be applied.[17]

Because of God's inspiration of Scripture, believe that what you are reading was meant for you—at least in some Christ-related way—as well as for the first recipients of the message. Without that attitude you'll rarely perceive the application of a passage of Scripture to your personal situation.

Understand the Text

A misunderstanding about the meaning of a verse leads to misguided applications of it. For instance, some have applied the injunction of Colossians 2:21—"Do not handle, Do not taste, Do not touch"—to prohibit just about everything imaginable. And while there may be good reasons to abstain from some of the things this verse has been used against, the text is misapplied when used that way because its meaning is misunderstood. When taken in context, it's clear that these words were actually the slogans of an ascetic group the apostle Paul was denouncing as an enemy of the gospel. So if you were reading this verse and thought it could apply to your need to lose weight, you might be pleased to know that's an invalid application from an incorrect interpretation. (However, a different diet might be the personal application the Holy Spirit would lead you to from 1 Corinthians 9:27.)

Watson was right when he said, "Take every word as spoken to yourselves." But we cannot do that until we understand how it was intended for those who heard it first. If you take every word of God's call to Abram in Genesis 12:1-7 as spoken to yourself, you'll soon be moving to Israel. But if you understand that particular call as unique to Abram, you can still discover the timeless truths within it and apply every word to yourself. Have you followed the call of God to come to Christ? Are you willing to obey the will of God wherever He might call you—to a new job, a new location, the mission field, and so on?

We must understand how a passage applied when it was first given before we can understand how it applies now. When Jesus said, "Today you will be with me in paradise" (Luke 23:43), its immediate application was for the thief on the cross beside Him. Because these words are part of Scripture, however, and because "all Scripture is breathed out by God and profitable" (2 Timothy 3:16), the Lord intends for them to have application to all believers. Obviously, the contemporary application is not that each Christian will die today and be with Jesus in paradise. But one way we can apply this text is in terms of preparing for death. We realize that it is possible for death to come today and then examine ourselves about our readiness for it. We also can apply the text regarding the presence of Christ. As Christians, Christ is always present within us, thus He is with us today even though we are not yet in paradise. How does a fresh awareness of Christ's presence affect your prayers or your outlook on the rest of the day?

Jesus' promise to the thief is an example of how not every promise is meant to be applied today in exactly the same way as it was originally. Yet many other promises are general, universal, and perpetual in their application. One obvious example is John 3:16. Another is Romans 10:9. How can we know which passages should be applied somewhat differently than when first given? Here is where a growing knowledge of Scripture through hearing, reading, and, in particular, studying the Bible pays dividends. For the better we understand the Bible, the better equipped we will be to apply it.

Having said all that, I maintain that most of Scripture is plain and straightforward in its basic meaning. Our problem continues to be more of a lack of action than comprehension. The words of Scripture must be understood to be applied, but until we apply them, we don't really understand them.

Meditate to Discern Application

We've already noted that meditation isn't an end in itself. Nevertheless, deep thinking on the truths and spiritual realities of Scripture is the often-neglected key to putting them into practice. It is by means of meditation that the facts of biblical information transform into practical application.

If we read, hear, or study God's Word without meditating on it, we shouldn't be surprised that applying Scripture to concrete situations is so difficult. Perhaps we could even train a parrot to learn every verse of Scripture that we ourselves have memorized, but if we don't apply those verses to life they won't be of much more lasting value to us than to the parrot. How does the Word memorized become the Word applied? It happens through meditation.

Most information, even biblical information, passes through our minds like water through a sieve. There's usually so much information coming in each day that we retain very little. But when we meditate, the truth remains and percolates. We can smell its aroma more fully and taste it better. As it brews in our brain, the insights come. The heart is warmed by meditation, and cold truth is melted into passionate action.

Psalm 119:15 puts it this way: "I will meditate on your precepts and fix my eyes on your ways." It was through meditation on God's Word that the psalmist discerned how to regard God's ways for living, that is, how to be a doer of them. It's no different for us. The way to determine how any Scripture applies to the real situations of life is to meditate on that Scripture.

Ask Application-Oriented Questions of the Text

As we noticed earlier, asking questions of the text is one of the best ways to meditate. The more questions you ask and answer about a verse of Scripture, the more you will understand it and the more clearly you will see how to apply it.

Here are some examples of application-oriented questions that can help you become a doer of God's Word:

- Does this text reveal something I should believe about God?
- Does this text reveal something I should praise or thank or trust God for?
- Does this text reveal something I should pray about for myself or others?
- Does this text reveal something I should have a new attitude about?
- Does this text reveal something I should make a decision about?

- Does this text reveal something I should do for the sake of Christ, others, or myself?

There are times when a verse of Scripture will have such evident application for your life that it will virtually jump off the page, take you by the shoulders, and urge you to do what it says. More often than not, however, you must interview the verse, patiently asking questions of it until a down-to-earth response becomes clear.

Respond Specifically

An encounter with God through His Word should result in at least one specific response. In other words, after you have concluded your time of Bible intake, you should be able to name at least one definite response you have made or will make to what you have encountered. That response may be an explicit act of faith, worship, praise, thanksgiving, or prayer. It may take the form of asking someone's forgiveness or speaking a word of encouragement. The response may involve forsaking a sin or showing an act of love. Regardless of the nature of that response, consciously commit yourself to at least one action to take following the intake of God's Word.

How important is this? How often have you closed your Bible and suddenly realized you can't remember a thing you've read? How many Bible studies have you participated in and how many sermons have you heard where you left without any imprint of Scripture on your life at all? I've known people who were in as many as six Bible studies per week, and yet they grew only in knowledge and not in Christlikeness because they were not applying what they were learning. Despite all their Bible intake, their prayer life wasn't strong, they weren't influencing lost people with the gospel, and their family life was strained. If we will begin to discipline ourselves to determine at least one specific response to the text before walking away from it, we will much more rapidly grow in grace. Without this kind of application, we aren't doers of God's Word.

MORE APPLICATION

Will you begin a plan of memorizing God's Word? If you've been a Christian for very long, you probably have already memorized much more Scripture than you realize. One of the verses you may know is Philippians 4:13: "I can do all things through him who strengthens me." Do you believe this verse is true? Do you believe that the "all" mentioned there includes Scripture memory? Since you *can* do it, will you do it? When will you begin?

Will you cultivate the Discipline of meditating on God's Word? Occasional Godward thoughts are not meditation. "A man may think on God every day," said William Bridge, "and meditate on God no day."[18] God calls us through the Scriptures to develop the practice of dwelling on Him in our thoughts.

By now I'm sure you realize that cultivating the Discipline of meditation involves a commitment of time. Bridge, one of the older but best-ever evangelical writers on meditation, anticipated this problem of making time for meditation:

> Oh, saith one, I would think on God, and I would meditate on God with all my heart, but meditation work is a work of time, it will cost time, and I have no time; my hands are so full of business, and so full of employment, I have no time for this work. Meditation is not a transient thought, but it is a work of time, and will ask time, and I have no time. Mark therefore what David saith in Psalm [119], "Lord incline my heart unto thy testimonies," how so? "Turn away mine eyes from beholding vanity." The way to have one's heart inclined to the testimonies of God, is to turn away one's eyes from these outward vanities. Would you therefore meditate on God and the things of God, then take heed that your hearts, and your hands, be not too full of the world and the employments thereof. . . .
>
> Friends, there is an art, and a divine skill of meditation,

which none can teach but God alone. Would you have it, go then to God, and beg of God these things.[19]

Here's the question we naturally tend to ask at this point: "Will the Discipline of meditation be worth this commitment of my time?" I cannot answer better than Bridge:

It is a help to knowledge, thereby your knowledge is raised. Thereby your memory is strengthened. Thereby your hearts are warmed. Thereby you will be freed from sinful thoughts. Thereby your hearts will be tuned to every duty. Thereby you will grow in grace. Thereby you will fill up all the chinks and crevices of your lives, and know how to spend your spare time, and improve that for God. Thereby you will draw good out of evil. And thereby you will converse with God, have communion with God, and enjoy God. And I pray, is not here profit enough to sweeten the voyage of your thoughts in meditation.[20]

When you consider what the Scriptures say about meditation, and when you weigh the testimonies of some of the godliest men and women of Christian history, the importance and value of Christian meditation for progress in Christian growth is undeniable.

Ponder one more quotation on the subject. It presents a challenge about meditation from Richard Baxter, the most practical of all Puritan writers. I join him in making this challenge to you regarding the cultivation of the Discipline of meditation:

If, by this means, thou dost not find an increase of all thy graces, and dost not grow beyond the stature of common Christians, and art not made more serviceable in thy place, and more precious in the eyes of all discerning persons; if thy soul enjoy not more communion with God, and thy life be not fuller of comfort, and hast it not readier by thee at a dying hour: then cast away these directions, and exclaim against me for ever as a deceiver.[21]

Will you prove yourself an "applier" of the Word? You have read many verses from the Word of God in this chapter. What will you do in response to these passages of Scripture?

Most of us would consider ourselves to be doers of the Word and not merely hearers. But "prove it," as one widely respected translation of the Bible (NASB) renders the beginning of James 1:22—"Prove yourselves doers of the word." How will you prove that you are a doer of the Word of God as it's been presented to you here?

The Discipline of Bible intake—especially the Discipline of applying God's Word—will often be difficult, and for many reasons, not the least of which is spiritual opposition. J. I. Packer makes that sobering point:

> If I were the devil, one of my first aims would be to stop
> folk from digging into the Bible. Knowing that it is the
> Word of God, teaching men to know and love and serve
> the God of the Word, I should do all I could to surround it
> with the spiritual equivalent of pits, thorn hedges, and man
> traps, to frighten people off. . . . At all costs I should want
> to keep them from using their minds in a disciplined way
> to get the measure of its message.[22]

Despite the difficulty and spiritual opposition, are you willing, at all costs, to begin using your mind "in a disciplined way" to feed on the Word of God "for the purpose of godliness"?

CHAPTER 4

PRAYER . . .
FOR THE PURPOSE OF GODLINESS

We Protestants are an undisciplined people.
Therein lies the reason for much of the dearth of spiritual
insights and serious lack of moral power.

ALBERT EDWARD DAY

The largest radio receiver on earth is in New Mexico. Pilots call it "the mushroom patch." Its real name is the Karl G. Jansky Very Large Array. The "VLA" is a series of twenty-seven huge satellite disks on thirty-eight miles of railways. Together the dishes mimic a single telescope the size of Washington, DC. Astronomers come from all over the world to analyze the optical images of the heavens composed by the VLA from the radio signals it receives from space. Why is such a giant apparatus needed? Because the radio waves, often emitted from sources millions of light-years away, are very faint. The total energy of all radio waves ever recorded barely equals the force of a single snowflake hitting the ground.

What great lengths people will go to in search of a faint message from space even as God has spoken so clearly through His Son and His Word! Straining through the eyes of telescopes and the electronic ears of the VLA, they search the infinite darkness for a possible word from somewhere in the universe. And all the while, "we have the prophetic word more fully confirmed, to which you will do well to pay attention as to a lamp shining in a dark place, until the day dawns and the morning star rises in your hearts" (2 Peter 1:19).

But God not only has spoken clearly and powerfully to us through Christ and the Scriptures, He also has a Very Large Ear continuously open to us. He will hear every prayer of His children, even when our prayers are weaker than a snowflake. That's why, of all the Spiritual Disciplines, prayer is second only to the intake of God's Word in importance.

Despite the penultimate importance of prayer, however, statistical surveys and experience seem to agree that a large percentage of professing Christians spend little time in sustained prayer. While they may offer a sentence of prayer here and there throughout their day, they rarely spend more than a very few minutes—if that— alone in conversation with God.

It's very easy to make people feel guilty about failure in prayer, and that's not the intent of this chapter. But we must come to grips with the fact that to be like Jesus we must pray.

PRAYER IS EXPECTED

I realize that to say prayer is expected of us may make the children of a nonconformist, anti-authoritarian age bristle a bit. Those who have been brought under the authority of Christ and the Bible, however, know that the will of God is for us to pray. But we also believe that His will is good.

Jesus Expects Us to Pray

Don't think of prayer as an impersonal requirement. Realize that it is a person, the Lord Jesus Christ, with all authority and with all love, who expects us to pray. These excerpts from His words show that He Himself expects us to pray:

- Matthew 6:5, "And when you pray . . ."
- Matthew 6:6, "But when you pray . . ."

- Matthew 6:7, "And when you pray . . ."
- Matthew 6:9, "Pray then like this: . . ."
- Luke 11:9, "And I tell you, ask . . . ; seek . . . ; knock."
- Luke 18:1, "And he told them a parable to the effect that they ought always to pray."

Suppose Jesus appeared to you personally, much as He did to the apostle John on the Isle of Patmos in Revelation 1, and said that He expected you to pray. Wouldn't you become more faithful in prayer, knowing specifically that Jesus expected that of you? Well, the words of Jesus quoted above are as much His will for you as if He spoke your name and said them to you face-to-face.

God's Word Makes It Clear

In addition to the words of Jesus, the unmistakable expectation of God from the rest of the New Testament is that we pray.

Colossians 4:2, "Continue steadfastly in prayer." People who "continue steadfastly in prayer" have devoted themselves to pursuing a Christlike life where prayer is an ongoing priority. When you make something a priority, when you sacrifice for it, when you give time to it, you know you are devoted to it. God expects Christians to be devoted to prayer.

First Thessalonians 5:17, "Pray without ceasing." While "continue steadfastly in prayer" emphasizes prayer as an activity, "pray without ceasing" reminds us that prayer is also a relationship. Prayer is in one sense an expression of a Christian's unbroken relationship with the Father.

This verse, then, doesn't mean that we should do nothing but pray, for the Bible expects many other things of us besides prayer, including times of rest when we could not consciously pray. But it does mean that if talking with and thinking of God can't be in the forefront of your mind, it should always be just to the side and ready to take the place of what you are concentrating on. You might think of praying without ceasing as communicating with God on

one line while also taking calls on another. Even while you are talking on the other line, you never lose your awareness of the need
to return your attention to the Lord. So praying without ceasing
means you never really stop conversing with God; you simply have
frequent interruptions.

I could have chosen other New Covenant passages indicating
that God expects us to pray, but these two are especially significant
because they are direct commands. This means too little time, too
many responsibilities, too many kids, too much work, too little desire, too little experience, and so on are not excuses that exempt us
from the expectation to pray. God gives us seasons of life where
priorities change as well as the time available for them;[1] nevertheless, in every season God expects every Christian to be devoted to
prayer and to pray without ceasing.

A praying man as well as reformer of the church, Martin Luther
expressed God's expectation of prayer this way: "As it is the business of tailors to make clothes and of cobblers to mend shoes, so it
is the business of Christians to pray."[2]

But we must see the expectation to pray not only as a divine
summons, but also as a royal invitation. As the writer of Hebrews
told us, "Let us then with confidence draw near to the throne of
grace, that we may receive mercy and find grace to help in time of
need" (4:16). We can be prayer pessimists and see the expectation
to pray merely as obligation, or we can be optimists who view the
command to pray as an opportunity to receive the mercy and grace
of God.

My wife, Caffy, expects me to call her when I travel. But that expectation is an expectation of love. She requires that I call because
she wants to hear from me. God's expectation that we pray is like
that. His command to pray is a command of love. In His love He
desires to communicate with us and to bless us.

God also expects us to pray just as a general expects to hear
from his soldiers in the battle. One writer reminds us that "prayer is
a walkie-talkie for warfare, not a domestic intercom for increasing

our conveniences."[3] God expects us to use the walkie-talkie of prayer because that is the means He has ordained not only for godliness, but also for the spiritual warfare between His kingdom and the kingdom of His Enemy. To abandon prayer is to fight the battle with our own resources at best, and to lose interest in the battle at worst.

And let's not forget that this expectation to pray is a gospel expectation. In other words, prayer is not so much a duty as a privilege, and not so much a privilege as it is an expression of life. We expect children to communicate—even if all they can do is cry—because they are alive. So God expects His children to communicate because they have been given eternal life and "have received the Spirit of adoption as sons, by whom we cry, 'Abba! Father!'" (Romans 8:15). The apostle Paul reiterated this in Galatians 4:6: "And because you are sons, God has sent the Spirit of his Son into our hearts, crying, 'Abba! Father!'" The children of God, impelled by the impulses of the Holy Spirit, want to talk with their heavenly Father.

Moreover, we know this: Jesus prayed. Luke told us, "But he would withdraw to desolate places and pray" (Luke 5:16). If Jesus needed to pray, how much more do we need to pray? Prayer is expected of us because we need it. We will not be like Jesus without it.

Why, then, do so many believers confess that they do not pray as they should? Sometimes the problem is primarily a lack of discipline: Prayer is never planned; time is never allotted just for praying. While lip service is given to the priority of prayer, in reality it always seems to get crowded out by things more urgent.

Often we do not pray because we doubt that anything will actually happen if we pray. Of course, we don't admit this publicly. But if we felt certain of visible results within sixty seconds of every prayer, there would be holes in the knees of every pair of Christian-owned pants in the world. Obviously the Bible never promises this, even though God does promise to answer prayer. Since prayer involves communication in the spiritual realm, many prayers are answered in ways that cannot be seen in the material realm. Many prayers are answered in ways different from what we asked. For a variety of reasons, after we open our eyes we do not always see tangible evidence of our prayers. When we are not vigilant, this tempts us to doubt the power of God through prayer.

A lack of sensing the nearness of God may also discourage prayer. There are those wonderful moments when the Lord seems so near that we almost expect to hear an audible voice. No one needs to be prodded to pray in such times of precious intimacy with God. Usually, though, we don't feel like that. In fact, sometimes we can't sense the presence of God at all. While it's true that our praying (as well as all aspects of our Christian living) should be governed by the truth of Scripture rather than our feelings, nevertheless the frailty of our emotions frequently erodes our desire to pray. When the desire to pray is weakened, we can find many other things to do besides pray.

When there is little awareness of real need, there is little real prayer. Some circumstances drive us to our knees. But there are periods when life seems quite manageable. Although Jesus said, "Apart from me you can do nothing" (John 15:5), this truth hits home more forcefully at some times than at others. In pride and self-sufficiency we may live for days as though prayer were needed only when something comes along that's too big for us to handle on our own. Until we see the danger and foolishness of this attitude, God's expectation for us to pray may seem irrelevant.

When our awareness of the greatness of God and the gospel is dim, our prayer lives will be small. The less we think of the nature and character of God, and the less we are reminded of what Jesus Christ did for us on the cross, the less we want to pray. While driving today I heard a radio program where the guest, an astrophysicist, spoke of the billions of galaxies in the universe. In only a moment of meditation on this I automatically shifted into praise and prayer. Why? I became freshly aware of how great God really is. And when I think of what Christ has saved me from, when I recall the shame He endured so willingly for my sake, when I remember all that salvation means, prayer is not hard. When this kind of thinking is infrequent, meaningful prayer will also be infrequent.

PRAYER IS LEARNED

Another reason many Christians pray so little is because they haven't learned about prayer. If you are discouraged by the command to pray because you feel like you don't know how to pray well, the fact that prayer is learned should give you hope. That means that it's okay to start the Christian life with little knowledge or experience of prayer. No matter how weak or strong your prayer life is right now, you can learn to grow even stronger.

There is a sense in which prayer needs to be taught to a child of God no more than a baby needs to be taught to cry. But crying for basic needs is minimal communication, and we must soon grow beyond that infancy. The Bible says we must pray for the glory of God, in His will, in faith, in the name of Jesus, with persistence, and more. A child of God gradually learns to pray like this in the same way that a growing child learns to talk. To pray as expected, to pray as a maturing Christian, and to pray effectively, we must say with the disciples in Luke 11:1, "Lord, teach us to pray."

By Praying

If you've ever learned a foreign language, you know that you learn it best when you actually have to speak it. The same is true with the "foreign language" of prayer. There are many good resources for learning how to pray, but the best way to learn how to pray is to pray.

Andrew Murray,[4] South African minister and author of *With Christ in the School of Prayer*, wrote, "Reading a book about prayer, listening to lectures and talking about it is very good, but it won't teach you to pray. You get nothing without exercise, without practice. I might listen for a year to a professor of music playing the most beautiful music, but that won't teach me to play an instrument."[5]

The Holy Spirit teaches praying people how to pray better. That's one of the applications of John 16:13 where Jesus said, "When the

Spirit of truth comes, he will guide you into all the truth." Just as a plane is guided more easily when it's airborne than when it's on the ground with its engines off, so the Holy Spirit guides us in prayer better when we are airborne in prayer than when we are not.

By Meditating on Scripture

This is one of the most compelling concepts on prayer I've ever learned, and it reinforces the importance and value of meditation presented in the previous chapter. Here's the simple, but extraordinarily powerful truth: Meditation is the missing link between Bible intake and prayer. Too often disjointed, the two should be united. Typically, we read the Bible, close it, and then try to shift gears into prayer. But many times it seems as if the gears between the two won't mesh. In fact, after some forward progress during our time in the Word, shifting to prayer sometimes feels like suddenly slipping back into neutral or even reverse. Instead there should be a smooth, almost unnoticeable transition between Scripture input and prayer output so that we move even closer to God in those moments. This happens when we insert the link of meditation in between.

At least two Scriptures teach this by example. David prayed in Psalm 5:1, "Give ear to my words, O LORD; consider my groaning." The Hebrew word rendered as "groaning" may also be translated "meditation." In fact, this same word is used with that meaning in another passage, Psalm 19:14: "Let the words of my mouth and the meditation of my heart be acceptable in your sight, O LORD, my rock and my redeemer." Notice that both verses are prayers, pleas to God that consisted of David's "words" (as we'd expect in prayer), but they also involve "meditation." In each case meditation was a catalyst that catapulted David from considering the truth of God into talking with God. In 5:1 he had been meditating and then David asked the Lord to give ear to and to consider his meditation. In Psalm 19 we find one of the best-known statements about Scripture written anywhere, beginning with the famous words of verse 7, "The law of the LORD is perfect, reviving the soul." This section continues through verse 11, and David formed his prayer in verse 14 as a result of these words and his meditation.

The process works like this: After the input of a passage of Scripture, meditation allows us to take what God has said and think deeply on it, digest it, and then speak to God about it in meaningful prayer. As a result, we pray about what we've encountered in the Bible, now personalized through meditation. And not only do we have something substantial to say in prayer, as well as the confidence that we are praying God's thoughts to Him, but we transition smoothly into prayer and with more passion for what we're praying about.

When enlivened by meditation, prayer becomes more like a real conversation with a real person—which is exactly what prayer is. God speaks to us in His Word, and we speak to Him in response to what He has said.[6] Then, when we've finished, we listen to the other person speak again—just like in a real conversation—meaning that we look to the next words God has spoken in His Word. And so the process continues, each part guided by the ever-fresh words of Scripture and without the repetition of worn phrases from previous prayers, until we must close that time of prayer.[7]

Those who seem to have known this secret best were the English Puritans who lived from about 1550 to 1700. Permit me to quote from several Puritan writers, not only to show how remarkably common this now uncommon connection between meditation and prayer was among them, but also to secure its truth firmly into your prayer life. There's much to hold on to in this collection of well-driven nails.

Richard Baxter, pastor and author of the still-printed classic *The Reformed Pastor*, wrote,

> In our meditations, to intermix soliloquy and prayer; some-
> times speaking to our own hearts, and sometimes to God,
> is, I apprehend, the highest step we can advance to in this
> heavenly work. Nor should we imagine it will be as well to

take up with prayer alone, and lay aside meditation; for they are distinct duties, and must both of them be performed. We need the one as well as the other, and therefore we shall wrong ourselves by neglecting either. Besides, the mixture of them, like music, will be more engaging; as the one serves to put life into the other. And our speaking to ourselves in meditation, should go before our speaking to God in prayer.[8]

John Owen, chaplain to Oliver Cromwell and the most influential theologian of the Puritans, said, "Pray as you think. Consciously embrace with your heart every gleam of light and truth that comes to your mind. Thank God for and pray about everything that strikes you powerfully."[9]

Puritan pastor and Bible commentator Matthew Henry remarked about Psalm 19:14, "David's prayers were not his words only, but his meditations; as meditation is the best preparation for prayer, so prayer is the best issue of meditation. Meditation and prayer go together."[10]

One of the most prolific Puritan preacher-writers was Thomas Manton. In a message on Isaac's meditation in the field (see Genesis 24:63), he pointed directly to meditation as the link between Bible intake and prayer. He wrote,

Meditation is a middle sort of duty between the word and prayer, and hath respect to both. The word feedeth meditation, and meditation feedeth prayer. These duties must always go hand in hand; meditation must follow hearing and precede prayer. To hear and not to meditate is unfruitful. We may hear and hear, but it is like putting a thing into a bag with holes. . . . It is rashness to pray and not to meditate. What we take in by the word we digest by meditation and let out by prayer. These three duties must be ordered that one may not jostle out the other. Men are barren, dry, and sapless in their prayers for want of exercising themselves in holy thoughts.[11]

William Bates, a Puritan minister of "distinguished talents and piety,"[12] said, "What is the reason that our desires like an arrow shot by a weak bow do not reach the mark? but only this, we do not meditate before prayer. . . . The great reason why our prayers are ineffectual, is because we do not meditate before them."[13]

Among the best of the practical Puritan writings came from the pen of William Bridge. On meditation he asserted the following:

> As it is the sister of reading, so it is the mother of prayer. Though a man's heart be much indisposed to prayer, yet, if he can but fall into a meditation of God, and the things of God, his heart will soon come off to prayer. . . . Begin with reading or hearing. Go on with meditation; end in prayer. . . . Reading without meditation is unfruitful; meditation without reading is hurtful; to meditate and to read without prayer upon both, is without blessing.[14]

A modern British writer, Peter Toon, in his book *From Mind to Heart*, summarized the teaching of the Puritans on these things:

> To read the Bible and not to meditate was seen as an unfruitful exercise: better to read one chapter and meditate afterward than to read several chapters and not to meditate. Likewise to meditate and not to pray was like preparing to run a race and never leaving the starting line. The three duties of reading Scripture, meditation, and prayer belonged together, and though each could be done occasionally on its own, as formal duties to God they were best done together.[15]

About two hundred years after the Puritans came the man recognized as one of the most God-anointed men of prayer ever seen by the world, George Müller. During the last two-thirds of the nineteenth century he operated an orphanage in Bristol, England. Solely on prayer and faith, without advertising his need or entering into debt, he fed, clothed, housed, and educated more than ten thousand orphans—as many as two thousand at a time—and supported mission work throughout the world. Hundreds of millions of dollars (in today's value) came through his hands unsolicited, and his tens of thousands of recorded answers to prayer are legendary.

Anyone who has heard the story of George Müller ponders the secret of his effectiveness in prayer. Although some argue for one thing as Müller's "secret" and others argue for another, I believe we must ultimately attribute his unusually successful prayer life to the sovereignty of God. But if we look for something transferable from his life to ours, my vote goes for something I've never heard credited as his "secret."

In the spring of 1841, George Müller made a discovery regarding the relationship between meditation and prayer that transformed his spiritual life. He described his new insight this way:

> Before this time my practice had been, at least for ten years previously, as an habitual thing, to give myself to prayer after having dressed in the morning. Now, I saw that the most important thing was to give myself to the reading of God's Word, *and to meditation on it*, that thus my heart might be comforted, encouraged, warned, reproved, instructed; and that thus, by means of the Word of God, *whilst meditating on it*, my heart might be brought into experimental[16] communion with the Lord.
>
> I began therefore to *meditate* on the New Testament from the beginning, early in the morning. *The first thing I did*, after having asked in a few words of the Lord's blessing upon His precious Word, *was to begin to meditate on the Word of God*, searching as it were into every verse to get blessing out of it; not for the sake of the public ministry of the Word, not for the sake of preaching on what I had meditated upon, but for the sake of obtaining food for my own soul.
>
> The result I have found to be almost invariably this, that

after a few minutes my soul has been led to confession, or
to thanksgiving, or to intercession, or to supplication; so
that, though I did not, as it were, give myself to prayer, *but
to meditation*, yet it turned almost immediately more or
less to prayer. When thus I have been for a while making
confession or intercession or supplication, or have given
thanks, I go on to the next words or verse, turning all,
as I go on, into prayer for myself or others, as the Word
may lead to it, but still continually keeping before me that
food for my own soul is the object of my *meditation. The
result of this is that there is always a good deal of confession,
thanksgiving, supplication, or intercession mingled with
my meditation*, and that my inner man almost invariably
is even sensibly nourished and strengthened, and that by
breakfast time, with rare exceptions, I am in a peaceful if
not happy state of heart.

The difference, then, between my former practice and
my present one is this: formerly, when I rose, I began to
pray as soon as possible, and generally spent all my time
till breakfast in prayer, or almost all the time. At all events
I almost invariably began with prayer. . . . But what was the
result? I often spent a quarter of an hour, or half an hour, or
even an hour on my knees before being conscious to myself
of having derived comfort, encouragement, humbling of
soul, etc.; and often, after having suffered much from wandering of mind for the first ten minutes, or quarter of an
hour, or even half an hour, I only then really began to pray.

I scarcely ever suffer now in this way. For my heart being
nourished by the truth, being brought into experimental
fellowship with God, I speak to my Father and to my Friend
(vile though I am, and unworthy of it) about the things that
He has brought before me in His precious Word. It often
now astonishes me that I did not sooner see this point. . . .
And yet now, since God has taught me this point, it is as

plain to me as anything that the first thing the child of God has to do morning by morning is to obtain food for his inner man.

Now what is food for the inner man? *Not prayer, but the Word of God; and here again, not the simple reading of the Word of God, so that it only passes through our minds, just as water passes through a pipe, but considering what we read, pondering over it and applying it to our hearts.*

When we pray we speak to God. Now prayer, in order to be continued for any length of time in any other than a formal manner, requires, generally speaking, a measure of strength or godly desire, and the season therefore when this exercise of the soul can be most effectually performed is after the inner man has been nourished *by meditation on the Word of God,* where we find our Father speaking to us, to encourage us, to comfort us, to instruct us, to humble us, to reprove us. We may therefore profitably *meditate* with God's blessing though we are ever so weak spiritually; nay, the weaker we are, the more we need *meditation* for the strengthening of our inner man. Thus there is far less to be feared from wandering of mind than if we give ourselves to prayer without having had time previously for *meditation.*

I dwell so particularly on this point because of the immense spiritual profit and refreshment I am conscious of having derived from it myself, and I affectionately and solemnly beseech all my fellow believers to ponder this matter. By the blessing of God, I ascribe to this mode the help and strength which I have had from God to pass in peace through deeper trials, in various ways, than I have ever had before; and having now above fourteen years tried this way, I can most fully, in the fear of God, commend it.[17]

How do we learn to pray? How do we learn to pray like David, the Puritans, and George Müller? We learn to pray by meditating on Scripture, for meditation is the missing link between Bible intake and prayer.

By Praying with Others

The disciples learned to pray, not only by hearing Jesus teach about prayer, but also by being with Him when He prayed. Let's not forget that the words "Lord, teach us to pray" didn't just come as a random idea. This request followed a time when the disciples accompanied Jesus in prayer (see Luke 11:1). In a similar way, we can learn to pray by praying with other people who can model true prayer for us.

And I don't mean just picking up new words and phrases to use in prayer. As with all learning by example, we can acquire some bad habits as well as good ones. I've heard people who never seem to pray an original prayer. Every time they pray they say the same things. It's obvious they merely mouth shiny phrases picked like fruit from the prayers of others here and there throughout the years. But Jesus said, "Do not heap up empty phrases" when praying (Matthew 6:7). Prayers piled with heaps of empty phrases rarely seem heartfelt. God is not the audience being addressed. In reality, simply fulfilling a function or impressing others in the room directs the prayer.

Other believers can teach us much when we pray with them. But we pray with them to learn principles of prayer, not phrases for prayer. One fellow Christian may model giving biblical reasons to the Lord why a prayer should be answered. Another might show us by example how to pray through passages of Scripture. By praying with a faithful intercessor we might learn how to pray for missions. Praying regularly with others can be one of the most enriching adventures of your Christian life. Many of the great movements of God can be traced to a small group of people He called together to begin praying.

By Reading about Prayer

Reading about prayer instead of praying simply will not do. But reading about prayer in addition to praying enriches your education in prayer. "Iron sharpens iron," says Proverbs 27:17, "and one man sharpens another." Read the lessons learned by veterans of the trenches of prayer and let them sharpen your weapons of the warfare of prayer. "Whoever walks with the wise becomes wise," Proverbs 13:20 reminds us. Reading the books of wise men and women of prayer gives us the privilege of "walking" with them and learning the insights God gave them on how to pray.

We've learned from experience how others can see things in a passage of Scripture we cannot, or how they can explain a familiar doctrine in a fresh way that deepens our understanding of it. In the same way, reading what others have learned about prayer from their study of Scripture and their pilgrimage in grace can be God's instrument of teaching us what we'd otherwise never learn on our own. Who hasn't learned about praying in faith after reading of George Müller's prayer life, or been motivated to pray after reading David Brainerd's life and diary? Hopefully the reading of this very chapter on the Discipline of prayer convinces you that you can learn to pray by reading about prayer.

Let me add a word of encouragement. No matter how difficult prayer seems for you now, if you will persevere in learning how to pray you can always enjoy the hope of an even stronger and more fruitful prayer life ahead of you.

PRAYER IS ANSWERED

I love how David addressed the Lord in Psalm 65:2: "O you who hear prayer."

Perhaps no principle of prayer is more taken for granted than this one—that prayer is answered. Try to read this promise of Jesus as though for the first time: "Ask, and it will be given to you; seek, and you will find; knock, and it will be opened to you. For everyone who asks receives, and the one who seeks finds, and to the one who knocks it will be opened" (Matthew 7:7-8).

Andrew Murray comments boldly, but I think rightly, on Christ's pledge:

"Ask and you shall receive; everyone that asks, receives."
This is the fixed eternal law of the kingdom: if you ask and
receive not, it must be because there is something amiss
or wanting in the prayer. Hold on; let the Word and Spirit
teach you to pray aright, but do not let go the confidence
He seeks to waken: Everyone who asks receives. . . . Let
every learner in the school of Christ therefore take the
Master's word in all simplicity. . . . Let us beware of weak-
ening the Word with our human wisdom.[18]

Because God answers prayer, when we "ask and receive not"
we must consider the possibility that there is "something amiss
or wanting" in our prayer. Perhaps God has indeed answered, but
not in an obvious way. And possibly our prayers show nothing
amiss, but we don't yet see the answer only because God intends
for us to persevere in praying about the matter awhile longer. Still,
we must learn to examine our prayers. Are we asking for things
outside the will of God or that would not glorify Him? Are we
praying with selfish motives? Are we failing to deal with the kind
of blatant sin that causes God to put all our prayers on hold?
Despite what we see in response to our prayers, however, let's not
become so accustomed to our shortcomings in prayer and to the
perception of asking without receiving that our faith in the force
of Jesus' promise is diminished. Prayer *is* answered.

My wife, Caffy, ministers as an artist and freelance illustrator
from a studio in our home. Although she's produced hundreds of
illustrations for a variety of Christian organizations, all her jobs
are on an occasional basis. Frequently we pray for the Lord to
open doors of opportunity for her artwork. Because she had nothing on the drawing board, I recently said to her that we should
start praying for some new projects. Before lunch the very next
morning Caffy called me and said, "Please stop praying for the
Lord to provide art work for me! I've had so many callers commissioning work this morning that it's going to take months to

get it all done!" She never had so much work come her way so quickly. There were any number of things I had been praying for (regarding not just myself, but my church and others) that the Lord could have chosen to answer. I don't know why it pleased Him to choose that particular request. Were these multiple opportunities really answers to prayer or just a collection of providential coincidences? Only God knows for sure. But I agree with the man who said, "If it is coincidence, I sure have a lot more coincidences when I pray than when I don't."

God doesn't mock us with His promises to answer prayer. C. H. Spurgeon said,

> I cannot imagine any one of you tantalizing your child by exciting in him a desire that you did not intend to gratify. It were a very ungenerous thing to offer alms to the poor, and then when they hold out their hand for it, to mock their poverty with a denial. It were a cruel addition to the miseries of the sick if they were taken to the hospital and there left to die untended and uncared for. Where God leads you to pray, He means you to receive.[19]

By the Scriptures about prayer and by His Spirit, God does lead His people to pray. He does not lead us to pray in order to frustrate us by slamming heaven's door in our face. Let's discipline ourselves to pray and to learn about prayer so that we may be more like Jesus in experiencing the joy of answered prayer.

MORE APPLICATION

Because prayer is expected, will you pray? I challenge you with this directly because I think we need to make some conscious decisions about our prayer lives. It's time for general intentions about prayer to become specific plans. One pastor who agrees writes the following:

> Unless I'm badly mistaken, one of the main reasons so many of God's children don't have a significant prayer life

is not so much that we don't want to, but that we don't plan to. If you want to take a four-week vacation, you don't just get up one summer morning and say, "Hey, let's go today!" You won't have anything ready. You won't know where to go. Nothing has been planned. But that is how many of us treat prayer. We get up day after day and realize that significant times of prayer should be a part of our life, but nothing's ever ready. We don't know where to go. Nothing has been planned. No time. No place. No procedure. And we all know that the opposite of planning is not a wonderful flow of deep, spontaneous experiences in prayer. The opposite of planning is the rut. If you don't plan a vacation you will probably stay home and watch TV. The natural, unplanned flow of spiritual life sinks to the lowest ebb of vitality. There is a race to be run and a fight to be fought. If you want renewal in your life of prayer you must plan to see it.[20]

For the purpose of godliness, will you pray? Today? Will you plan to pray tomorrow? The days after that?

Since prayer is learned, will you learn to pray? Learning more about prayer often helps improve your prayer life. But just as with the practice of prayer, learning about prayer also takes some planning. Will you learn to pray by linking your Bible reading to prayer via meditation? Do you have a plan for praying with others? Are you willing to learn more about prayer by reading? What will you read? Books on the subject, as well as biographies of great prayer warriors, abound. In addition to considering some of the sources quoted in this chapter, consult your pastor or prayerful Christian friend for recommendations. Now, when will you start?

Since prayer is answered, will you persistently pray? Remember that the words *ask*, *seek*, and *knock* in Matthew 7:7-8 in the original Greek language of the text are in the present, continuous tense. That means we often must pray persistently before the answers come. Starting in Luke 18:1, Jesus told an entire parable "to the effect that they ought always to pray and not lose heart." Sometimes a failure to persist in prayer betrays a lack of seriousness about our request in the first place. At other times God wants us to persist in prayer in order to strengthen our faith in Him. Faith would never grow if all prayers were answered immediately. Persistent prayer tends to develop deeper gratitude as well. As the joy of a baby's birth is greater because of the months of anticipation, so is the joy of an answer after long and persistent praying. And as much as a generation that measures time in nanoseconds hates to admit its need for it, God crafts Christlike patience in us when He requires persistence in prayer.

George Müller observed,

> The great fault of the children of God is, they do not continue in prayer; they do not go on praying; they do not persevere. If they desire anything for God's glory, they should pray until they get it. Oh, how good, and kind, and gracious, and condescending is the One with Whom we have to do! He has given me, unworthy as I am, immeasurably above all I had asked or thought![21]

Do we hear such testimonies so infrequently because so few persevere in prayer? A persevering pursuit of God in prayer promises to reward any amount of frustration and discouragement with prayer. Don't let the Enemy tempt you to a silent cynicism about God's willingness and ability to answer. Let a love for God cause you to prevail in prayer to Him who loves you, even when His judgments are unsearchable and His ways inscrutable (see Romans 11:33).

Let's pause and get our bearings. Although God hears everything, including every prayer and every thought, He does not hear our prayers with a view to answering them (see Isaiah 59:2) until we repent and come to Him through faith in Jesus Christ and what He has done (see John 14:6). Instead of relying on our sincerity or spirituality to turn the ear of God, we trust in the righteousness of Christ. The gospel teaches us that God welcomes us "in the Beloved" (Ephesians 1:6), and so we always come to our Father in the name of His Son, praying with the help of the Holy Spirit. Prayer must still remain a Discipline, for even with the God-given desire to pray it's easy to be distracted from habits of prayer by the crush of responsibilities. But thanks to the grace of God in the gospel, our prayers are always welcome.

Ultimately, though, this appeal to discipline ourselves to pray is "for the purpose of godliness." Where there is prayerfulness there is godliness. Typically picturesque, Spurgeon said it this way: "Even as the moon influences the tides of the sea, even so does prayer . . . influence the tides of godliness."[22]

Prayerful people become godly people, for prayerfulness with God cultivates godliness in all of life. My ministerial experience concurs with the words of J. C. Ryle: "What is the reason that some believers are so much brighter and holier than others? I believe the difference, in nineteen cases out of twenty, arises from different habits about private prayer. I believe that those who are not eminently holy pray *little*, and those who are eminently holy pray *much*."[23]

Would you be like Christ? Then do as He did—discipline yourself to be a person of prayer.

CHAPTER 5

WORSHIP . . .
FOR THE PURPOSE OF GODLINESS

*True spiritual self-discipline holds believers in bounds but
never in bonds; its effect is to enlarge, expand and liberate.*

D. G. KEHL

One of the saddest experiences of my childhood happened on my
tenth birthday. Invitations to the celebration were mailed days in
advance to eight friends. It would be my best birthday ever. They
all came to my house right after school. We played football and
basketball outside until dark. My dad grilled hot dogs and ham-
burgers while my mother put the finishing touches on the birthday
cake. After we had eaten all the icing and ice cream and most of the
cake, it was time for the presents. Honestly, I can't recall even one
of the gifts today, but I do remember the great time I was having
with the guys who gave them. Since I had no brothers, the best
part of the whole event was just hanging out with the other boys.

The climax of this grand celebration was a gift from me to
them. Nothing was too good for my friends. Cost was immaterial.
I was going to pay their way to the most exciting event in our small
town—the high school basketball game. I can still see us spilling
out of my parents' station wagon with laughter on that cool evening

and running up to the gymnasium. Standing at the window, paying for nine 25-cent tickets and surrounded by my friends—it was one of those simple but golden moments in life. The picture in my mind was the perfect ending to a ten-year-old boy's perfect birthday. With four friends on one side and four on the other, I would sit in the middle while we munched popcorn, playfully punched each other, and cheered our high school heroes. As we went inside, I remember feeling happier than Jimmy Stewart in the closing scene of *It's a Wonderful Life*.

Then the golden moment was shattered. Once in the gym, all my friends scattered and I never saw them again the rest of the night. There was no "Thanks" for the fun, the food, or the tickets. Not even a "Happy birthday, but I'm going to sit with someone else." Without a word of gratitude or good-bye, they all left and didn't look back. So I spent the rest of my tenth birthday in the bleachers by myself, growing old alone. As I recall, it was a miserable ball game.

I tell that story, not to gain sympathy for a painful childhood memory, but because it reminds me of the way we often treat God in worship. Though we come to an event where He is the Guest of Honor, it is possible to give Him a routine gift, sing a few customary songs to Him, and then totally neglect Him while we focus on others and enjoy the performance of those in front of us. Like my ten-year-old friends, we may leave without any twinge of conscience, without any awareness of our insensitivity, convinced we have fulfilled an obligation well.

Jesus Himself reemphasized and obeyed the Old Testament command, "Worship the Lord your God" (see Matthew 4:10). It is the duty (and privilege) of all people to worship their Creator. "Oh come, let us worship and bow down," says Psalm 95:6, "let us kneel before the LORD, our Maker!" God clearly expects us to worship. It's our purpose! Godliness without the worship of God is unthinkable. But those who pursue godliness must realize that it is possible to worship God in vain. Jesus quoted another Old Testament passage to warn of worshiping God vainly: "This people honors me with their lips, but their heart is far from me; in vain do they worship me" (Matthew 15:8-9). Note that God called their activity "worship." And "this people" believed they were honoring God. But God rejected their worship as worship "in vain."

How can we worship God without worshiping Him in vain? How can we instead "offer to God acceptable worship" (Hebrews 12:28)? We must learn an essential part of pursuing Christlikeness—the Spiritual Discipline of biblical worship.

WORSHIP IS . . .
FOCUSING ON AND RESPONDING TO GOD

Worship is difficult to define well. Let's observe it first. In John 20:28, when the resurrected Jesus appeared to Thomas and showed him the scars in His hands and side, worship happened when Thomas said to Him, "My Lord and my God!" In Revelation 4:8, we read of four creatures around the throne who worship God day and night without ceasing and say, "Holy, holy, holy, is the Lord God Almighty, who was and is and is to come!" Then in verse 11 the twenty-four elders around the throne of God in heaven worship Him by casting their crowns at His feet, falling down before Him, and saying, "Worthy are you, our Lord and God, to receive glory and honor and power, for you created all things, and by your will they existed and were created." In the next chapter, thousands and thousands of angels, elders, and living creatures around the heavenly throne of Jesus Christ, the Lamb of God, cry out with a loud voice in worship, "Worthy is the Lamb who was slain, to receive power and wealth and wisdom and might and honor and glory and blessing!" (5:12). Immediately following comes worship from "every creature" saying, "To him who sits on the throne and to the Lamb be blessing and honor and glory and might forever and ever!" (5:13).

Now let's describe what we've seen. The word *worship* descends from the Saxon word *weorthscype*, which later became *worthship*. To worship God means to ascribe the proper worth to God, to magnify His worthiness of praise, or better, to approach and address God as He is worthy. As the holy and almighty God, the Creator and Sustainer of the universe, the Sovereign Judge to whom we must give an account, He is worthy of all the worth and honor we can give Him and then infinitely more. Notice, for instance, how those around the throne of God in Revelation 4:11 and 5:12 addressed God as "worthy" of so many things.

The more we focus on God, the more we understand and appreciate His infinite worth. As we understand and appreciate this, we can't help but respond to Him. Just as an indescribable sunset or a breathtaking mountaintop vista evokes a spontaneous response, so we cannot encounter the worthiness of God without the response of worship. If you could see God at this moment, you would so utterly understand His worthiness of worship that you would instinctively fall on your face and worship Him. That's why we read in Revelation that those around the throne who see Him fall on their faces in worship, and those creatures closest to Him are so astonished with His worthiness that throughout eternity they ceaselessly worship Him with the response of "Holy, holy, holy." So while I could nuance it at length, here's my simple definition: Worship is focusing on and responding to God.

But we are not yet in heaven to see the Lord this way and to focus on Him visually. So how does the invisible God reveal Himself to us here that we might focus on Him? First, He has revealed Himself in a general way through Creation (see Romans 1:20), thus the right response to the stunning sunset or the spectacular mountain view is worship of the Creator of such beauty and majesty. Second, and more specifically, God has flawlessly revealed Himself through His written Word, the Bible (see 2 Timothy 3:16; 2 Peter 1:20-21), and His incarnate Word, Jesus Christ (see John 1:1,14; Hebrews 1:1-2). In response we should seek God by means of Christ as revealed in the Bible. As we do so and the Holy Spirit opens the eyes of our understanding, we see God revealed in Scripture and respond with worship.

For example, we have just read in the Bible (see Revelation 4:8) that God is holy. As we meditate on this and begin to discover more of what it means for God to be holy, the Holy Spirit causes the desire to worship Him to overwhelm us. But exactly how do we discover more of what it means for God to be holy? The Bible, which is the most reliable and authoritative source on earth for information about the holiness of God, tells us. And to learn from the Bible more of what the holiness of God is like, among the places we look are the passages about Jesus, for the holy God is most clearly revealed in Jesus Christ, who is God in the flesh. If by means of meditation we will focus on the person and work of Christ as found in the Bible, we will understand more of the holy God, for Jesus "has made him known" (John 1:18). And to the degree we truly comprehend more of God, we will in turn respond to Him more in worship.

That's why all worship of God—public, family,[1] and private worship—should be based upon and include much of the Bible. The Bible reveals God to us so that we may focus on Him, and to the extent we focus on Him we will worship Him. So if there's little revelation of God, there is little focus on God. And if there is little focus on God, there is little worship of God. Conversely, much revelation of God fosters much focus on God, which in turn evokes much worship of God.

Bible reading and preaching are central in public worship because they are the clearest, most direct, most extensive presentations of God in the gathering. For the same reasons, Bible intake and meditation are the heart of private worship. In worship we should also sing biblically saturated songs[2] as both a musical declaration of God's truth and a biblical response (praise and thanksgiving) to the revelation of God. Prayer expresses in a biblical way our worshipful devotion to and dependence on God as He is revealed in Scripture; so does giving. God has ordained baptism and the Lord's Supper as elements of public worship, and in a visual way they, too, proclaim and remind us of divinely revealed truth.

All the elements of worship prescribed in Scripture help us to focus on God.

Since worship is focusing on and responding to God, regardless of what else we are doing we are not worshiping if we are not thinking about God. You may be listening to a biblically sound sermon, but if you aren't mindful of what it says about God or from God to you, you aren't worshiping. You may be singing "Holy, holy, holy," but if you aren't thinking about God while singing it, you are not worshiping. You may be listening to someone pray, but if you aren't praying with him or her and thinking of God, you aren't worshiping. In one sense we can say that all things done in obedience to the Lord, even everyday things at work and at home, are acts of worship. But these do not substitute for the directly focused, exclusive-of-any-other-activity, biblically based worship of God.

Worship often includes words and actions, but it goes beyond them to the focus of the mind and heart. Worship is the God-centered focus and response of the soul; it is being preoccupied with God. So no matter what you are saying or singing or doing at any moment, you are worshiping God only when He is the center of your attention. But whenever you do focus on the infinite worth of God, you will respond in worship as surely as the moon reflects the sun. This kind of worship is not in vain. Worship is also not in vain when . . .

WORSHIP IS . . . DONE IN SPIRIT AND TRUTH

The most profound passage on worship in the New Testament is John 4:23-24. There Jesus said, "But the hour is coming, and is now here, when the true worshipers will worship the Father in spirit and truth, for the Father is seeking such people to worship him. God is spirit, and those who worship him must worship in spirit and truth."

Before we can worship in spirit and truth we must have within us the One who is the "Spirit of truth" (John 14:17), that is, the Holy Spirit. He lives only within those who have come to Christ in repentance and faith. Without Him true worship will not happen. As 1 Corinthians 12:3 declares, "No one can say 'Jesus is Lord' except in the Holy Spirit." That doesn't mean a person cannot speak the words "Jesus is Lord" apart from the Holy Spirit, for anyone who can talk can utter the phrase. Rather, it means no one can say "Jesus is Lord" as a genuine confession of their worshipful submission to Christ apart from the regenerating power and indwelling presence of the Holy Spirit. He is the One who reveals God to us, who convicts us of our sin against God, and who makes Christ and His saving power irresistible. The Holy Spirit opens minds to the truth of Scripture and awakens hearts that were dead toward God. He causes souls that were cold in worship to flame with passion for Christ.

Having the Holy Spirit residing within does not guarantee that we always *will* worship in spirit and truth, but His presence does mean we *can*. To worship God in spirit involves worship from the inside out. It also necessitates sincerity in our acts of worship. No matter how spiritual the song you are singing, no matter how poetic the prayer you are praying, if it isn't sincere then it isn't worship; it's hypocrisy.

The balance to worshiping in spirit is to worship in truth. Worship in truth is worship according to the truth of Scripture. First, we worship God as He is revealed in the Bible, not as we might want Him to be. We worship Him according to the truth of who He says He is: a God of both mercy and justice, of love and wrath, who both welcomes into heaven and condemns into hell. Second, worship according to the truth of Scripture means to worship God in the ways to which He has given His approval in Scripture. In other words, we should do in the worship of God what God says in the Bible we should do in worship.[3]

Having made a case for worshiping God in response to the truth of Scripture, I want to move from that and say more about worshiping in spirit. Whether engaged in public, family, or private worship, realize that unless the heart is plugged in, there's no electricity for worship. One pastor and author put it bluntly: "Where feelings for God are dead, worship is dead."[4] Here's how he illustrated that:

> Worship is a way of gladly reflecting back to God the radiance of His worth. This cannot be done by mere acts of duty. It can be done only when spontaneous affections arise in the heart.
>
> Consider the analogy of a wedding anniversary. Mine is on December 21. Suppose on this day I bring home a dozen long-stemmed roses for Noël. When she meets me at the door I hold out the roses, and she says, "O Johnny, they're beautiful, thank you," and gives me a big hug. Then suppose I hold up my hand and say matter-of-factly, "Don't mention it; it's my duty."
>
> What happens? Is not the exercise of duty a noble thing? Do not we honor those we dutifully serve? Not much. Not if there's no heart in it. Dutiful roses are a contradiction in terms. If I am not moved by a spontaneous affection for her as a person, the roses do not honor her. In fact, they belittle her. They are a very thin covering for the fact that she does not have the worth or beauty in my eyes to kindle affection. All I can muster is a calculated expression of marital duty. . . .
>
> The real duty of worship is not the outward duty to say or do the liturgy. It is the inward duty, the command— "Delight yourself in the Lord!" (Psalm 37:4). . . .
>
> The reason this is the real duty of worship is that this honors God, while the empty performance of ritual does not. If I take my wife out for the evening on our anniversary and she asks me, "Why do you do this?" the answer that honors her most is, "Because nothing makes me happier tonight than to be with you."
>
> "It's my duty," is a dishonor to her.
>
> "It's my joy," is an honor.

How shall we honor God in worship? By saying, "It's my duty"? Or by saying, "It's my joy"?[5]

So we must worship in both spirit and truth, with both heart and head, with both emotion and thought. If we worship with too much emphasis on spirit we will be mushy and weak on the truth, worshiping mainly according to feelings. That can lead anywhere from a lazy, unthinking tolerance of anything in worship at one extreme to uncontrollable spiritual wildfire on the other. But if we overemphasize worship in truth and minimize worship in spirit, then our worship will be taut, grim, and icily predictable.

Actually, these balancing truths of worshiping in spirit and truth complement each other. It helps to realize this because frankly, every Christian sometimes attempts to offer the sacrifice of worship but finds no fire on the altar of the heart. Meditation on the truth, rightly done, can kindle the emotions of worship and help us worship in spirit. Conversely, the right kind of heart for God, ready to worship in spirit, loves God's truth and longs to be guided by the truth. So even if individually we incline more toward spirit or truth in worship, we must have both. Jesus said something very similar in Mark 12:30 when He declared that the greatest commandment involved loving God with all the heart as well as with all the mind. Worship arising from truth-kindled hearts and expressed by heartfelt thoughts toward God will not be rejected as worship in vain.

But what if we endure a long period of spiritual dryness where practically every supposed worship experience seems little more than an exercise in hypocrisy? Why continue the discipline if we feel ourselves stuck on a treadmill of vain worship? Should we stop attending worship or discontinue daily devotions if we can't seem to maintain the proper balance of spirit and truth?

No, we should not stop engaging in the forms of worship even though we don't have the feelings of worship. There are some things in which we must persevere even when we don't feel like it, just because it is the right thing to do. Remember that even our "best" worship is imperfect in some ways, however minuscule those imperfections might appear. But we don't advocate the cessation of worship because it is somehow flawed. More importantly, the "breakthrough" in restoring the joy and freedom of worship will most likely happen in the context of worship. People frequently tell me that they didn't feel like coming to church for a particular service, but they disciplined themselves to attend and something happened during that time that refreshed them and restored their spiritual perspective.

Every believer must cross a few spiritual deserts in his or her pilgrimage to the Celestial City. Some arid places may be traversed in an hour or a few days. Occasionally, however, you may be required to travel for weeks with an almost withered soul. Press on in worship. Cry out to God for a renewed awareness of the "rivers of living water" (referring to the Holy Spirit) that Jesus in John 7:38 promised would flow in every believer. But don't stop worshiping. Never give up in the desert. You don't know how wide it is, and you may be almost across.

WORSHIP IS . . .
EXPECTED BOTH PUBLICLY AND PRIVATELY

According to Hebrews 10:25, God expects His people to participate regularly in worship gatherings with other believers, warning specifically about "not neglecting to meet together, as is the habit of some." So the core of the Discipline of worship involves developing the habit of faithfully assembling with other Christians where the primary purpose is to worship God.

The church of Jesus Christ is not a collection of isolationists. The New Testament describes the church with metaphors like "flock" (Acts 20:28), "body" (1 Corinthians 12:12), "structure" (Ephesians 2:21), and "household" (Ephesians 2:19), each of which implies a relationship between individual units and a larger whole. To express and experience Christianity almost always on the individual level (that is, to the exclusion of the group dynamic) means you will needlessly and sinfully miss much of the blessing and power of God. Hebrews 10:25 teaches that those who neglect the disciplined "habit" of assembling with other believers have developed an unchristian habit.

To "meet together" undeniably means to gather in the physical presence of other believers. Not only do the words themselves permit no other interpretation, but when this letter was written to the Hebrews there was no other way the phrase could be construed. So we cannot persuade ourselves that we "meet together" with other Christians when by electronic means we watch them worship elsewhere. Good reasons support the idea of providing both live and recorded distance video access to church worship, but none of those reasons includes the idea of substituting media ministry for church attendance by those who are able.

Furthermore, the blessing of a consistent, high-quality, personal devotional life doesn't exempt you from worshiping with other believers. Your devotional experiences may rival those of Jonathan Edwards or George Müller, but you need corporate worship as much as they and these Jewish Christians in Hebrews 10:25 did. There's an element of worship and the Christian life that can never be experienced in private worship or by watching worship. There are some graces and blessings that our Father gives only when we "meet together" with other believers as His family.

The Puritan preacher David Clarkson explained this in an instructive sermon on "Public Worship to Be Preferred Before Private":

> The most wonderful things that are now done on earth are wrought in the public ordinances [that is, public worship], though the commonness and spiritualness of them makes them seem less wonderful. . . . Here the Lord speaks life unto dry bones, and raises dead souls out of the grave and sepulchre of sin. . . . Here the dead hear the voice of the Son of God and his messengers, and those that hear do live. Here he gives sight to those that are born blind;

it is the effect of the gospel preached to open the eyes of sinners, and to turn them from darkness to light. Here he cures diseased souls with a word, which are otherwise incurable by the utmost help of men and angels. . . . Here he dispossesses Satan, and casts unclean spirits out of the souls of sinners that have been long possessed by them. Here he overthrows principalities and powers, vanquishes the powers of darkness, and causes Satan to fall from heaven like lightning. Here he turns the whole course of nature in the souls of sinners, makes old things pass away, and all things become new. Wonders these are, and would be so accounted, were they not the common work of the public ministry. It is true indeed, the Lord has not confined himself to work these wonderful things only in public; yet the public ministry is the only ordinary means whereby he works them.[6]

On the other hand, no matter how fulfilling or sufficient our regular public worship celebration seems, there are experiences with God that He gives only in our private worship. Jesus participated faithfully in the public worship of God at the synagogue each Sabbath (see Luke 4:16) and at the stated assemblies of Israel at the temple in Jerusalem. In addition to that, however, Luke observed that Jesus "would withdraw to desolate places and pray" (5:16). As the familiar Puritan commentator Matthew Henry put it, "Public worship will not excuse us from secret worship."[7]

How can we worship God publicly once each week when we do not care to worship Him privately throughout the week? Can we expect the flames of our worship of God to burn brightly in public on the Lord's Day when they barely flicker for Him in secret on other days? Could it be that our corporate worship experience often dissatisfies us because we do not pursue satisfying worship in private? "There is no way," says Welsh pastor Geoffrey Thomas, "that those who neglect secret worship can know communion with God in the public services of the Lord's Day."[8]

We must not forget, however, that God expects us to worship privately so He can bless us. We minimize our joy when we neglect the daily worship of God in private. What an incredible blessing that God does not limit our access to Him and the enjoyment of His presence to only one day per week! Every day the strength, guidance, encouragement, forgiveness, joy, and all that God is awaits us. You will never live a day, Christian, without an invitation to grow in intimacy with Jesus Christ Himself that day.

Think of it: The Lord Jesus Christ stands ready to meet with you privately for as long as you want; willing—even eager—to meet with you every day! Suppose you had been one of the thousands who followed Jesus around for much of the last three years of His earthly life. Can you imagine how excited you would have been if one of His disciples said, "The Master sent me to tell you that He is willing to meet with you in private whenever you're ready, and for as much time as you want to spend, and He'll be expecting you most every day"? What a privilege! Who would have complained about this expectation? Well, that marvelous privilege and expectation actually does belong to you—today, tomorrow, and always. Exercise this privilege and fulfill this expectation for the glory and enjoyment of God forever.

WORSHIP IS . . .
A DISCIPLINE TO BE CULTIVATED

Jesus said, "Worship the Lord your God" (Matthew 4:10). To worship God throughout a lifetime requires discipline. Without discipline, our worship of God will be thin and inconsistent. Certainly worship must be much more than discipline, more than simply the proper expression of the correct words and forms. So when I say that worship is focusing on and responding to God, I hope to convey my conviction that true worship always exudes evidence of "heartprints." Worship can't be calculated or produced. Instead it is evoked; it's the response of a heart evoked by the beauty, glory, and allure of the object of your mental focus—holy God. And yet, we also consider worship a Discipline, a Discipline that must be cultivated, just as all relationships must be in order for them to remain healthy and grow.

Worship is a Spiritual Discipline insofar as it is both an end and a means. The worship of God is an *end* in itself because to worship, as we've defined it, is to focus on and respond to God. No higher goal or greater spiritual pleasure exists than focusing on and responding to God. But worship is also a *means* in the sense that it is a means to godliness. The more we truly worship God, the more—through and by means of worship—we become like Him.

The worship of God makes believers more godly because people become like their focus. We emulate what we think about. Children pretend they are the heroes they dream about. Teenagers dress like the sports stars or popular musicians they admire. But these tendencies don't disappear when we become adults. Those who concentrate on "making it to the top" read the books of those "at the top," then copy their business style and "secrets" of success. To illustrate the point on a more crude level, those who focus on pornography tend to mimic what they see. Focusing on the world more than on the Lord makes us more worldly than godly. But if we would be godly, we must focus on God. Godliness requires disciplined worship.

"But I've tried it," someone screams in frustration, "and it doesn't work for me! I faithfully attend church. I've tried a daily routine of Bible reading and prayer, but I didn't experience the results I expected. Despite all I'm doing I don't seem to be growing much in godliness."

The rigid rehearsal of a routine is not the same as rightly practicing a Spiritual Discipline. Reading the Bible every day doesn't automatically make me godly any more than reading *The Wall Street Journal* every day makes me a businessman. And a failure to experience the spiritual growth we want when we want it doesn't disprove the effectiveness of God's means (that is, the Spiritual Disciplines) to Christlikeness. So if you are discouraged by the snail's pace of your sanctification, get counsel from those who do seem to be growing in godliness through public and private worship. Talk to a mature Christian who has a meaningful devotional life. Review some of the earlier sections of this book, particularly the ones on meditation and prayer. The development of any discipline, from hitting a golf ball to playing the piano, almost always requires outside help from those with more experience. So don't be surprised that you need help in the development of the Disciplines that lead to Christlikeness, and don't be afraid to ask for it.

Describing contemporary man, someone has said, "He worships his work, works at his play, and plays at his worship." In defiance of this, will you cultivate the Discipline of worship?

MORE APPLICATION

Will you commit yourself to the Discipline of daily worship? "If you will not worship God seven days a week," said A. W. Tozer, "you do not worship Him on one day a week."[9] Let's not fool ourselves. True worship, as a once-a-week event, does not exist. We can't expect worship to flow from our lips on the Lord's Day if we keep it dammed in our hearts throughout the week. The waters of worship should never stop flowing from our heart, for God is always God and always worthy of worship. But the flow of worship should be channeled at least daily into a distinct worship experience.

A growing number seem content to practice the personal Spiritual Disciplines and neglect worship with other believers. They believe their private devotional life is superior to anything they experience in corporate worship, so they neglect the public ministry of God's Word. Be alert to the danger of such imbalance. In my pastoral ministry, however, I have encountered many more professing Christians who tilt to the opposite extreme. They faithfully discipline themselves to attend corporate worship, but they disregard the regular practice of privately worshiping God. More fall into this pitfall than perhaps any other on the path to godliness. They progress little in Christlikeness simply because they fail to discipline themselves at this very point. Don't let it happen to you.

Will you put actual worship into your acts of worship? What David Clarkson says about public worship applies to all acts of worship, both public and private:

> What you do in public worship, do it with all your might. Shake off that slothful, indifferent, lukewarm temper, which is so odious to God. . . . Think it not enough to present your bodies before the Lord. . . . The worship of the body is but the carcass of worship; it is soul worship that is the soul of worship. Those that draw near with their lips only shall find God far enough from them; not only lips, and mouth, and tongue, but mind, and heart, and affections; not only knee, and hand, and eye, but heart, and conscience, and memory, must be pressed to attend upon God in public worship. David says, not only "my flesh longs for Thee," but "my soul thirsts for Thee." Then will the Lord draw near, when our whole man waits on Him; then will the Lord be found, when we seek Him with our whole heart.[10]

The act of worship without actual worship is a miserable, hypocritical experience. So if worship wearies you, you aren't really worshiping. God is not wearisome. Imagine one of the perpetually worshiping creatures around the throne of God complaining, "I'm tired of this!" That thought never once crossed their minds throughout all eternity past, nor will it ever in all eternity to come. Instead we read that they are so endlessly overwhelmed with the glory of God that "day and night they never cease" worshiping Him (Revelation 4:8). Obviously we cannot yet see and experience in worship all that they are privileged to enjoy, but we can learn from them that meaningless worship is a contradiction in terms. Since the object of our worship is the glorious and majestic God of heaven, when worship becomes empty, the problem lies somewhere with the subject (us), not the object (God).

So "come, let us worship" (Psalm 95:6) the one, true God who has ordained the Spiritual Discipline of worshiping Him—in public, in the family, and in private—as one of the most bountiful means of receiving the grace to grow in Christlikeness. For as we grow in the worship of God, we grow in the likeness of Christ.

Do remember, though, that Christ, who is indeed the example of everything God wants us to grow toward, is much more than our example. It was necessary for Him to live and die to make us worshipers with whom God is pleased. Only as we come to God by faith in Jesus' righteousness does our worship become acceptable. Thus by faith in God's Christ and according to God's Word, as Hebrews 12:28 exhorts us, "let us offer to God acceptable worship," not the worship Jesus condemned as "worship in vain."

CHAPTER 6

EVANGELISM . . .
FOR THE PURPOSE OF GODLINESS

*Disciplined faith is a faith that is likely to survive
and lead to faith in others.*
ALISTER E. MCGRATH

Only the sheer rapture of being lost in the worship of God is as exhilarating and intoxicating as telling someone about Jesus Christ.

Some of the most rewarding times of my life have been during mission trips when I have done nothing but talk about Christ, on the streets and in homes, with one individual or group after another, all day long. Likewise in my own locale—nothing so excites me as a conversation about Christ with someone who does not know Him. But my experience is not unusual; talking to a person about Jesus can be an intensely rewarding experience for any believer.

And yet nothing causes an eye-dropping, foot-shuffling anxiety more quickly among a group of Christians like myself than talking about our responsibility to evangelize. I know many believers who feel confident they are obeying the Lord when it comes to their intake of Scripture or to their giving or serving, but I don't know a single Christian who would boldly say, "I am as evangelistic as I should be."

Evangelism is a broad subject, and I won't attempt to be comprehensive about it in this chapter. The main idea I want to

communicate here is that godliness requires that we discipline ourselves in the practice of evangelism. I'm convinced that the main
reason many of us don't witness for Christ in ways that would be
effective and relatively fear-free is simply because we don't discipline ourselves to do it.

EVANGELISM IS EXPECTED

Most of those reading this book will not need convincing that Jesus
expects evangelism of each of His followers. He does not expect
all Christians to use the same *methods* of evangelism, but He does
expect all Christians to evangelize.

Before we go further, let's define our terms. What is evangelism?
If we want to define it thoroughly, we could say that *evangelism*
is presenting Jesus Christ in the power of the Holy Spirit to sinful people, in order that they may come to put their trust in God
through Him, to receive Him as their Savior, and to serve Him as
their King in the fellowship of His church.[1]

If we want something more concise, we could define New Testament evangelism as communicating the gospel. Anyone faithfully
relating the essential elements of God's salvation through Jesus
Christ is evangelizing. Evangelism occurs whether the words of
the gospel are spoken, written, or recorded; delivered to one person
or to a crowd.

The Lord Jesus Christ Himself has commanded us to witness.
Consider His authority in the following:

- "Go therefore and make disciples of all nations, baptizing
  them in the name of the Father and of the Son and of
  the Holy Spirit, teaching them to observe all that I have
  commanded you. And behold, I am with you always, to the
  end of the age." (Matthew 28:19-20)
- "He said to them, 'Go into all the world and proclaim the
  gospel to the whole creation.'" (Mark 16:15)
- "[He] said to them, '. . . that repentance and forgiveness

of sins should be proclaimed in his name to all nations, beginning from Jerusalem.'" (Luke 24:46-47)
- "Jesus said to them again, 'Peace be with you. As the Father has sent me, even so I am sending you.'" (John 20:21)
- "You will receive power when the Holy Spirit has come upon you, and you will be my witnesses in Jerusalem and in all Judea and Samaria, and to the end of the earth." (Acts 1:8)

These commands weren't given to the apostles only. For example, those of us in the United States can say that the apostles never came to *this* nation. For the command of Jesus to be fulfilled and for America to hear about Christ, the gospel had to come here by other Christians who understood that they, too, were charged with going to "all nations." And the apostles will never come to your home, your neighborhood, or to the place where you work. For the Great Commission to be fulfilled there, for Christ to have a witness in that "remote part" of the earth, a Christian like you must discipline yourself to do it.

Some Christians believe that evangelism is a gift and the responsibility only of those with that gift. They appeal to Ephesians 4:11-12 for support: "He gave the apostles, the prophets, the evangelists, the shepherds and teachers, to equip the saints for the work of ministry, for building up the body of Christ." God does gift some for ministry as evangelists, but He calls all believers to be His witnesses and provides them with both the power to witness and a powerful message. Thus while God calls every believer to be a witness, He calls only a few witnesses to the vocational ministry of an evangelist. Just as each Christian, regardless of spiritual gift or ministry, is to love others, so each believer is to evangel*ize* whether or not his or her gift is that of evangel*ist*.

Think of our responsibility for personal evangelism from the perspective of 1 Peter 2:9: "But you are a chosen race, a royal priesthood, a holy nation, a people for his own possession." Many Christians are familiar with this part of the verse, but do you know the rest? It goes on to say that these privileges are yours, Christian, so "that you may proclaim the excellencies of him who called you out of darkness into his marvelous light." We normally think of this verse as establishing the doctrine of the priesthood of all believers. But we may equally identify it as one that exhorts us to a kind of prophethood of all believers. God expects each of us to "proclaim the excellencies" of Jesus Christ.

EVANGELISM IS EMPOWERED

If it is so obvious to almost all Christians that we are to evangelize, how come almost all Christians seem to disobey that command so often?

Some believe they need months of specialized training to witness effectively. They fear speaking with someone about Christ until they feel confident in the amount of their Bible knowledge and their ability to deal with any potential question or objection. That confident day, however, never comes. What if the blind man whom Jesus healed in John 9 had thought that way? Would he ever have felt ready to witness to the scholarly, critical Pharisees? And yet within hours, perhaps minutes, of meeting Jesus, he bravely told them what he knew of Jesus.

Sometimes we fail to speak of Christ because we fear that people will think us strange and reject us. In law school I became friends with a fellow student. When I realized he was not a Christian, I became burdened to share the gospel with him. I did my best to model the character of Christ around him and prayed for opportunities to witness to him. One day near the end of the school year, just as the first bell rang he surprised me by asking, "Why are you always so happy?" Although class was about to start, I could have given my friend a clear testimony, even if it were only one sentence. I could have answered, "Because of Jesus Christ." Or I might have said, "I'd like to tell you why after class." But when the opportunity I'd prayed for finally came, I froze in fear that he might think less of me for my faith and said, "I don't know."

In some cases we can trace our evangelophobia to the method of witnessing we're asked to use. If it requires approaching someone we've never met and striking up a conversation about Christ, most people will be terrified and indicate it by their absence. Although a few enjoy it, most people tremble at the thought of going door-to-door to share the gospel. Even methods that call for witnessing to friends or family, if they involve a forced, confrontational, or unnatural approach, fill us with fear at sharing the best news in the world with the people we love the most.

I've never heard it expressed, but I think the seriousness of evangelism is the main reason it frightens us. We realize that in talking with someone about Christ, heaven and hell are at stake. The eternal destiny of the person looms before us. And even when we rightly believe that the results of this encounter rest in God's hands and that we bear no accountability for the person's response to the gospel, we still sense a solemn duty to communicate the message faithfully, as well as a holy dread of saying or doing anything that might rise as a stumbling block to this person's salvation. Many Christians feel too unprepared for such a challenge, or simply have too little faith and falter at entering into such an eternally important conversation.

One researcher offers another explanation for Christians' fear of evangelism:

> One dominant reason underlying the increasing reluctance of Christians to share their faith with non-Christians pertains to the faith sharing experience itself. In asking Christians about their witnessing activities, we have found that nine out of ten individuals who attempt to explain their beliefs and theology to other people come away from those experiences feeling as if they have failed. . . . The reality of human behavior is that most people avoid those activities in which they perceive themselves to be failures. As creatures seeking pleasure and comfort, we emphasize

those dimensions and activities in which we are most capable and secure. Thus, despite the divine command to spread the Word, many Christians redirect their energies into areas of spiritual activity that are more satisfying and in which they are more likely to achieve success.[2]

What is success in evangelism? When the person you witness to comes to Christ? Certainly that's what we want to happen. But if we measure evangelistic success only by conversions, are we failures whenever we share the gospel and people refuse to believe? Was Jesus an "evangelistic failure" when people like the rich young ruler turned away from Him and His message (see Mark 10:21-22)? Obviously not. Then neither are we when we present Christ and His message and people turn away in unbelief. We need to learn that sharing the gospel *is* successful evangelism. We ought to have an obsession for souls, and tearfully plead with God to see more people converted, but only God can produce the fruit of evangelism called conversion.

In this regard we are like the postal service. They measure success by the careful and accurate delivery of the message, not by the response of the recipient. Whenever we share the gospel (which includes the summons to repent and believe), we have succeeded. In the truest sense, *all* biblical evangelism is successful evangelism, regardless of the results.

The power of evangelism is the Holy Spirit. From the instant that He indwells us He gives us the power to witness. Jesus stressed this in Acts 1:8 when He said, "But you will receive power when the Holy Spirit has come upon you, and you will be my witnesses in Jerusalem and in all Judea and Samaria, and to the end of the earth." Jesus expects evangelism of every Christian because the Spirit empowers every Christian to evangelize. But Christians often misunderstand this power. The Spirit does not empower all Christians to evangelize in the same way; rather, all believers have been given power to be witnesses of Jesus Christ. And the evidence that you've been given the power to witness is a changed life. The same Holy Spirit power that changed your life for Christ is the power to witness for Christ. So if God by His Spirit has transformed you into a follower of Jesus, be confident of this: God has given you Acts 1:8 power. This means that in ways and methods compatible with your personality, spiritual gift, opportunities, and so on, you do have the power to share the gospel with people. Having Acts 1:8 power also means God will empower your life and words in the sharing of the gospel in ways you will often not perceive. To put it another way, the Holy Spirit may grant much power to your witness in an evangelistic encounter without giving you any *feeling or sense* of power in it.

The Holy Spirit not only empowers people who share the gospel, the gospel we share is itself embedded with the power of the Holy Spirit as well. "I am not ashamed of the gospel," said the apostle Paul in Romans 1:16, "for it is the power of God for salvation to everyone who believes, to the Jew first and also to the Greek." That's why people can be converted whether they hear the gospel from a teenage teacher of a vacation Bible school class or a seminary-trained evangelist with a PhD; whether they read it in a book by an Oxford scholar like C. S. Lewis or in a simple tract. It is *the gospel* God blesses like no other words.

That does not mean the gospel is a kind of magic wand we can wave over unbelievers and the power of God will automatically spring from it and convert all who hear. You are probably like me in that you heard the gospel many times before you were saved. Doubtless you can think of several people who have heard the gospel repeatedly and have not experienced the new birth. God must also grant faith (Ephesians 2:8-9) with the hearing of the gospel, "for it is the power of God for salvation to everyone who *believes*" (emphasis added). Nevertheless, it is *through the gospel* that God gives the power to believe. That's the meaning of Romans 10:17: "So faith comes from hearing, and hearing through the word of Christ." When you speak the gospel, you share "the power of God for salvation to everyone who believes." Sharing the gospel is like walking around in a thunderstorm and handing out lightning rods. You don't know when the lightning will strike or who it will strike, but you know what it will strike—the lightning rod of the gospel. And when it does, that person's lightning rod will be charged with the power of God and he or she will believe.

That's why we can be confident that some will believe if we will faithfully and tenaciously share the gospel. The gospel is the power of God for salvation and not our own eloquence or persuasiveness. God has His elect whom He will call and whom He has chosen to call *through the gospel* (see Romans 8:29-30; 10:17). Otherwise we would despair when people reject the gospel, and their unbelief would convince us to stop evangelizing. But the power for people to be made right with God comes through the message of God's Son. If we will give that message, we can be assured some will respond.

Living a life openly devoted to Christ also manifests a power that augments evangelism. This power, strange as it may sound, can be illustrated by one of my favorite barbecue restaurants. Its best advertising isn't the typical media variety aimed at the eye or ear. Its best advertising is directed to the *nose*. They barbecue the seasoned beef and pork where its tangy smoke can waft across the four-lane highway. Every day, people driving by become interested in the "message" of the restaurant simply because of its fragrant aroma.

Paul described the power of godliness that way in 2 Corinthians 2:14-17:

> Thanks be to God, who in Christ always leads us in triumphal procession, and through us spreads the fragrance of the knowledge of him everywhere. For we are the aroma of Christ to God among those who are being saved and among those who are perishing, to one a fragrance from death to death, to the other a fragrance from life to life. Who is sufficient for these things? For we are not, like so many, peddlers of God's word, but as

men of sincerity, as commissioned by God, in the sight of God we speak in Christ.

The Lord empowers the life (see verses 14-16) and the words (see verse 17) of the faithful believer with a power of spiritual attraction, making them like a fragrant aroma that attracts people to the message about His Son.

The most powerful ongoing Christian witness has always been the speaking of God's Word by one who is living God's Word. A few years ago, Caffy started a women's Bible study in our home at the encouragement of two new believers. To the second meeting they brought Janet, a mutual friend who was very cynical about the whole thing. In a song about her spiritual pilgrimage, she later wrote, "Sex and drugs and rock-and-roll [were] my trinity." Her thinking had been further blurred by involvement in a cult. But something began that night that only Janet knew about. Months afterward, she said that from their initial meeting an aroma from Caffy's Christian living, especially in her own home, combined with the meat of God's Word in the Bible study made her want to taste more. She couldn't get enough of the aromatic message that had changed these people's lives so beautifully. Today Janet is a fresh and living "aroma of Christ to God among those who are being saved and among those who are perishing."

Because of the nature of the Holy Spirit and the Holy Scriptures, evangelism is empowered.

EVANGELISM IS A DISCIPLINE

Evangelism is a natural overflow of the Christian life. Every Christian should be able to talk about what the Lord has done for him or her and what He means to him or her. But evangelism is also a *Discipline* in that we must discipline ourselves to get into situations where evangelism can occur, that is, we must not just wait for witnessing opportunities to happen.

Jesus said in Matthew 5:16, "Let your light shine before others, so that they may see your good works and give glory to your Father who is in heaven." To "let" your light shine before others means more than simply, "Don't do anything to keep your light from shining." Think of His exhortation as more proactive, as in, "Let there be the light of good works shining in your life; let there be the evidence of God-honoring change radiating from you. Let it begin! Make room for it!"

Why, then, don't we witness more actively? As mentioned earlier, some place the blame on the lack of adequate training to share their faith. Indeed, I wish many more could enjoy the advantages of some good instruction about the specifics of sharing the gospel. But as we think again about the blind man Jesus healed in John 9:25, we realize that we cannot attribute our failure to witness to a lack of training. Though he had been a believer in Jesus only for a few minutes and obviously had no evangelism training at all, he was willing to tell others what Jesus had done for him ("One thing I do know, that though I was blind, now I see"). So any Christian who has heard biblical preaching, participated in Bible studies, and read the Scriptures and Christian literature for any time at all should have at least enough understanding of the basic message of Christianity to share it with someone else. Surely if we have understood the gospel well enough ourselves to be converted, we should know it well enough (even if as yet we know nothing else about the faith) to tell someone else how to be converted.

We should also acknowledge the common objection that people do not witness because of the lack of time. Between job, family, and church responsibilities, there simply isn't enough time to "go witnessing." Before we adopt this objection to evangelism, let's ponder this: Do we really want to say that we are too busy to fulfill the Great Commission of Jesus Christ to make disciples (see Matthew 28:19-20)? Do we expect that at the Judgment Jesus will excuse us from the single most important responsibility He gave us because we say, "I didn't have time"?

Let's work from the assumption that God has given us most,

even all, of our time-consuming responsibilities. And, for the sake of argument, let's accept as fact the statement that we don't have room on our calendar for one more regularly scheduled activity. Even if God did put everything on our to-do list, He is also the Author of the Great Commission. He still intends for each of His followers to find ways to share the gospel with unbelievers. In whatever context the Lord places us to live our lives, He calls us to find ways to fulfill the Great Commission there, however limiting the context might be. Raising children in the "discipline and instruction of the Lord" (Ephesians 6:4) is one way of fulfilling the Great Commission. Supporting the work of a church and its missionaries financially is another. But what about those unbelievers outside our families? And who will do the evangelistic ministry of a church but people like you who comprise the membership of that church?

Isn't the main reason we don't witness the simple lack of *disciplining* ourselves to do it? Yes, there are those wonderful, unplanned opportunities God appoints to give the "reason for the hope that is in you" (1 Peter 3:15). Nevertheless, I maintain that apart from making evangelism a Spiritual Discipline, most Christians will seldom share the gospel.

As a minister, I could spend twenty-four hours a day, seven days a week with Christians and never finish the work. With sermon preparation, counseling, committee meetings, Bible studies, hospital visits, and the like, I could invest all my time exclusively with professing believers (except for large group settings or in cases where unbelievers ask to meet with me privately). And since my ongoing ministry with God's people never finishes, I could "justify" as easily as anyone my lack of individual contact with non-Christians. But what potential for winning unbelievers to Christ would I have if I was never with unbelievers? None. When would I share the gospel with a lost person except when it's part of my job? Never. That can't be right.

Ministers and others who work daily in churches and in Christian organizations and institutions aren't the only ones in this situation. The Christian homemaker, for example, who rarely has the opportunity to see anyone except her children and her friends from church, may live with the same dilemma.

"That's not my problem!" says someone. "At work I'm surrounded all day long by the most worldly people you can imagine." Assuming you don't try sharing the gospel with them on company time, when will you? The point is not so much how many unbelievers you see every day but rather how often you are with them in an appropriate context for sharing the gospel. Despite the important work-related discussions you may have throughout the day, how often do you have the kinds of meaningful conversations with co-workers where spiritual issues can be raised? If you never have an opportunity to talk about Jesus, it doesn't matter how many non-Christians you are around—your potential for evangelism is little better than mine might be.

That's why I say evangelism is a Spiritual Discipline. Unless we discipline ourselves for evangelism, we can easily excuse ourselves from ever sharing the gospel with anyone.

Notice in Colossians 4:5-6 the terminology indicating that disciplined thought and planning should go into evangelism: "Walk in *wisdom* toward outsiders, *making the best use* of the time. Let your speech always be gracious, seasoned with salt, so that you may *know* how you ought to answer each person" (emphasis added). We must think about evangelism whenever we talk with outsiders—wisely "making the most of the opportunity" (verse 5, NASB). Knowing how to respond to people as individuals implies reflection and preparation. These principles can be applied in as many specific ways as we have witnessing opportunities. But in general they support the idea that in addition to its spontaneous element, evangelism is a Spiritual Discipline.

For me that means I discipline myself to be with unbelievers. Sometimes Caffy and I schedule a meal with neighbors who don't know Christ. We make sure to take food or a housewarming gift to the new family on the street and spend time getting to know them, or check in on a neighbor in crisis. I try to focus on outsiders at social events in our church, even though I have more in common with the Christians there and usually enjoy the conversations with them more. Again, the goal is not just to rub shoulders with unbelievers, but to dialogue with them in such a way that their hearts and minds might be opened to the gospel.

Disciplined evangelism might also involve having coffee or lunch with neighbors or coworkers periodically and learning to ask good questions about the personal side of their lives. The same kinds of opportunities might arise at company-sponsored athletic or social events, or during informal times while traveling on business with fellow workers. Through conversation and good listening, you will discover their felt needs and, hopefully, explore with them their deepest need, their need for Christ.

Whether with someone you're around frequently or with someone you've met for the first time, the best way I've found to turn the conversation toward spiritual matters is to ask the person how you can pray for him or her. Although such a question is common to the Christian, most non-Christians don't know of anyone who prays for them. I've often seen unbelievers deeply moved by this unusual (to them) expression of concern. I had a neighbor for more than seven years with whom I'd been unsuccessful in discussing the things of God. But the first time I told him I frequently prayed for him and wanted to know how I could pray more specifically, he began to disclose some family problems I never knew existed. I once went through my neighborhood asking for needs our church could pray for that night in a special service. At almost every home I was amazed by people's responses and their unprecedented openness to talk about spiritual issues. A few days or weeks afterward they were open to a follow-up inquiry about their prayer request, which in turn often led to an opportunity to share the gospel.

But the point in all these possibilities is that you will have to discipline yourself to bring them about. They won't just happen. You'll have to discipline yourself to ask your neighbors how you can pray for them or when you can share a meal with them. You'll have to discipline yourself to get with your coworkers during off-hours. Many such opportunities for evangelism will never take place if you wait for them to occur spontaneously. The world, the flesh, and the Devil will do their best to see to that. You, however, backed by the invincible power of the Holy Spirit, can make sure that these enemies of the gospel do not win.

As mentioned earlier, I don't want to leave the impression that the Discipline of evangelism requires that we all share the gospel in exactly the same ways. Throughout this chapter you may have had a picture of certain methods of evangelism that seem terrifying to you. But the preconceived style of evangelism you fear may not rank among the best ways for you to help make disciples for Christ.

In his first letter, the apostle Peter divided all spiritual gifts into the two broad categories of serving gifts and speaking gifts (see 1 Peter 4:10-11). Some find that they evangelize better through serving, others more through speaking. Evangelistic serving might involve hosting a meal and living the gospel in front of your guests. As they see the distinctives in your home and family life, immediate or eventual opportunities to voice the gospel may arise. Perhaps you might cook a meal or grill some burgers to provide an open door for your spouse to share his or her faith. I'm told that every family averages a "crisis" once every six months. During that time of illness, job change, financial crunch, birth, death, and so on, being a Christlike servant to that family frequently demonstrates the reality of your faith in a way that piques their interest. Through serving, you may have a chance to give a Bible or some evangelistic literature, or to initiate a gospel conversation in some imaginative way.

I know a church well where people have hosted home evangelism meetings. They invite neighbors, coworkers, and friends into their homes for the expressed purpose of hearing a guest talk about Jesus Christ and answering their questions about Christianity and the Bible. The hosts may not feel confident about their ability to articulate the gospel, especially to groups of people, but by serving through hospitality, they provide an opportunity for evangelism by someone whose strength *is* a verbal presentation of the gospel. By opening their homes and working with other believers, evangelism takes place that wouldn't have happened otherwise. But this kind of evangelistic serving still requires as much discipline as any other. It still requires the discipline to put the date on the calendar, to invite the people, to prepare the meal, to pray for the gathering, and so on. Without such discipline, evangelistic serving never happens.

On the other hand, some are more adept at communicating the gospel directly. As I've pointed out, if you're better at speaking than serving, you may be able to work with someone who specializes in evangelistic serving in ways that will provide more witnessing opportunities than you've had before. However, just as servers may need to serve in order to open a door for speaking the gospel themselves, so those whose strength is in speaking may need to discipline themselves to serve more so they will have chances to speak. In short, speakers often need to serve first so they can verbalize the gospel, and evangelistic servers must eventually speak the words of the gospel. Regardless of how shy or unskilled we may feel about evangelism, we must not convince ourselves that we cannot or will not verbally share the gospel under any circumstances.

I heard the story of a man who became a Christian during an evangelistic emphasis in a city in the Pacific Northwest. When he told his boss about it, his employer responded with, "That's great! I am a Christian and have been praying for you for years!"

But the new believer was crestfallen. "Why didn't you ever tell me you were a Christian? You were the very reason I have not been interested in the gospel all these years."

"How can that be?" the boss wondered. "I have done my very best to live the Christian life around you."

"That's the point," explained the employee. "You lived such a model life without telling me that it was Christ who made the difference, I convinced myself that if you could live such a good and happy life without Christ, then I could too."

The Bible says in 1 Corinthians 1:21 that "it pleased God through the folly of what we preach to save those who believe." Often it is the message of the Cross *lived and demonstrated* that God uses to open a heart to the gospel, but it is the message of the Cross *proclaimed* (by word or page) through which the power of God saves those who believe its content. No matter how well we live the gospel (and we must live it well, else we hinder its reception), sooner or later we must communicate the *content* of the gospel before a person can become a disciple of Jesus. The *example* of Christianity saves no one; rather it is the *message* of Christianity—the gospel—that "is the power of God for salvation" (Romans 1:16).

Before closing this section, I want to emphasize that the Discipline of evangelism also applies to the support of missions. For the same reasons we should discipline ourselves for sharing the message of Christ with those around us, we also should discipline ourselves to help those who are fulfilling the Great Commission in places far from us. Disciplining ourselves to support missions by giving, praying, informing ourselves, and being open to go if God calls (or to let our children go if God calls them) is a part of the pursuit of godliness.

MORE APPLICATION

Because evangelism is expected, will you obey the Lord and witness? In one sense, of course, every Christian constantly witnesses. By our words and lives, at every moment we testify—well or poorly—to the power of Jesus Christ. But I am speaking now of witnessing by design, not by default.

Are you willing to obey Jesus Christ and to witness *intentionally*? Intentional evangelism will necessarily be customized by your spiritual gift, talents, personality, schedule, family situation, location, and so on. But having taken all that into consideration, every believer must realize that it is sinful not to seek ways to spread the message about our Lord Jesus.

Please don't get the impression that because I've written this chapter and shared some experiences that I consistently model bold, dynamic evangelism. Besides the failure I've admitted in the previous pages, I could list many other occasions when I should have spoken about Jesus and did not, usually because of fear. But I believe we can find long-term solutions to our inconsistency and frequent lack of witnessing if we will discipline ourselves for evangelism.

Because evangelism is empowered, will you believe God can use your words in the salvation of others? God blesses words, the words of the gospel. It was the *words* of the Lord Jesus, the *words* of Peter, and the *words* of Paul that God blessed in the conversion of people in New Testament times, and words are what He still blesses today. He will bless *your* words when they contain the words of His powerful gospel.

Some fear witnessing because they don't feel confident enough in their persuasive powers or their ability to answer all imaginable objections to the gospel. But the power for evangelism is not in our ability; it resides in His gospel. You may have never imagined that an unbeliever could actually be born again by hearing of Christ from your lips. But that's not humility; it's doubt, a denial of God's blessing upon His gospel just because you were the speaker. Don't doubt the power of God to add His blessing upon your words when you speak of Christ.

Throughout his life, John Bunyan, author of *The Pilgrim's Progress*, insisted that overhearing the conversation of some poor women, talking of the things of God while sitting in a sunlit doorway, was a critical turning point in his coming to Christ. Believe that in the same way the Lord can use what you say as the catalyst in a conversion.

Let's pause and make sure we're not taking something for granted: Do you know the words of the gospel? Try this experiment first on yourself and then, if you dare, in your church, class, or small group to reveal their clarity on the gospel. Distribute paper, then ask people how many times they think they've heard the gospel.

Some, if they've professed faith in Christ for many years, may answer that they've heard it hundreds or even thousands of times.

"Good!" you say. "Now, please write the gospel on that piece of paper."

Then watch people freeze, and stare at you as though you've asked them to list the capitals of every country in the world.

"Didn't you just say that you've heard the gospel many times? And to become a Christian you had to hear the gospel and believe it so as to be saved, right? For you can't be saved by a gospel you don't understand and believe. So please, simply write down in a paragraph or so the message people must hear to be made right with God and go to heaven."

Be prepared for an uncomfortable silence and for many blank sheets of paper—despite the presence of some of your best, most devoted members.

How would *you* do? Can you speak simply, but clearly about how all people have broken the Law of a holy God who created them and are under His condemnation because of their sin? Can you tell them of how in His mercy God sent His Son, Jesus, who perfectly kept the Law of God and was willing to offer to others the credit for His obedience? Can you speak of how Jesus was willing to sacrifice Himself on the cross as a substitute for sinners? Can you talk of how God raised Jesus from the dead, demonstrating His acceptance of Jesus' sacrifice and validating all that Jesus said and did? Can you urge people to repent of their sin and of living for themselves and to believe that Jesus' life and death can make them right with God and give them eternal life? If you have believed these things for yourself, you can share them so others can believe them.

I think there are many Christians who can clearly articulate the gospel and want to speak to others about the Lord, but do not for fear that the observable, daily sin in their lives undermines the integrity of their witness. *How can I ever witness to my boss,* such thinking goes, *after I angered him so much?* Or, *I'll never be able to tell my neighbor about the power of Christ now that she's seen me yell at my children.*

If God does not use people like these—like us!—as His witnesses, there will be no human witnesses. Since there are no perfect people, there are no perfect witnesses. This does not change the fact that the more Christlike our lives, the more convincing our words about Christ. We need to do what we can to eliminate any sin that makes our words sound hollow. But while attempting to do that, we must be convinced that we cannot delay our witnessing until we reach sinless perfection. Otherwise, we would never share the gospel. Part of the beauty of our message is that God saves sinners, sinners like us. In fact, the Holy Spirit can make it possible to turn an occasion of sin into an opportunity to talk about the Savior. I've known Christians who returned to those who observed their sin or were victims of it, and by confessing the sin and asking forgiveness were then able to give a powerful witness. Such evidence of a changed life gets an unbeliever's attention. That boss supervises other people who anger him; that neighbor sees other people yell at their children. But when you humble yourself and acknowledge that you were wrong and ask forgiveness, you make a distinction between yourself and others who angered their boss or yelled at their children. The practice of consistent Christian living does empower evangelism, but a Christian recovery from your own *un*christian living confirms your witness in another, very believable way. Through your failures and weaknesses, the life-changing power of Christ can be made visible and strong.

Because evangelism is a Discipline, will you plan for it? While preaching to his London congregation in 1869 about the responsibility of evangelism, C. H. Spurgeon said,

> If I never won souls, I would sigh till I did. I would break my heart over them if I could not break their hearts. Though I can understand the possibility of an earnest sower never reaping, I cannot understand the possibility of an earnest

sower being content not to reap. I cannot comprehend any
one of you Christian people trying to win souls and not
having results, and being satisfied without results.[3]

If you are not content with your reaping of souls for Christ's
sake, will you plan for more disciplined sowing? Will you calendar
an event designed for evangelism? Could you set up a lunch meeting at work or with a neighbor? How about discussing with your
pastor a home evangelistic meeting? Where can you get some evangelistic literature to give away? Who can you ask to pray for? Will
you commit yourself to *at least one way* of intentional evangelism
in the near future?

Evangelism is not often mentioned in books on spirituality and
Christlikeness. So is evangelism really that important as a Spiritual
Discipline? The following adaptation of 1 Corinthians 13 reminds us:

> Though I speak with the tongues of scholarship, and though
> I use approved methods of education, and fail to win others
> to Christ, or to build them up in Christian character, I am
> become as the moan of the wind in a Syrian desert.
>
> And though I have the best of methods and understand
> all mysteries of religious psychology, and though I have
> all biblical knowledge, and lose not myself in the task of
> winning others to Christ, I become as a cloud of mist in an
> open sea.
>
> And though I read all Sunday School literature, and
> attend Sunday School conventions, institutes, and summer
> school, and yet am satisfied with less than winning souls to
> Christ and establishing others in Christian character and
> service, it profiteth nothing.
>
> The soul-winning servant, the character-building
> servant, suffereth long and is kind; he envieth not others
> who are free from the servant's task; he vaunteth not
> himself, is not puffed up with intellectual pride.

Such a servant doth not behave himself unseemly between Sundays, seeketh not his own comfort, is not easily provoked. Beareth all things, believeth all things, hopeth all things.

And now abideth knowledge, methods, the Message, these three: but the greatest of these is the Message.[4]

Yes, there is a correlation between the pursuit of godliness and a passion for God's message. The more we pursue Christ, the more we want to proclaim Christ. But without discipline, our best evangelistic intentions often go unspoken. May we discipline ourselves to live so that we can say with the apostle Paul, "I do all things for the sake of the gospel, so that I may become a fellow partaker of it" (1 Corinthians 9:23, NASB).

CHAPTER 7

SERVING . . .
FOR THE PURPOSE OF GODLINESS

Ministering hearts are disciplined to labor,
for they regularly move beyond their comfort zones,
they put themselves in vulnerable spots, they make
commitments which cost, they get tired for Christ's sake,
they pay the price, they encounter rough seas.
But their sails billow full of God's Spirit.

R. KENT HUGHES

It's been gone since 1861, yet people still recognize the name. The Pony Express was a private express company that carried mail by an organized relay of horseback riders across a series of 184 stations. The eastern end was St. Joseph, Missouri, and the western terminal was in Sacramento, California. The cost of sending a half-ounce letter by Pony Express varied from $25 to $125 in today's dollars, depending upon when during the life span of the service it was sent. If the horses held out, and the weather and the Indians held off, that letter would complete the nearly two-thousand-mile journey in a speedy eight to ten days, as did the report of Lincoln's Inaugural Address.

It may surprise you that the Pony Express was in operation only from April 3, 1860, until November 18, 1861—just nineteen months. When the telegraph line was completed between the two cities, the horseback service was no longer needed.

Being a rider for the Pony Express was a tough job. You were expected to cover seventy-five to one hundred miles a day, riding hard day and night, changing horses every ten to fifteen miles. Other than the mail, you carried little else besides a revolver and a knife. In order to travel light, and to increase speed and mobility during Indian attacks, the men rode in shirtsleeves whenever possible, sometimes even during the fierce winter weather.

How would you recruit volunteers for this hazardous job? Bolivar Roberts, superintendent for the western end of the Express, is said to have placed this ad in a San Francisco newspaper in March 1860: "Wanted—young, skinny, wiry fellows not over 18. Must be expert riders willing to risk death daily. Orphans preferred."[1]

Those were the honest facts of the service required, but the Pony Express never suffered a shortage of riders.

We need a similar honesty with the facts about the Discipline of serving God. Like the Pony Express, serving God is not a job for the casually interested. It's costly service. God asks for your life. He requires that service to Him become a priority, not a pastime. He doesn't want servants who offer Him the leftovers after their other commitments. And serving God isn't a short-term responsibility either, for unlike the Pony Express, His kingdom will never end, regardless of the technological advances in the world.

The mental picture we have of the Pony Express probably compares with the one imagined by the young men of 1860 who read that newspaper ad. Scenes of excitement, camaraderie, and the thrill of adventure filled their heads as they swaggered over to the Express office to apply. Yet few of them envisioned that excitement would only occasionally punctuate the routine of the long, hard hours and loneliness of the work.

The Discipline of serving is like that. Although no more spiritually grand and noble way of life can be found than living in response to Christ's summons to serve, the daily realities of such a life often appear as lowly and pedestrian as washing someone's feet. In *The Cost of Discipleship*, Dietrich Bonhoeffer famously declared, "When Christ calls a man, he bids him come and die."[2] Such a call to serve Christ summons up images of legendary martyrs, fearless in the face of persecution, or of a triumphant death after a lifetime of planting the flag of the gospel among unreached peoples. Instead, it seems that far more commonly Christ's call is to a death by degrees, washing feet in obscurity. We're drawn to the appeal of service when it holds out the promise of bold adventure, but repelled when it means—as it more often does—feeling banished to serve Christ in a dreary corner of a seemingly inconsequential place. To have served Jesus by walking with Him during His three-year ministry would have been a glorious adventure; to have served Him three years earlier as His sweeper and saw-sharpener in the carpenter's shop wouldn't have been as appealing.

The ministry of serving may be as public as preaching or teaching, but more often it will be as sequestered as nursery duty. It may be as visible as singing a solo, but usually it will go as unnoticed as operating the sound equipment to amplify the solo. Serving may be as appreciated as a powerful testimony in a worship service, but typically it's as thankless as washing dishes after a church social. Most service, even that which seems the most appealing, we perceive as we would the tip of an iceberg. Only the eye of God sees the larger, hidden part of it.

Beyond the church walls, serving can manifest itself as baby-sitting for neighbors, taking meals to families in flux, running errands for the homebound, providing transportation for the one whose car breaks down, helping with lawn or home maintenance, feeding pets and watering plants for vacationers, and—hardest of all—displaying a servant's heart in the home. Serving typically looks as unspectacular as the practical needs it seeks to meet.

That's why serving must become a Spiritual Discipline. The flesh connives against its hiddenness and sameness. Two of the deadliest of our sins—sloth and pride—loathe serving. They paint glazes on our eyes and put chains on our hands and feet so that we don't serve as we know we should or even as we want. If we don't discipline ourselves to serve for the sake of Christ and His kingdom and for the purpose of godliness, we'll "serve" only occasionally or when it's convenient or self-serving. The result will be a quantity and quality of service we'll regret when the Day of Accountability for our service comes.

Not every act of service will, or even should, be disciplined serving. Most of the time our service should spring simply from our love for God and love for others. Like our worship and evangelism, so also our service should often flow from within—without any need of discipline—as a result of the life-transforming presence and work of the Holy Spirit. But because the Spirit of Jesus within us causes us to yearn to be more like Jesus, and also because of the persistent gravitational tendencies toward selfishness in our hearts, we must also discipline ourselves to serve. And those who do will find serving one of the most sure and practical means of growth in grace.

But lest we begin to think that serving is merely an option, let's chisel this into the cornerstone of our Christian life.

EVERY CHRISTIAN IS EXPECTED TO SERVE

When God calls His elect to Himself, He calls no one to idleness. When we are born again and our sins forgiven, the blood of Christ cleanses our conscience, according to Hebrews 9:14, in order for us to "serve the living God." Every believer's Bible exhorts him or her to "serve the LORD with gladness" (Psalm 100:2, NASB). God's Word has no place for spiritual unemployment or spiritual retirement or any other description of a professing Christian *not* serving God.

Of course, motives matter in the service we offer to God. The Bible mentions at least six motives for serving.

Motivated by Obedience

In Deuteronomy 13:4 Moses wrote, "You shall walk after the LORD your God and fear him and keep his commandments and obey his voice, and you shall serve him and hold fast to him." Everything in that verse relates to obedience to God. In the midst of this cluster of commands on obedience we find the mandate to "serve him." We should serve the Lord because we want to obey Him.

John Newton, the slave trader who became a pastor following his conversion to Christ and wrote such hymns as "Amazing Grace," illustrates obedient service as follows:

> If two angels were to receive at the same moment a commission from God, one to go down and rule earth's grandest empire, the other to go and sweep the streets of its meanest village, it would be a matter of entire indifference to each which service fell to his lot, the post of ruler or the post of scavenger; for the joy of the angels lies only in obedience to God's will.[3]

Can you imagine one of those angels refusing to serve? It's unthinkable. Likewise, how can any professing Christian think it acceptable to sit on the spiritual sidelines and watch others do the work of the kingdom? Any true Christian would say that he or she *wants* to obey God. But we disobey God when we do not actively serve Him. We sin when we refuse to serve God.

Motivated by Gratitude

The prophet Samuel exhorted the people of God to service with these words: "Only fear the LORD and serve him faithfully with all your heart. For consider what great things he has done for you" (1 Samuel 12:24). When serving God seems like a burden, remembering the "great things he has done for you" vaporizes the burden.

Do you remember what it's like *not* to know Christ, to be without God and without hope? Do you remember how it feels to be guilty before God and unforgiven? Do you remember the terror of knowing you have offended God and that His anger burns toward you? Do you remember the horror of knowing you're only a heartbeat away from hell? Now do you remember the experience of seeing Jesus Christ with the eyes of faith, and of understanding for the first time who He really is and what He has done by His life, death, and resurrection? Do you remember the joy of your first awareness of forgiveness and deliverance from judgment and hell? Do you remember the initial, incomparable realization of your assurance of heaven and eternal life? When the fire of service to God grows cold, consider what great things the Lord has done for you.

God has never done anything greater for anyone, nor could He do anything greater for you, than what He has done in bringing you to Himself. Suppose He put ten million dollars into your bank account every morning for the rest of your life, but He didn't save you? Suppose He gave you the most beautiful body and face of anyone who ever lived, a body that never aged for a thousand years, but then at death shut you out of heaven and sent you into hell for eternity? What has God ever given anyone that could compare with the salvation He has given to you as a believer? Do you see that God could never do anything for you or give anything greater to you than the gift of Himself? If we cannot be grateful servants of Him who is everything and in whom we have everything, what *will* make us grateful?

Motivated by Gladness

The inspired command of Psalm 100:2 is, "Serve the LORD with gladness" (NASB). God expects His servants to serve—not grudgingly, grimly, or glumly—but gladly.

In the courts of ancient kings, servants were often executed for nothing more than looking sad in the service of the king. Nehemiah, in 2:2 of the book that bears his name, was grieving over the news he'd heard that Jerusalem was still in ruins despite the return of many Jews from the Babylonian exile. As he was serving food to King Artaxerxes one day, the king said, "Why is your face sad, seeing you are not sick? This is nothing but sadness of the heart." Because of what that could mean for him, Nehemiah wrote, "Then I was very much afraid." That's because you don't mope or sulk when you serve a king. Not only does it give the appearance that you serve reluctantly, it also reveals your dissatisfaction with the way he's running things.

The person who can't serve the Lord with gladness contradicts with his heart what he professes with his lips. I can understand why the person who serves God only out of obligation doesn't serve with gladness. I can understand why the person who serves God in an attempt to earn his way to heaven doesn't serve with gladness. But the Christian who gratefully acknowledges what God has done for him or her for eternity should be able to serve God cheerfully and with joy.

A believer does not look upon serving God as a burden, but as a privilege. Suppose God let you choose anyone in the world to serve and know intimately, but wouldn't let you serve Him? Suppose He allowed you to serve in any political or business position in the world, but barred you from serving in His kingdom? Or suppose He permitted you to serve yourself, doing anything you wanted with your life and with no needs or worries, but you could never know Jesus? Even the best of these things becomes a miserable slavery in comparison with the immeasurable privilege of serving God. That's why the psalmist could say, "For a day in your courts is better than a thousand elsewhere. I would rather be a doorkeeper in the house of my God than dwell in the tents of wickedness" (Psalm 84:10).

Do you serve on that church committee with gladness or with gloom? Do you serve your neighbors willingly or reluctantly? Do your kids get the impression from you that you really enjoy serving God or that you merely endure it?

Motivated by Forgiveness, Not Guilt

In Isaiah's famous vision of God, notice his response once God had forgiven him:

> One of the seraphim flew to me, having in his hand a
> burning coal that he had taken with tongs from the altar.

And he touched my mouth and said: "Behold, this has touched your lips; your guilt is taken away, and your sin atoned for." And I heard the voice of the Lord saying, "Whom shall I send, and who will go for us?" Then I said, "Here I am! Send me." (6:6-8)

Like a dog on a leash, Isaiah was straining out of his skin to serve God in some way, *any* way. Because he felt guilty? No! Because God had taken his guilt *away*!

That pulpit lion of London, C. H. Spurgeon, moved with some of Isaiah's emotion, said in a sermon on September 8, 1867,

The heir of heaven serves his Lord simply out of gratitude; he has no salvation to gain, no heaven to lose; . . . now, out of love to the God who chose him, and who gave so great a price for his redemption, he desires to lay out himself entirely to his Master's service. O you who are seeking salvation by the works of the law, what a miserable life yours must be! . . . you have that if you diligently persevere in obedience, you may perhaps obtain eternal life, though, alas! none of you dare to pretend that you have attained it. You toil and toil and toil, but you never get that which you toil after, and you never will, for, "by the works of the law there shall no flesh living be justified." . . . The child of God works not for life, but from life; he does not work to be saved, he works because he is saved.[4]

The people of God do not serve Him in order to *be* forgiven but because we *are* forgiven. When believers serve only because they feel guilty, they serve with a ball and chain dragging from their hearts. There is no love in that kind of service, only labor. No one feels joy in it, only obligation and drudgery. Christians should not act like grudging prisoners, sentenced to serve in God's kingdom because of guilt. We can serve willingly because Christ's death freed us from guilt.

Motivated by Humility

Jesus was the perfect Servant. He revealed His greatness in the lowliness He embraced so He could serve the most basic needs of His twelve friends.

> When he had washed their feet and put on his outer garments and resumed his place, he said to them, "Do you understand what I have done to you? You call me Teacher and Lord, and you are right, for so I am. If I then, your Lord and Teacher, have washed your feet, you also ought to wash one another's feet. For I have given you an example, that you also should do just as I have done to you. Truly, truly, I say to you, a servant is not greater than his master, nor is a messenger greater than the one who sent him." (JOHN 13:12-16)

With astonishing humility, Jesus, their Lord and Teacher, washed His disciples' feet as an example of how all His followers should serve with humility.

In this world, Christians will always live with an affinity for sin (the Bible calls it "the flesh") that will say, "If I have to serve, I want to get something for it. If I can be rewarded, or gain a reputation for humility, or somehow turn it to my advantage, then I'll give the impression of humility and serve." But this isn't Christlike service. This is hypocrisy. Hypocritical "servants" will not serve without recognition, without "some return on their investment" of time. They may desire the recognition of applause, public acknowledgment, appreciation via social media, assured results, honor for their example, or, most subtle of all, development of a reputation as holy, sacrificial, or exceptionally spiritual. Hypocrites do this because they feel no inclination for the kind of service that God alone can see and reward. So if necessary, they will devise clever, yet religiously acceptable and falsely humble ways to ensure some sort of human notice. If this fails, they will attempt to negotiate at least some form of reciprocity for their service. By the power of the Holy Spirit we must reject this self-righteous, hypocritical service as a sinful motivation, and serve "in humility," considering "others more significant" than ourselves (Philippians 2:3).

Can you serve your boss and others at work, helping them to succeed, and can you be happy, even when they receive the promotions and you get overlooked? Can you work to make others look good without envy filling your heart? Can you minister to the needs of those whom God exalts and men honor when you yourself seem neglected? Can you pray for the ministry of others to prosper when it would cast yours in the shadows? If God places you there, will you, like your Master, serve for years in your own equivalent of an obscure, village carpentry shop if that's where God wants to grow you in godliness and deepen your knowledge of Him?

In the Discipline of service, God looks not only for a job well done, for even the world serves well when it leads to profit. He also calls us to serve with humility, because that leads to Christlikeness.

Motivated by Love

At the heart of service, according to Galatians 5:13, should be love: "For you were called to freedom, brothers. Only do not use your freedom as an opportunity for the flesh, but through love serve one another."

No fuel for service burns longer and provides more energy than love. I do some things in the service of God that I would not do for money, but I am willing to do them out of love for God and others. I read of a missionary in Africa who was asked if he really liked what he was doing. His response was shocking. "Do I like this work?" he said. "No. My wife and I do not like dirt. We have reasonably refined sensibilities. We do not like crawling into vile huts through goat refuse. . . . But is a man to do nothing for Christ he does not like? God pity him, if not. Liking or disliking has nothing to do with it. We have orders to 'Go,' and we go. Love constrains us."

When Christ's love controls or constrains people, they "no longer live for themselves but for him who for their sake died and was raised" (2 Corinthians 5:15). They serve God and others, motivated by love for God and others. Jesus said in Mark 12:28-31 that the greatest commandment is to love God with all you are, and the next most important one is to love your neighbor as you love yourself. In light of these words, surely the more we love God the more we will live for Him and serve Him, and the more we love others the more we will also serve them.

EVERY CHRISTIAN IS GIFTED TO SERVE

Spiritual Gifts

At the moment of salvation, when the Holy Spirit comes to live within you, He brings a gift with Him. We read in 1 Corinthians 12:4,11 of different varieties of gifts, and that the Holy Spirit determines by His sovereign will which gift goes to which believer: "Now there are varieties of gifts, but the same Spirit. . . . All these are empowered by one and the same Spirit, who apportions to each one individually as he wills." Equally important, 1 Peter 4:10 certifies that each Christian receives a special gift, a gift intended for use in service: "As each has received a gift, use it to serve one another, as good stewards of God's varied grace."

You may already know that the subject of spiritual gifts sparks ongoing controversy in many parts of the church. The primary passages on this topic are Romans 12:4-8; 1 Corinthians 12:5-11, 27-31; 1 Corinthians 14; Ephesians 4:7-13; and 1 Peter 4:11. I encourage you to read them all prayerfully. Regardless of your theology of spiritual gifts, the two most important points about them remain those given in 1 Peter 4:10, namely, (1) if you are a Christian you definitely have at least one spiritual gift, and (2) God gave you that gift for the purpose that you serve with it for His kingdom.

Perhaps you have heard little about spiritual gifts, or for whatever reason never identified your spiritual gift. Relax. Many Christians serve God faithfully and fruitfully for a lifetime without ascertaining their specific gift. I'm not suggesting you shouldn't try to discover your gift; I'm saying that you aren't relegated to benchwarmer status in the kingdom of God until you can name your gift. Study the biblical material on spiritual gifts and carefully choose some of the best books from the torrent of tomes written on the subject. But by all means, don't be discouraged from serving, for you may still serve effectively without knowing the name of your gift. J. I. Packer reminds us, "The most significant gifts in the church's life in every era are ordinary natural abilities sanctified."[5]

Stay in balance. God has given you a spiritual gift, and it is not the same as a natural ability. That natural talent, rightly sanctified for God's use, often points toward the identity of your spiritual gift. But you should find out the special gift God has given you while you're serving as diligently as you can without that definite information. In fact, in addition to the study of Scripture, the best way to discover and confirm which spiritual gift is yours is through serving. If you have an inclination to teach, you may never know if your gift is teaching until you accept that class and try. You may discover through a ministry to people who are hurting that your gift is mercy. On the other hand, through involvement in a particular ministry you may confirm what your gift is not. Years ago I thought I had one gift until through serving it became painfully clear that I had an entirely different gift.

I encourage you to discipline yourself to serve in a regular, ongoing ministry in your local church. You don't necessarily have to serve in a recognized or elected position. But find a way to defeat the temptation to serve only when it's convenient or exciting. That's not disciplined service. Those with a servant's heart and eyes will find themselves compelled by love to serve in ways and times beyond the expectations of their "official" ministry in the church, but in doing so they will not neglect the ongoing ministry of the local body of Christ.

You may feel overlooked, you may feel limited by an unusual

schedule, you may be physically incapacitated, but you can still find ways to serve. People with unusual schedules or physical limitations often make powerful intercessors in a prayer ministry. Despite their restrictions, those with hearts to serve always find ways to serve.

A flight attendant in our church works overseas routes. When she's on the job she's gone for several days at a time. And she's not on a regular Monday-through-Friday schedule. She had always been one who wrote letters of encouragement and gave away books as a ministry; however, when she joined our fellowship she looked for a disciplined way to serve along with other believers rather than just individually. But how to do this with her schedule? It soon became apparent that her spiritual gift is service, that is, meeting practical needs. She also excels at hospitality. Now she belongs to a ministry team in our church that specializes in hospitality. Because it is a group ministry, the work doesn't require her presence every time they serve. When in town, she contributes her part.

God gives spiritual gifts for use in service. If He intended no use for your gift, there would no longer be any purpose for your life. Why would God allow us to live beyond any usefulness to Him? In His wisdom and providence, He gifts each believer to serve and keeps each believer alive as long as He wants him or her to serve.

The point of this chapter, however, is a call for *disciplined* serving, with the goal that we become more like Jesus. Some spiritual gifts incline toward ministries conducted out of the spotlight and which often go unappreciated by the masses. And yet, like Jesus, no matter how much public recognition we gain in ministry, God calls us to times of service in the shadows as well. Regardless of your gifts or talents, determine to employ them for Christ and His kingdom. "Some have the gift of helping, and these actions [of service] come more naturally," writes Jerry White. "For most Christians, serving requires a conscious effort."[6] Or to put it another way: "Serving requires discipline."

Serving Is Often Hard Work

Some teach that once you discover and employ your spiritual gift, then serving becomes nothing but effortless joy. That's not New Testament Christianity. The apostle Paul wrote in Ephesians 4:12 about "the equipping of the saints for the *work* of service" (NASB, emphasis added). Sometimes serving God and others is nothing less than hard work.

Scripture describes Christians not only as children of God, but also as servants of God. Recall how Paul typically started his letters by referring to himself as a servant of God, as in Romans 1:1. Every Christian is a servant of God, and servants *work*.

Paul described his service to God with these words in Colossians 1:29: "For this I toil, struggling with all his energy that he powerfully works within me." The word *toil* means "to work to the point of exhaustion," while from the Greek word translated "struggling" comes our word *agonize*. So for Paul to serve God was "to agonize to the point of exhaustion." That doesn't mean his ministry was miserable toil; in fact, the reason Paul worked so hard was because the only thing he loved more than serving God was God Himself. God supplies us with the desire and power to serve Him, then we struggle in service "with all his energy that he powerfully works" in us. True ministry is never forced out by the strength of the flesh. But do not misunderstand: The result of His power working mightily in us frequently feels like "toil."

That means when you serve the Lord in a local church or in any type of ministry, it will often be hard. Like Paul, sometimes your service will also be agonizing and exhausting. It will take your time. It will often prove more stressful or less enjoyable than other ways you could invest your life. And if for no other reason, serving God is hard work because it means serving people. Despite all that, remember: Service that costs nothing accomplishes nothing.

And even though serving God can be agonizing and exhausting work, it is also the most *fulfilling and rewarding* kind of work.

In John 4 we read where Jesus had been talking with the woman of Samaria. He'd been walking all day. He was tired, thirsty, and hungry. And it was all because He'd been serving His Father. While He was resting at the well near Sychar, this Samaritan woman came to the well. They talked and her life was changed forever. As she went back into Sychar to tell others about Jesus, His disciples returned from buying food there. When they offered some to Him, He said, "My food is to do the will of him who sent me and to accomplish his *work*" (4:34, emphasis added).

Jesus found the work of serving God so satisfying that He called it His food. Serving God sometimes so physically exhausted Him that He could sleep in a boat even as waves crashed over the sides. It once meant forty days without eating. For Jesus, service meant frequent nights of sleeping outside on the ground. It meant getting up before daylight to have any time alone. But in the midst of all the weariness, hunger, thirst, pain, and inconvenience, Jesus said that the work of serving God was so fulfilling that it was like food. It nourished Him; it strengthened Him; it satisfied Him; and He devoured it. Serving God is work, but there's no work so gratifying.

Disciplined service is also the most *enduring* kind of work. Unlike some things we may do, service to God is never valueless. The same Paul who agonized to the point of exhaustion while serving God reminded us, "Therefore, my beloved brothers, be steadfast, immovable, always abounding in the work of the Lord, knowing that in the Lord your labor is not in vain" (1 Corinthians 15:58).

You don't have to serve God long before you're tempted to think your work actually is in vain. Thoughts come that your service is a waste of time. You see few, if any, results. God promises, however, that regardless of what you think and see, your work for Him is never in vain. That doesn't mean you won't frequently feel as though nothing has resulted from all your efforts, nor does it mean that you'll someday enjoy all the fruit you'd hoped and prayed for. But the Lord's promise does mean that even if you can't see the proof, your service to God is *never* in vain.

God sees and knows of all your service to Him, and He will never forget it. He will reward you in heaven for it because He is a faithful and just God. I love Hebrews 6:10: "For God is not unjust so as to overlook your work and the love that you have shown for his name in serving the saints, as you still do."

Disciplined service to God is work—hard and costly labor sometimes—but it will endure for all eternity.

MORE APPLICATION

Worship empowers serving; serving expresses worship. Godliness requires a disciplined balance between the two. Those who can maintain service without regular private and congregational worship are serving in the flesh. Regardless of their length of service or how well others think they serve, they are not striving according to God's power, as Paul did, but their own.

In worship, our experience with God and His truth refreshes our reasons and desires to serve. Isaiah didn't say, "Here I am! Send me" (6:8) until after his vision of God. That's the order— worship, then worship-empowered service. As A. W. Tozer put it, "Fellowship with God leads straight to obedience and good works. That is the divine order and it can never be reversed."[7] We cannot long endure the demands of service without receiving the power for them through worship.

At the same time, one measure of the authenticity of worship (again, both personal and interpersonal) is whether it results in a desire to serve. Isaiah (quoted above) is the classic example here also. Tozer again says it best: "No one can long worship God in spirit and in truth before the obligation to holy service becomes too strong to resist."[8]

Therefore, we must maintain that the pursuit of godliness requires that we discipline ourselves for both worship and service. To engage in one without the other is to experience neither.

You are expected to serve and gifted to serve, but are you willing to serve? The Israelites knew without a doubt that God *expected* them to serve Him, but Joshua once looked them in the eye and challenged them on their *willingness* to serve: "If it is evil in your eyes to serve the LORD, choose this day whom you will serve. . . . But as for me and my house, we will serve the LORD" (Joshua 24:15).

When I think of a faithful willingness to serve, I remember a quiet little man from a church where I was a staff member. On Sundays his arrival always went unnoticed, for he came long before anyone else. Nevertheless, he burrowed his old car into an obscure corner of the parking lot to leave the best places for others. He unlocked all the doors, got the bulletins, and then waited outside. When you walked up he'd give you a bulletin and a big smile. But he couldn't talk. He was embarrassed when newcomers asked him questions. Something had happened to his voice long ago. When I met him he was into his sixties and living alone. When he experienced car trouble, which was often, he told no one and walked more than a mile to the church. Because of his vulnerability, he was robbed and beaten several times, at least twice during the three years I was in that church. Some longtime church members told me they suspected he lost his voice as the result of being beaten years before. Extensive arthritis stooped his shoulders, prevented him from turning his neck, and made hard work of simply unlocking doors and handing out bulletins. But he was always there, always smiling, even though he couldn't speak a word. Everything about his life worked to keep him unheralded and in the background, even his name—Jimmy Small. Yet despite his drawbacks, setbacks, handicaps, and a plethora of potential excuses, he willingly served God. And he served in a disciplined way, which in the sight of God was neither small nor in vain.

The gospel of Christ creates Christlike servants. The Lord Jesus was always the servant, the servant of all, the servant of servants, *the Servant.* He said, "I am among you as the one who serves" (Luke 22:27). Jesus is our great example of servanthood. But He did not come to earth, live, and die just to make us more servant-hearted, for we needed much more than that. Because of our sin, we needed to be reconciled to God, and no one makes himself or herself acceptable to God by trying to emulate Jesus' example of service. No one can serve so much or so well that he or she becomes sufficiently righteous before God. We must understand and believe the gospel of God to be right with God.

The gospel of Jesus Christ transforms sinners against God into servants of God. The Holy Spirit works through the gospel to turn those who serve their idols (such as wealth, career, sports, sex, house, land, education, hobby, drugs, politics, and so on) into servants of God, just as He did in the apostle Paul's day when the missionary wrote to some relatively new Christians, "You turned to God from idols to serve the living and true God" (1 Thessalonians 1:9). Those who believe the gospel of Jesus receive the Christlike hearts of servants. So one of the clearest indications that people have truly believed the gospel of Jesus is that a new, Christlike desire to serve begins to overcome their selfish desire to be served. They start looking for ways to do something for Christ and His church, especially ways that will serve the gospel. Has the gospel you believed given you a servant's heart? Is your service rooted in the gospel?

Still, it is true that if gospel-transformed, servant-hearted people are to grow more like Christ, they must *discipline* themselves to serve as Jesus served. Will you?

WANTED: Gifted volunteers for difficult service in the local expression of the kingdom of God. Motivation to serve should be obedience to God, gratitude, gladness, forgiveness, humility, and love. Service will rarely be glorious. Temptation to quit place of service will sometimes be strong. Volunteers must be faithful in spite of long hours, little or no visible results, and possibly no recognition—except from God for all eternity.

CHAPTER 8

STEWARDSHIP . . .
FOR THE PURPOSE OF GODLINESS

How often do we hear about the discipline of the Christian
life these days? How often do we talk about it? How often
is it really to be found at the heart of our evangelical
living? There was a time in the Christian church when
this was at the very centre, and it is, I profoundly believe,
because of our neglect of this discipline that the church is
in her present position. Indeed, I see no hope whatsoever
of any true revival and reawakening until we return to it.

D. MARTYN LLOYD-JONES

Think for a moment: What events produced the greatest stress
in your life today? This past week? Haven't they involved some
feeling of being overloaded with responsibilities at home, work,
school, church, or all the above? How about stress related to paying bills? Running late for an appointment? Going with too little
rest? Juggling your finances? Waiting in a traffic jam on the highway or runway? Facing unexpected car repair or medical expenses?
Running short of cash before payday?

Each of these anxiety-producers, like so many other daily issues,
relates to either time or money. The clock and the dollar are such
substantial factors in so many parts of life that we must consider
their role in any serious discussion of godly living.

THE DISCIPLINED USE OF TIME
Godliness is the result of a biblically disciplined spiritual life. But at
the heart of a disciplined spiritual life is the disciplined use of time.

To be like Jesus, we must see the use of our time as a Spiritual Discipline. Having so perfectly ordered His moments and His days, at the end of His earthly life Jesus was able to pray to the Father, "I glorified you on earth, having accomplished the work that you gave me to do" (John 17:4). As with Jesus, God gives us both the gift of time and work to do during that time. The more we grow *like* Jesus, the more we understand *why* the disciplined use of the time God gives us is so important. Here are ten biblical reasons (many of which were made clear to me in the reading of Jonathan Edwards' sermon on "The Preciousness of Time and the Importance of Redeeming It"[1]) to use time wisely.

Use Time Wisely "Because the Days Are Evil"

To use time wisely "because the days are evil" is a curious phrase embedded in the inspired language of the apostle Paul in Ephesians 5:15-16: "Look carefully then how you walk, not as unwise but as wise, making the best use of the time, because the days are evil." Paul may have exhorted the Christians at Ephesus to make the most of their time because he and/or the Ephesians were experiencing persecution or opposition (such as in Acts 19:23–20:1). In any case, we too need to wisely use every moment "because the days are evil" still.

Even without the kind of persecution or opposition known by the Christians of Paul's day, the world we live in makes it difficult to use time wisely, especially for purposes of biblical spirituality and godliness. In fact, our days are days of *active* evil. Great thieves of time serve as minions of the world, the flesh, and the Devil. They may range in form from high-tech, socially acceptable preoccupations to simple, idle talk or ungoverned thoughts. But the natural course of our minds, our bodies, our world, and our days leads us toward evil, not toward Christlikeness.

Thoughts must be disciplined, otherwise, like water, they tend to flow downhill or stand stagnant. That's why in Colossians 3:2 we're urged, "Set your minds on things that are above." Without this conscious, active, disciplined setting of the direction of our thoughts, they'll be unproductive at best, and evil at worst. Our *bodies* incline to ease, pleasure, gluttony, and sloth. Unless we practice self-control, our bodies will tend to serve evil more than God. We must carefully discipline ourselves in how we "walk" in this *world*, else we will conform more to its ways than to the ways of Christ. Finally, our *days* are days of active evil because so many temptations and evil forces are so extremely active in our days. The use of time is important because time is the stuff of which days are made. If we do not discipline our use of time for the purpose of godliness in these evil days, these evil days will keep us from becoming godly.

Wise Use of Time Is the Preparation for Eternity

You must prepare for eternity in time. You can take that statement either of two ways. One means that during time (that is, in this life) you must prepare for eternity, for there will be no second chance once you cross eternity's timeless threshold.

I recently had an unforgettable dream that soberly reminded me of this reality. (I place no great weight or prophetic value on the dream; I mention it only because it illustrates my point.) Along with some other Christians, I was in a place of persecution. After a sham trial we were escorted to a room where our persecutors began putting each believer to death by lethal injection. While waiting my turn I was overcome by the awareness that in moments I would enter eternity, and all my preparation for that event was now done. I dropped to my knees and began to pray my last prayers of this life, committing my spirit to the Lord Jesus Christ. At this point in the dream I snapped awake with the adrenaline rush of a man seconds from execution. My first conscious thought after realizing it was but a dream was that one day it would *not* be a dream. Regardless of when or how death occurs, there is a specific day on the calendar when all my preparation for eternity will indeed be over. And since that day could be any day, I should use my time wisely, for it's all the time I have to prepare for where I will endlessly live beyond the grave.

Do you realize that whether you experience unending joy or eternal agony depends on what happens in moments of your life just like this one? What, then, is more precious than time? As a relatively small rudder determines the direction of a great ocean liner, so that which we do in the small span of time influences all eternity.

That leads to the other meaning of the statement "You must prepare for eternity in time," namely that you must prepare for eternity before it is too late. The classic scriptural alert is, "Behold, now is the favorable time; behold, now is the day of salvation" (2 Corinthians 6:2). Right now is the right time to prepare for where you will spend eternity. If that is an uncertain or unsettled matter with you, take the time to settle it now. You possess no guarantee of any more time than this moment to prepare for eternity. Don't delay responding to the One who made you and gives you this time.

Prepare for eternity by coming in faith to the eternal Son of God, Jesus Christ. Come to Him in time, and He will bring you to Himself in eternity.

Time Is Short

The more scarce something is, the more valuable it is. Gold and diamonds would be worthless if you could pick them up like pebbles beside the road. Likewise, time would not be so precious if we never died. But since we live never more than a breath away from eternity, the way we use our time has eternal significance.

Although decades of life might remain, the fact is, "You are a mist that appears for a little time and then vanishes" (James 4:14). Even the longest life is brief in comparison to eternity. In spite of all the time that's passed, you probably can remember happy or tragic events of your childhood or teenage years as vividly as if they happened yesterday. The reason you can is not simply the strength of your memory, but also because it really hasn't been that long ago. When you think of an entire decade as only 120 months, a great chunk of life suddenly seems short. So regardless how much time remains for you to develop more Christlikeness, it really isn't much. Use it well.

Time Is Passing

Not only is time short, but what does remain is fleeting. Time is not like a bag of ice in the freezer, out of which you can use a bit when you want and save the rest for later. Instead, time is very much like the sands in an hourglass—what's left is continuously slipping away. The apostle John put it bluntly: "The world is passing away along with its desires" (1 John 2:17). Passing away along with the world is our time in it.

We speak of saving time, buying time, making up time, and so on, but those are illusions, for time is always passing. We should use our time wisely, but even the best use of time cannot put pages back on the calendar.

As a child, time seemed to drag. Now I increasingly find myself saying what I remember my parents saying: "I can't believe another year is over! Where has the time gone?" The older I get, the more I feel as though I'm paddling on the Niagara—the closer I get to the end, the faster it comes. If I don't discipline my use of time for the purpose of godliness now, it won't be any easier later.

The Remaining Time Is Uncertain

Not only is time short and passing, but we do not even know how short it actually is nor how long before it all passes away. That's why the wisdom of Proverbs 27:1 advises, "Do not boast about tomorrow, for you do not know what a day may bring." Thousands entered eternity today, including many much younger than you, who just hours ago had no idea that today was their last day. Had they known that, their use of time would have become far more important to them.

Regardless of when you read this, you can probably recall the recent death of some college or professional athlete, or a famous member of the music or film industries. Likely you can still sense the shock of the unexpected death of a child or teenager known to you. These remind us that neither youth nor strength, stardom nor stature obligates God to give us one more hour. Regardless of how long we want to live or expect to live, our times are in His hands (see Psalm 31:15).

Obviously, we must make some types of plans as though many more years remain. But a proper recognition of reality calls us to use our time for the purpose of godliness as though it were uncertain we would live tomorrow, for that is a very certain uncertainty.

Time Lost Cannot Be Regained

Many things can be lost, but then regained. Many a man has declared bankruptcy, only to amass an even greater fortune later. Time is different. Once gone, it is gone forever and can never be regained. If you could galvanize every person on earth into the purpose of regaining time, the entire world's efforts, wealth, and technology could not bring back one minute.

God offers you this present time to discipline yourself for the purpose of godliness. Jesus said in John 9:4, "We must work the works of him who sent me while it is day; night is coming, when no one can work." The time for the works of God, that is, godly living, is now while it is "day." For each of us "night is coming," and none of us can stop or slow the approach of that night. If you misuse the time God offers to you, He never offers that time again.

Many reading these lines may grieve the loss of wasted years. Despite your misuse of time in the past, you can improve the time that remains. The will of God for you now resides in the words of the apostle Paul: "Forgetting what lies behind and straining forward to what lies ahead, I press on toward the goal for the prize of the upward call of God in Christ Jesus" (Philippians 3:13-14). Through the work of Christ to repentant believers, God will forgive every millisecond of misused time. And it pleases Him for you to discipline the balance of your time for the purpose of godliness.

You Are Accountable to God for Your Time

There's hardly a more sobering statement in Scripture than Romans 14:12: "So then each of us will give an account of himself to God." The words "each of us" apply to Christians and non-Christians alike. And though believers will be saved by grace and not by works, once in heaven our reward there will be determined on the basis of our works. The Lord will cause "each one's work [to] become manifest," and for each it will be either that "he will receive a reward" or "he will suffer loss, though he himself will be saved, but only as through fire" (1 Corinthians 3:13-15). So not only will we be held accountable for our use of time, but our eternal reward will be directly related to it.

Hebrews 5:12 illustrates something of how God will hold us accountable at the Judgment for our use of time in disciplining ourselves for the purpose of godliness. In this passage God chastised these Jewish Christians for failing to use their time in a way that develops spiritual maturity: "For though by this time you ought to be teachers, you need someone to teach you again the basic principles of the oracles of God. You need milk, not solid food." If, as here, He holds believers still on earth responsible for not disciplining their time for godliness, He will undoubtedly do so at the Judgment in heaven.

Jesus said, "I tell you, on the day of judgment people will give account for every careless word they speak" (Matthew 12:36). If we must give an account to God for every word spoken, surely we must give an account for every hour spent carelessly (that is, wastefully, negligently). And He said in Matthew 25:14-30 that we are accountable for all the talents we have received and how we use them for the sake of our Master. If God will hold us accountable for the talents He has given us, then certainly He will hold us accountable for the use of so precious a gift as time. The wise response to such truth is to evaluate your use of time now and spend it in a way that you will not regret at the Judgment. And if you cannot answer your conscience regarding how you use your time in the growth of Christlikeness now, how will you be able to answer God then?

Deciding to discipline yourself to use your time for the purpose of godliness is not a matter for delay and deliberation. Each hour that passes is another for which you must give an account.

Time Is So Easily Lost

Except for the "fool," no other character in the book of Proverbs draws the scorn of Scripture like the slothful "sluggard." The reason? His lazy and wasteful use of time. When it comes to finding excuses for avoiding his responsibilities and failing to improve his time, the sluggard's creative brilliance is unsurpassed. "The sluggard says," according to Proverbs 26:13-14, "'There is a lion in the road! There is a lion in the streets!' As a door turns on its hinges, so does a sluggard on his bed." The contemporary sluggard won't go to places he should go (such as church), saying, "It's too dangerous out there on the highways!" Or he might say, "If I discipline my time for the purpose of godliness, I might miss important things on TV or the Internet, or become so busy I won't get enough rest!" And he plops down on the couch or rolls back over in bed.

The sluggard never has time for the things that really matter, especially things that require discipline. And before he realizes it, his time and opportunities expire. As Proverbs 24:33-34 observes, "A little sleep, a little slumber, a little folding of the hands to rest, and poverty will come upon you like a robber, and want like an armed man." Notice that it's just a "little" sleep, a "little" slumber, a "little" folding of the hands to rest that brought the ruin of lost time and opportunity. It's so easy to lose so much, just a little at a time. You don't have to do anything to lose time.

Many people value time as silver was appraised in the days of Solomon. First Kings 10:27 reports, "The king made silver as common in Jerusalem as stone." Time appears so plentiful that losing much of it seems inconsequential. People waste money easily as well, but if people threw away their money as thoughtlessly as some throw away their time, we would think them insane. Yet time is infinitely more precious than money because money can't buy time. You can, however, at least minimize the loss and waste of time by disciplining yourself for the purpose of godliness.

We Value Time at Death

As the person out of money values it most when it is gone, so do we at death value time most when it is gone.

This assessment comes more tragically for some than for others, especially in the case of those who reject Christ. In his dying words, the famous French infidel Voltaire said to his doctor, "I will give you half of what I am worth if you will give me six-months' life." So desperate were his cries when his time was gone that the nurse who attended him said, "For all the wealth in Europe I would not see another infidel die."[2] Similarly, the last words of the English skeptic Thomas Hobbes were, "If I had the whole world, I would give it to live one day."[3]

The most important thing to learn from death scenes like these, as mentioned earlier, is to come to Christ while you still can. Those who have already given their lives to Christ should understand this: If additional years were given to us at death, they would profit nothing unless we made a change in how we used our time. So the moment to value time is now, and not just at death. The time to pursue godliness is now, and the way that God has provided this for those who stand forgiven by grace is through diligence in the Spiritual Disciplines.

Most pursue a course of life based more on pleasure than on the joy found in the way of God's Disciplines. God warns them through His Word of the regrets that will gash their hearts when their time runs out. Imagine the heartache of dying this way: "At the end of your life you groan, when your flesh and body are consumed, and you say, 'How I hated discipline, and my heart despised reproof! I did not listen to the voice of my teachers or incline my ear to my instructors'" (Proverbs 5:11-13). If, as this man, you suddenly realized you had no more time, would you likewise regret how you've spent your time in the past and present? The way you have used your time can instead provide great comfort to you in your last hour. You will surely regret some events, but won't you be pleased then for all the times of Spirit-filled living, for all the occasions when you obeyed Christ? Won't you be glad then for every moment you spent reading the Scriptures, praying, worshiping, evangelizing, serving, fasting, and so on for the purpose of becoming more like the One before whom you are about to stand in judgment (see John 5:22-29)? Pursue the kind of life Jonathan Edwards determined to live: "Resolved, that I will live so as I shall wish I had done when I come to die."[4]

Why not do something about it while you still have time?

Time's Value in Eternity

I doubt that in heaven we experience regret, but if we did it would be for not using our earthly time more for the glory of God and for growth in His grace. Hell, by contrast, will howl forever with agonizing laments over time so foolishly squandered.

In Luke 16:22-25, the Bible portrays this anguish over a wasted lifetime in the story of the rich man who went to Hades and of the poor beggar, Lazarus, who went to "Abraham's side." Jesus told how the rich man, being in torment, lifted his eyes and saw Lazarus far away, living in joy with Abraham. The rich man asked Abraham to send Lazarus with water, but Abraham responded, "Child, remember that you in your lifetime received your good things, and Lazarus in like manner bad things; but now he is comforted here, and you are in anguish."

What value would those like this man, who have lost all opportunity for eternal life, place on the time you have right now? Puritan writer Richard Baxter asked, "Doth it not tear their very hearts for ever, to think how madly they consumed their lives, and wasted the only time that was given them to prepare for their salvation? Do those in Hell now think them wise that are idling or playing away their time on earth?"[5] If those in the merciless side of eternity owned a thousand worlds, they would give them all (if they could) for one of our days. They have learned the value of time by experience—but only after it's too late. Let us learn it by encountering the truth, and discipline our time for the purpose of godliness. After all, if you have given your life to Christ, "You are not your own, for you were bought with a price" (1 Corinthians 6:19-20). "Your" life and "your" time belong to God now. The best and most joy-filled way to spend them is to use them the way God wants.

THE DISCIPLINED USE OF MONEY

The Bible relates not only the use of time to our spiritual condition, but also our use of money. The disciplined use of money requires that we manage it in such a way that our needs and those of our families are met. In fact, the Bible denounces as a hypocrite any professing Christian who fails to care for the physical needs of his family because of financial irresponsibility, slothful mismanagement, or waste. "If anyone does not provide for his relatives, and especially for members of his household," 1 Timothy 5:8 says firmly, "he has denied the faith and is worse than an unbeliever." So how we use money for ourselves, for others, and especially for the sake of God's kingdom is from first to last a spiritual issue.

Why does God consider a biblical use of money and resources a crucial part of our growth in godliness? For one thing, it's a matter of sheer obedience. A surprisingly large amount of Scripture speaks to the use of wealth and possessions. If we ignore it or take it lightly, our "godliness" will be a fraud. But as much as anything else, the reason our use of money and the things it buys indicates our spiritual maturity and godliness is that we exchange such a great part of our lives for it. Because we invest most of our days working in exchange for money, in a very real sense our money represents *us*. Therefore, how we use it reveals who we are, for it manifests our priorities, our values, and our heart. To the degree we use our money and resources Christianly, we prove our growth in Christlikeness.

All of the truths about the disciplined use of time also apply to the use of money and possessions (with the exception that, unlike time, these things when lost may be replaced). Reviewing each of those truths regarding time and relating them here to the general use of money would be redundant. Instead, let's consider how the Scriptures teach us to discipline ourselves "for the purpose of godliness" in the specific area of giving our money for the sake of Christ and His kingdom.

Growth in godliness will express itself in a growing understanding of these ten New Testament principles of giving.

God Owns Everything You Own

In 1 Corinthians 10:26, the apostle Paul quoted Psalm 24:1, which reads, "The earth is the Lord's, and the fullness thereof." God owns everything, including everything you possess, because He created everything. "All the earth is mine," the Lord said in Exodus 19:5. He declared it again in Job 41:11: "Whatever is under the whole heaven is mine."

That means we are managers or, to use the biblical word, *stewards* of the things God gives to us. As a slave, Joseph was a steward when Potiphar placed him over his household (see Genesis 39:5-6). Since slaves own nothing, Joseph owned nothing. But he managed everything Potiphar owned on his behalf. The management of Potiphar's resources included the use of them to meet his own needs, but Joseph's main responsibility was to use them for Potiphar's interests. That's our task. God wants us to use and enjoy the things He permits us to have, but as stewards of them we must remember that they all belong to Him and should be used for His kingdom.

The house or apartment you live in, then, is God's house or apartment. The trees in your yard are God's trees. The grass that you mow is God's grass. The garden that you have planted is God's garden. The car you drive is God's car. The clothes you are wearing and those hanging in your closet belong to God. The food in your cabinets belongs to God. The books on your shelves are God's books. All your furniture and everything else inside your home belongs to God.

We own nothing. God owns everything, and we are His managers. For most of us, the house we now call "my house" was called "my house" by someone else a few years ago. And a few years from now, someone else will call it "my house." Do you own any land? A few years from now, someone else will call it "my land." We just temporarily steward things that belong eternally to God. You probably believe that in theory already, but your giving will reflect how much you genuinely believe it.

God has specifically said that He owns not just the things we possess, but even the money under our name in the bank and the currency in our wallets. He said in Haggai 2:8, "'The silver is mine, and the gold is mine,' declares the LORD of hosts." So the question is not, "How much of my money should I give to God?" but rather, "How much of God's money should I keep for now?"

When we give to the Lord's work, we should give with the belief that *all* we have belongs to God and with the commitment that we will use *all* of it as *He* wants.

Giving Is an Act of Worship

In Philippians 4:18, the apostle Paul thanked the Christians in the Grecian city of Philippi for the financial gift they gave to support his missionary ministry. He wrote, "I have received full payment, and more. I am well supplied, having received from Epaphroditus the gifts you sent, a fragrant offering, a sacrifice acceptable and pleasing to God." He called the money they gave "a fragrant offering, a sacrifice acceptable and pleasing to God," comparing it to an Old Testament sacrifice people gave in worship to God. In other words, Paul said that their act of giving to the work of God was an act of worshiping God.

Have you ever thought of giving as worship? You know that praying, singing praises to God, observing the Lord's Supper, thanksgiving, and listening to Him speak through His Word are all worship, but do you realize that giving to God is one of the biblical and tangible ways of adoring and worshiping Him?

In his book *The Gift of Giving*, Wayne Watts wrote,

> While researching the Biblical principles of giving, I considered the subject of worship. Frankly, I had never before studied worship in detail to find out God's point of view. I have come to the conclusion that giving, along with our thanksgiving and praise, is worship. In the past I made pledges to my church to be paid on a yearly basis. Once a month, I would write a check while in church and drop it in the collection plate. Sometimes I would mail a check from my office. My objective was for the church to get the total pledge before the end of the year. Though I had already experienced the joy of giving, the act of making my gift had little relationship to worship. While I was writing this book God convicted me to begin giving every time I went to church. The verse that spoke to me about this was Deuteronomy 16:16—"Do not appear before Me empty-handed." When I started doing this, if a check were not handy, I gave cash. At first I thought about keeping up with the money given. Then God convicted me again. He seemed to say, "You do not need to keep up with the amount of cash. Give to Me simply out of a heart of love, and see how much you enjoy the service." I made this change in giving habits, and it has greatly enhanced my joy in our worship services.[6]

This awakened me to a better way in my own giving. In my church tradition, people attending the small-group Bible study before the worship service commonly make their gifts to the church then rather than during the worship gathering. If you have a similar pattern, you might discover as I have that your giving seems more like worship when you give in the context of a worship service instead.

Many people give to the Lord's work as many times each month as they get paid. In other words, if they get paid on the first of the month, they give once a month, likely on the first Sunday of the month. If they are paid on the first and the fifteenth, they give twice each month. Like Watts suggests and I commend, each week you might want to give part of your overall offering, rather than all of it only on the Sunday immediately after each payday. Of course, the danger with not giving all at once is spending some of the money you had intended to give the next Sunday. Some people avoid this by preparing in one sitting all their gifts for that pay period. Then, every Sunday their hands have something tangible to give as part of their worship to the Lord. Those who must give electronically or outside the congregational worship experience should ensure that the time of the offering in the worship service remains a moment of worship for them, and not a time of wandering thoughts. While others give, they could offer thanks to the Lord for His goodness and gifts, and otherwise express their worship in prayer.

Giving goes beyond a duty or obligation. Biblical giving displays a heart worshiping God.

Giving Reflects Faith in God's Provision

The proportion of your income that you give back to God testifies to how much you trust Him to provide for your needs. The Bible presents a story of giving and uncommon faith by a poor and very common lady in Mark 12:41-44:

> [Jesus] sat down opposite the treasury and watched the people putting money into the offering box. Many rich people put in large sums. And a poor widow came and put in two small copper coins, which make a penny. And he called his disciples to him and said to them, "Truly, I say to you, this poor widow has put in more than all those who are contributing to the offering box. For they all contributed out of their abundance, but she out of

her poverty has put in everything she had, all she had to live on."

This poor widow gave "everything she had, all she had to live on" because she believed God would provide for her.

We, too, will give to the extent we believe God will provide for us. The greater our faith that God will provide for our needs, the greater will be our willingness to risk giving to Him. And the less we trust God, the less we will want to give to Him.

I have a pastor-friend who was convicted by the poor widow's faith of his own need to trust God more for the provision of his needs. So he decided with his wife to give an entire month's salary to the Lord and trust Him to provide for them. They were almost out of food when a woman came by with several sacks of groceries. "How did you know?" they asked, since they'd told no one of their plan. But she knew nothing of their situation. She simply sensed that the Lord wanted her to take groceries to her pastor. They trusted God, demonstrated their faith by their giving, and God provided.

Your giving, too, can be—and probably already is—a tangible indication of how much you believe that God will provide for your needs.

Giving Should Be Sacrificial and Generous

The widow whom Jesus commended illustrates the fact that giving to God is not just for those who, as the world would put it, can "afford it." The apostle Paul gave another such illustration in 2 Corinthians 8:1-5 when he told of how the poor Christians in Macedonia sacrificed to give generously:

> We want you to know, brothers, about the grace of God
> that has been given among the churches of Macedonia,
> for in a severe test of affliction, their abundance of joy
> and their extreme poverty have overflowed in a wealth
> of generosity on their part. For they gave according to

their means, as I can testify, and beyond their means, of their own accord, begging us earnestly for the favor of taking part in the relief of the saints—and this, not as we expected, but they gave themselves first to the Lord and then by the will of God to us.

Paul described these Macedonians as people living in "extreme poverty." And yet "their extreme poverty . . . overflowed in a wealth of generosity." They gave not only "according to their means," but "beyond their means." Like these people, our giving should be sacrificial and generous.

Let me remind you that giving isn't sacrificial unless you sacrifice to give. Many professing Christians give only token amounts to the work of God's kingdom. A much smaller number give well. Perhaps only a few actually give sacrificially.

Polls consistently show that the more money Americans make, the less sacrificially we give.[7] With each transition to a higher income bracket, the smaller the percentage of our income we give each year to churches, charities, and other nonprofit groups. Wouldn't you agree that if we are making more money than ever but giving a smaller percentage than before, then we are not giving sacrificially? We may be giving larger amounts, but actually sacrificing less financially for the kingdom of God.

I've never known anyone who gave sacrificially—whether through a one-time sacrificial gift or consistent sacrificial offerings—who regretted it. Sure, they missed having some of the things they could have enjoyed if they'd spent the money on themselves. But the joy and fulfillment they gained by giving away something they could not ultimately keep was more than worth the sacrifice. Such people tend to say, "I never made a sacrifice. I always got something greater in return than I gave."

Imagine a mom or dad seeing her or his child graduating from high school or college, or getting married to a godly spouse, or watching that child do something that makes his or her eyes moist with tears of joy. You say to that mom or dad, "Hey, think of all the sleepless nights you had with that child, all the dirty diapers, the tens of thousands of dollars that child cost you that you could've spent on things you needed. Think of all the time that raising the child required when you could have been doing something else you really wanted. Parenting was just one sacrifice after another." She or he would reply, "It was worth every so-called sacrifice I made, because what I got in return was worth it all." You feel the same way when you give sacrificially and generously of your resources to other facets of the Lord's work, too. You never regret it.

Giving Reflects Spiritual Trustworthiness

Jesus revealed this startling insight into the ways of God's kingdom in Luke 16:10-13:

> One who is faithful in a very little is also faithful in much, and one who is dishonest in a very little is also dishonest in much. If then you have not been faithful in the unrighteous wealth, who will entrust to you the true riches? And if you have not been faithful in that which is another's, who will give you that which is your own? No servant can serve two masters, for either he will hate the one and love the other, or he will be devoted to the one and despise the other. You cannot serve God and money.

Notice again verse 11, which says that your giving reflects your spiritual trustworthiness: "If then you have not been faithful in the unrighteous wealth, who will entrust to you the true riches?" If we are not faithful with the money God entrusts to us—and certainly that includes the giving of our money for Christ's kingdom—the Bible says God will deem us untrustworthy to handle spiritual riches.

Here's an analogy: Suppose the owner of a lumber company privately decides on a certain employee to take over the business someday. Of course, the owner wants to determine if this employee can handle the business properly. So he gives him a part of the company to manage—the ordering and inspecting of new lumber—to see if he can make it profitable. He watches very closely how the employee runs that department for several months, not primarily to protect the company's bottom line, but in order to determine his trustworthiness and abilities. If he doesn't prove trustworthy with this part of the lumber company, the owner certainly won't hand over the entire enterprise. But if he proves faithful with it, the owner will entrust him with the true riches of the company ownership.

How you manage the financial "department" of your life is one of the best ways of evaluating your relationship with Christ and your spiritual trustworthiness. If you love Jesus and the work of His kingdom more than anyone or anything, your finances will reflect that. If you are truly submitted to the lordship of Christ, willing to obey Him completely in every area of your life, your giving will reveal it. We will do many things before we will give to someone else—even to Jesus—the rights over every dollar we have and ever will have. But if you have surrendered those rights to Him, your giving will show it.

That's why your financial records tell more about you than almost anything else. If after your death, in order to gain insight into your commitment to Christ, a biographer or your children were to scan the record of what you did with your money, what would they conclude? Would your financial footprints prove your spiritual trustworthiness?

Giving—Love, Not Legalism

God does not send you a bill. The church does not send you a monthly statement. We don't give to God and to the support of the work of His kingdom to fulfill some supposed "eleventh commandment." Love to God should motivate giving to God. How much you give should reflect how much you love God.

In 2 Corinthians 8, the apostle Paul reported to the first recipients of this letter, the people of Corinth, how some of their fellow Greeks in Macedonia were such good and faithful givers. In verse 7 he told the Corinthians, "But as you excel in everything—in faith, in speech, in knowledge, in all earnestness, and in our love for you—see that you excel in this act of grace also." In other words, "See that you excel in this grace of giving like the Macedonians." Notice what he then said in verse 8: "I say this not as a command, but to prove by the earnestness of others that your love also is genuine." Paul did not exercise his authority as an apostle (special messenger) of Jesus and command the Corinthians to give. Instead of dictating a law of giving, he said that giving is a way of proving the genuineness of your love for God.

He made this principle even clearer in the next chapter. Notice the absence of religious demand as a motive for giving in the first part of 2 Corinthians 9:7—"Each one must give as he has decided in his heart." He said much the same thing to them in 1 Corinthians 16:2, where he taught that each person should give "as he may prosper." Paul never gave his readers an external, measurable standard of giving. Instead, he maintained that giving to God should be measured in the heart, and the standard of that measurement was the depth of their love for God.

Allow me to adapt an illustration used in the chapter on worship and apply it this time to our motivation in giving. Suppose I come to Caffy on Valentine's Day, pull from behind my back a dozen of her favorite yellow roses, and say, "Happy Valentine's Day!" She says, "Oh, they're beautiful! Thank you! You shouldn't have spent so much money!" I respond neutrally to her joy with, "Don't mention it. Today is Valentine's Day, and as your husband it's my duty to get a gift for you." How do you think she'd feel? Probably like sticking every rose up my nose, thorns and all! Now suppose I do the same thing but say instead, "There's nothing I'd rather do with my money than use it for you because I love you so much." Same money. Same gift. But one gift is motivated by duty, the other by love. And the motive makes all the difference.

In the same way, God wants you to give, not as a formality or an obligation, but as the overflow of your love for Him.

Give Willingly, Thankfully, and Cheerfully

Again the verse is 2 Corinthians 9:7: "Each one must give as he has decided in his heart, not reluctantly or under compulsion, for God loves a cheerful giver."

God doesn't want you to give with a grudge—that is, you give but you'd rather not. He takes no pleasure in gifts presented resentfully, regardless of the amount involved. God is not a celestial landlord tapping a greedy, outstretched palm, demanding His due, having no concern for how you feel about it. God doesn't want you to give to Him out of a reluctant acquiescence to the reality that He owns it all anyway. He wants you to give because you want to.

One man said, "There are three kinds of giving: grudge giving, duty giving, and thanksgiving. Grudge giving says, 'I have to'; duty giving says, 'I ought to'; thanksgiving says, 'I want to.'"[8]

God wants you to *enjoy* giving.

Some people give to God like they fork over to the IRS after an audit. Others give to God like they pay their electric bill. But a few people give to God like they give an engagement ring to their fiancée or like they give wrapped surprises to their ecstatic four-year-old on Christmas morning.

Some give because they know they can't keep it. Others give because they believe they owe it. And a happy few give because they say *they can't help it!*

I realize we need a reason to give thankfully and cheerfully. Otherwise, this sounds like a person who comes when you're down and blithely says, "Cheer up!" Well, when you're down you need a reason to cheer up. But you shouldn't have to think long or hard for reasons to give thankfully and cheerfully to God. When you consider how God has given you the greatest possible gift in His Son, Jesus Christ, when you recall the mercy and grace He applies to you, when you reflect on how He provides all you have, and when you remember that you are actually giving to *God*, you should be able to give thankfully and cheerfully.

If one Sunday morning your pastor announced, "The head of one of the world's largest drug cartels is here today, and we are going to take up an offering for his army," you would not give willingly or cheerfully. (You would not give at all, except possibly under the threat of violence from your "guest.") But if he said, "The Lord Jesus Christ is outside in the hallway, and everything you give today will be presented to Him and used by Him for His kingdom," probably the only thing lighter than your heart after that worship service would be your wallet, because of the realization that you gave to God Himself.

Do you "just give," or do you give to God? You don't give grudgingly or under compulsion when you believe you're giving to God. Instead you give willingly, thankfully, and cheerfully.

Giving—an Appropriate Response to Real Needs

There are times when genuine needs should be communicated to one's local church, so that the members of the church may give spontaneously in response to those needs.

Three instances of this occur in the book of Acts where the Christians gave through the church in response to specific needs. The first happened in the days just after the earthshaking events of Pentecost. In Acts 2:43-45 we read, "And awe came upon every soul, and many wonders and signs were being done through the apostles. And all who believed were together and had all things in common. And they were selling their possessions and belongings and distributing the proceeds to all, as any had need." At Pentecost, when the Holy Spirit filled followers of Jesus with an unprecedented desire and power to declare the gospel, there were thousands from all parts of the Roman Empire there in Jerusalem to celebrate that annual Jewish feast. Three thousand people, many of them from among the visitors in town, became Christians on Pentecost Sunday. Soon thousands more were added to the church. Many of these visitors delayed or canceled their plans to return home, staying in Jerusalem because of their new faith in Christ and the exciting joy of fellowship with other believers. They had no home there, they had no jobs in Jerusalem, and they didn't have the means to provide for their needs. So to meet that unique, immediate predicament, all who had believed pooled their resources, sold property, and provided for one another.

The situation is similar in Acts 4:32-35:

> Now the full number of those who believed were of one heart and soul, and no one said that any of the things that belonged to him was his own, but they had everything in common. And with great power the apostles were giving their testimony to the resurrection of the Lord Jesus, and great grace was upon them all. There was not a needy person among them, for as many as were owners of lands or houses sold them and brought the proceeds of what was sold and laid it at the apostles' feet, and it was distributed to each as any had need.

Real needs existed within the church. Church members giving to meet those needs was the appropriate response.

In the third example from Acts, the need wasn't a local one. Those who gave could not see and did not know the people in need. Read Acts 11:27-30:

> Now in these days prophets came down from Jerusalem to Antioch. And one of them named Agabus stood up and foretold by the Spirit that there would be a great famine over all the world (this took place in the days of Claudius). So the disciples determined, every one according to his ability, to send relief to the brothers living in Judea. And they did so, sending it to the elders by the hand of Barnabas and Saul.

The Christians in Antioch, three hundred miles to the north of Jerusalem, gave to help feed and meet other needs of their unknown, fellow Christians in Jerusalem. This example provides a biblical precedent for our taking special offerings in church, such as offerings for international and home missions, world hunger, disaster relief, and so on—even for taking a spontaneous offering for any appropriate need.

Notice that no one in these three cases from Acts felt either pressured to give or like they were mandated an amount to give.

We don't have the space to discuss other guidelines for giving in response to special needs, such as making sure you have the necessary facts, confirming the integrity and accountability of those using the money, and so on. But note that despite the biblical legitimacy of spontaneous giving, most of our giving probably should *not* be unplanned.

Giving Should Be Planned and Systematic

Notice how the apostle Paul directed the Christians to give in 1 Corinthians 16:1-2: "Now concerning the collection for the saints: as I directed the churches of Galatia, so you also are to do. On the first day of every week, each of you is to put something aside and store it up, as he may prosper, so that there will be no collecting when I come."

This "collection for the saints" was a special offering for the poor Christians suffering in Jerusalem because of a famine. But even though the offering targeted a specific need, Paul instructed the Corinthians to give toward that need on a weekly basis for quite some time in advance of his coming. He knew that in the long run, greater efficiency and effectiveness results from giving in a planned and systematic way than haphazardly whenever a need arises. Since many needs are ongoing—like missions, feeding the hungry, and maintaining the ministry of a local church—systematic giving will meet those needs more consistently than an unceasing series of special offerings.

Note three observations about this planned, systematic giving. To begin with, Paul told them to give "on the first day of every week." These people probably were paid every day, if not every week. Most of us get paid every week, every two weeks, or once a month. Perhaps there is biblical wisdom for us all in a "first day of every week" principle of giving. That could mean either systematically dividing your giving by the number of Sundays per pay period and giving equal amounts on the "first day of every week," or giving a small amount of pocket cash on the Sundays when you aren't giving your main gift.

Second, note that he said "each of you" should do this. All self-identified Christians should express their stewardship of God's money through giving. This means we can't excuse ourselves from giving financially on the grounds that we give of our time or our talents. To share from those resources is good and right stewardship of those things, but completely substituting them for financial giving contradicts the biblical teaching on the stewardship of money. Paul's phrase "each of you" also means we can't totally exempt ourselves from giving because we experience a difficult time financially, or because we are retired, or because we are teenagers, or because we work only part-time. Remember: God owns all we have, even if He hasn't given us much to manage, and He is the One who tells us how to use what He owns. Also remember: We'll be happiest when we use God's money God's way. God's way involves giving in a planned, systematic way.

Third, he says that each should give "as he may prosper." Generally, the more you prosper, the higher you should make the percentage of your income that you give. The Bible sets no percentage *goal* in giving. Giving 10 percent of your gross income does not necessarily mean you have fulfilled the will of God. Ten percent does not make a ceiling of giving at which to stop, but a floor from which to grow.

I never see what anyone gives, but from personal conversations with them I know that one family in our church gives almost 20 percent of its gross income to the Lord, and another regularly gives between 20 and 25 percent. Neither their neighbors nor others in the church would consider these families wealthy by local standards.

I think it likely that our membership contains a few more families who give like that. They have children, house payments, and all the bills common to most of us. They haven't always given like this, however. But over the years they determined to increase systematically the percentage of their giving as they prospered.

Caffy had an aunt who didn't own much, but didn't have many bills either, so she eventually lived on 10 percent of her income and gave 90 percent. By contrast, R. G. LeTourneau of Peoria, Illinois, became a very wealthy Christian businessman and manufacturer of earth-moving equipment. As the Lord continued to prosper him, he increased the proportion of his giving until he devoted 90 percent of his annual income to the work of God's kingdom. Do you think either of them in heaven regrets doing that?

George Müller asked,

> Are you giving *systematically* to the Lord's work, or are you leaving it to feeling, to impression made upon you through particular circumstances, or to striking appeals? If we do not give from principle *systematically*, we shall find that our one brief life is gone before we are aware of it, and that, in return, we have done little for that adorable One who bought us with His precious blood, and to whom belongs all we have and are.[9]

Whenever you get a raise, unless there are unusual circumstances, plan to give a greater percentage than you give now. The percentage increase may be a little or a lot, but set a goal to give systematically more to God every time you "prosper."

My parents taught me percentage giving as a little boy when they started giving me a weekly allowance of fifteen cents. They gave me three boxes—on one they marked "giving," on the second they printed "savings," and on the third they wrote "spending." Each week a nickel went into the "savings" box, a nickel went into the "giving" box—where it lay until I took it to church on Sunday—and the other nickel, well, it never went into the "spending" box. For I immediately rode my bike the mile to the variety store downtown and bought a package of baseball cards. But I learned systematic giving.

Hear Müller again:

> Therefore I may affectionately beseech and entreat my beloved Christian friends to take this to heart, and consider that hitherto they have been depriving themselves of vast spiritual blessings, because they have not followed the principle of giving systematically, and giving as God prospers them, and according to a plan; not merely just according to impulse, not as they are moved by a missionary or charity sermon, but systematically and habitually giving on principle, just as God enables them. If he entrusts to them one pound, to give accordingly a proportion; if they are left a legacy of a thousand pounds, to give accordingly; if he entrusts them with ten thousand pounds, or whatever it may be, to give accordingly. Oh, my brethren, I believe if we realized the blessing, we would give thus on principle; and, if so, we should give a hundred times more than we do now.[10]

Generous Giving Results in Bountiful Blessing

Our Lord Jesus said in Luke 6:38, "Give, and it will be given to you. Good measure, pressed down, shaken together, running over, will be put into your lap. For with the measure you use it will be measured back to you."

That's not an isolated idea in the New Testament. Go back to 2 Corinthians 9:6-8 and read this promise of God: "The point is this: whoever sows sparingly will also reap sparingly, and whoever sows bountifully will also reap bountifully. Each one must give as he has decided in his heart, not reluctantly or under compulsion, for God loves a cheerful giver. And God is able to make all grace abound to you, so that having all sufficiency in all things at all times, you may abound in every good work."

If you give to God, these texts say that God will give to you. If you give bountifully to Him, He will give bountifully to you.

I think the "prosperity theology" popular today is heresy. It perverts the gospel, misrepresents God, and misleads its adherents. I do not believe that if you give a lot to God He will make you financially rich here on earth. But I do believe passages like these and others indicate that earthly blessings of an unspecified nature will be given to those who are faithful stewards of God's money. The end of verse 8 talks about "having all sufficiency in all things at all times, you may abound in every good work." That's clearly speaking of earthly blessings. God never says that if you give faithfully He will give you a lot of money, or some other specific earthly blessing. But He does say He will bless you in this life if you love and trust Him enough to be generous in your giving to Him.

Beware, though, three enemies to generous giving. For one, the world wants God's money. Advertising makes that plain. Second, Christians possess the same sinful desire as everyone else—the Bible calls such desires "the flesh"—to spend money selfishly. Third, the Devil tempts us to waste money because he is our Enemy and the Enemy of God's kingdom, and he wants to ruin our lives and the work of God. But if God really loves us as He says (and He demonstrated the depth of His love at the Cross), then we must believe He will tell us how to use our money in ways that ultimately benefit us the most and will bring us more joy than we would receive using money our way.

Most of God's blessing for our giving, however, will not come in this life. And it takes faith to believe that giving money here on earth lays up treasure in heaven. It takes faith to believe Jesus rightly said, "It is more blessed to give than to receive" (Acts 20:35). But if these passages are true (and they are!), we can believe that at a definite time in a real place God is actually going to reward us bountifully for what we have given generously and cheerfully.

Regardless of your interpretation of these passages, regardless of how much God rewards you here for your giving and how much in heaven, the bottom line is clear: God will bless you bountifully if you give generously.

MORE APPLICATION

Are you prepared for the end of time? A popular musician-songwriter of the early 1970s was Jim Croce. One of his most famous recordings was "Time in a Bottle," a love song about his desire to save time in a bottle in order to spend it later with someone he loved. The eerie thing about that piece was when it became the number one best-selling song in America, Jim Croce was dead. Had he been able to save time in a bottle, I'm sure he would have used it to prolong his life. Of course, he wasn't able to do that. And even if he had, the time he bottled would have been used up long ago.

Only so many sands occupy everyone's hourglass, and sooner or later they all run out. Even while writing this chapter I was called to the home of someone whose father had just died. If Christ does not come back first, someday the last grain of time in your life will fall and you will go with it.

Are you prepared? You may have written your will, planned and paid for your funeral, and have plenty of insurance, but you are not prepared unless the account of your sins before God has been settled. You are not prepared—in fact, on your own you cannot be prepared—to give an account of the time you have wasted in living for yourself instead of God, the time you spent in disobedience to God, the time you squandered on worldly pursuits that were destined to perish with the world itself, time that you could have spent investing in the work of the kingdom of God.

You are not prepared to stand before God unless you have taken the time to come to Christ and confess the misuse of your entire life. You are not prepared for death until you have asked God to forgive you on the basis of the death of Christ. You are not prepared for time to stop unless you have given the control of the rest of your time to the risen Christ.

"Today, if you hear his voice," says Hebrews 4:7, "do not harden your hearts." Hell is full of people who hardened their hearts while they still had time to repent and believe in Christ. So many now in hell hardened their hearts because they thought they had plenty of time and would come to Christ later. But no one in hell would harden his heart if he was given the opportunity you have right now; if he had one more occasion as you do to respond to the gospel. A hellish chorus of millions cries out in anguished agreement with Hebrews 4:7 to those who are outside of Christ, "Today, if you hear his voice, do not harden your hearts."

Are you using your time as God would have you use it? Evaluate your use of time in each of these areas and ask yourself if you are spending your time in each as God would have it (remembering that there are extremes on both sides of these): family, work, church, work in and around your home, media, sports, the Lord's Day, hobbies, exercise, sleep, Bible intake, prayer, and physical preparation for the day. Any sore spots there? If so, could that be the Lord's nudge about a needed change?

Maybe your use of time requires some fine-tuning. Maybe God is calling for a major adjustment. But remember that a disciplined life is impossible without the Discipline of time. Let's also state it positively: A disciplined life *is* possible through the Discipline of time.

Let me insert a word here to correct some possible misunderstandings. The disciplined use of time described in these pages should not be understood as promoting a relentless, unresting, burnout-prone lifestyle. After reading several biographies of Jonathan Edwards, preacher of "The Preciousness of Time" sermon referenced earlier, I'm convinced he consistently lived in accordance with the biblical principles regarding the use of time described in this chapter. And yet his biographers never portray him as a distracted and breathless man, hurtling through his day, always behind schedule. Although he was an introvert and intent on what today we would call "producing," he welcomed all who called on him as pastor. His home was almost constantly occupied with long-term guests, usually ministers in training. At least once daily Edwards met with his wife, Sarah, besides the three meals he enjoyed at home each day with her and the rest of the household. He spent time with his eleven children and knew how to laugh with them. And he did all these things because he believed that they were a wise use of his time and that it pleased God for him to do them.

At the heart of the biblical Discipline of time is doing the will of God when it ought to be done. "For everything there is a season," says Ecclesiastes 3:1, "and a time for every matter under heaven." There is a time for the specific kinds of Disciplines mentioned in this book, but there is also a time to discipline ourselves to rest, to replenish our physical and emotional resources through the right kinds of recreation, and to cultivate relationships. Though Jesus often ministered long hours and frequently under conditions that produced great demands on Him, nevertheless He was a man who rested, relaxed (after all, He walked everywhere He went, and surely at least some of that was leisurely paced), and cultivated relationships. He never used an hour uselessly, yet we never read of Him acting rushed. And Jesus is our Model in the disciplined use of time.

A more Christlike life really is possible for you through a Spirit-filled Discipline of time. God doesn't dangle growth in grace before you like a spiritual lure that's always enticing but never enjoyed. He promises that actual progress in godliness is possible and the Spiritual Disciplines are the means. The practical step behind each of the Spiritual Disciplines is the Discipline of time.

Are you willing to accept God's principles for giving? You've read them and thought about them, but do you believe them and accept them as God's will for *you*?

Are you giving like you mean it? Does your use of money—that for which you exchange so much of your life—make clear that you follow Christ and pursue godliness? Will you resolve that from this day forward your giving will show that Jesus Christ is the center of your life?

An article entitled "A Gallery of the Greatest" appeared in the Centennial Edition of *The Wall Street Journal*.[11] It reviewed the careers of several men the *Journal* considered business and financial successes, men like Andrew Carnegie, Henry Ford, J. P. Morgan, and others. In spite of their multiple millions, in spite of all the benevolent and philanthropic uses they made of their wealth, most of the men in this article apparently did not use their money as God instructs in Scripture. But you can. It's too late for the "Gallery of the Greatest," but not for you. No matter how much or little you have, as a believer you can discipline yourself to use your money for the greatest purposes on earth: for the glory of God and "for the purpose of godliness."

CHAPTER 9

FASTING . . .
FOR THE PURPOSE OF GODLINESS

Self-indulgence is the enemy of gratitude, and
self-discipline usually its friend and generator. That
is why gluttony is a deadly sin. The early desert fathers
believed that a person's appetites are linked: full stomachs
and jaded palates take the edge from our hunger and thirst
for righteousness. They spoil the appetite for God.

CORNELIUS PLANTINGA JR.

Quick—what do people who fast look like? What kinds of people come to your mind? Do they appear a bit strange? Are they John the Baptist types? Legalists? Health nuts?

Does Jesus come to your mind when you think of fasting and "fasters"? Jesus both practiced and taught fasting, you know. And yet, fasting is the most feared and misunderstood of all the Spiritual Disciplines.

One reason many fear fasting is the belief that it will make us appear unnecessarily strange or cause undesirable consequences. We fear that fasting will make us hollow-eyed fanatics or odd for God. We worry that it will make us suffer dreadfully and give us a generally negative experience. For some Christians, fasting for spiritual purposes is as unthinkable as walking barefoot across a fire pit or handling poisonous snakes in order to prove their devotion.

Fasting is the most misunderstood Discipline because of the famine of contemporary awareness of it. Even though there's a renewal of interest in fasting today, how many people do you know who practice fasting? How many sermons have you heard on the subject? In most Christian circles you will rarely hear fasting mentioned, and few will have read anything about it. And yet it's mentioned in Scripture more times even than something as important as baptism (about seventy-seven times for fasting to seventy-five for baptism).

Christians in a gluttonous, denial-less, self-indulgent society may struggle to accept and begin the practice of fasting. Few Disciplines go so radically against the flesh and the mainstream of culture as this one. Nevertheless, we dare not overlook its biblical significance. Of course, some people, for medical reasons, cannot fast. Still, even those unable to fast from food can enjoy many applications of this Discipline. No Christian should ignore fasting's benefits in the disciplined pursuit of a Christlike life.

FASTING EXPLAINED

Christian fasting is a believer's voluntary abstinence from food for spiritual purposes. Other types of fasting—despite the benefits they may produce for the mind and body—could not be classified as *Christian* fasting, and fasting by a non-Christian obtains no eternal value. It is for *believers* in Christ, for the Discipline must be rooted in a relationship with Christ and practiced with the desire to become more like Christ. Believers should fast according to biblical teaching and with purposes that are God-centered. It is *voluntary* in that fasting should not be coerced. And fasting is more than just the ultimate crash diet for the body; it is *abstinence from food* for *spiritual* purposes.

Let me address first the fact that, strictly speaking, fasting is *abstinence from food*. There is a broader, yet often overlooked view of fasting in which, for spiritual purposes, a person abstains from or denies himself the enjoyment of something other than food. Sometimes, for example, we may perceive the need to "fast" from involvement with other people, or from the media, from a sport or hobby, from talking, from sleep, from sex,[1] and so on. The reason might be that we sense the activity is exerting too much influence on our hearts or our time and we need to fast from it to regain a more biblical perspective. Or it might be simply that we want the freedom to become more absorbed in a particular spiritual focus.

Martyn Lloyd-Jones affirms the acceptability of this wider definition of fasting:

> To make the matter complete, we would add that fasting, if we conceive of it truly, must not only be confined to the question of food and drink; fasting should really be made to include abstinence from anything which is legitimate in and of itself for the sake of some special spiritual purpose. There are many bodily functions which are right and normal and perfectly legitimate, but which for special peculiar reasons in certain circumstances should be controlled. That is fasting. There, I suggest, is a kind of general definition of what is meant by fasting.[2]

So while it's appropriate to speak of fasting from any legitimate freedom, technically the Bible uses the term only in its primary sense, that is, abstinence from food. In this chapter, I will limit my remarks to that kind of fasting.

To understand fasting *for spiritual purposes*, realize that the Bible distinguishes between several *kinds* of fasts. Although it doesn't use the labels we frequently employ today to describe these fasts, each of the following may be found:

A *normal* fast involves abstaining from all food, but not from water. Matthew 4:2 reports of Jesus, "After fasting forty days and forty nights, he was hungry." It says nothing about Him becoming thirsty. Furthermore, Luke 4:2 says that He "ate nothing during those days," but it does not say He drank nothing. Since the body can normally function only a few days without water, we assume He drank water during these weeks (unless, and it is possible, this was a supernatural fast as described below). To abstain from food but to drink water or perhaps other liquids is the most common kind of Christian fast.

A *partial* fast is a limitation of the diet, but not abstention from all food. For ten days Daniel and three other Jewish young men had only "vegetables to eat and water to drink" (Daniel 1:12). Matthew 3:4 says that, for the rugged prophet John the Baptist, "his food was locusts and wild honey" for an unknown period of time. Historically, Christians have observed partial fasts by eating much smaller portions of food than usual for a certain time and/or eating only a few simple foods. By this means, many of those who cannot safely observe a normal fast can fast nonetheless.[3]

An *absolute* fast is the avoidance of all food and liquid, even water. We're told that "Ezra withdrew . . . neither eating bread nor drinking water, for he was mourning over the faithlessness of the exiles" (Ezra 10:6). When Esther requested that the Jews fast and pray on her behalf, she said, "Go, gather all the Jews to be found in Susa, and hold a fast on my behalf, and do not eat or drink for three days, night or day" (Esther 4:16). After the apostle Paul was converted on the road to Damascus, Acts 9:9 tells us, "for three days he was without sight, and neither ate nor drank."

The Bible also describes a *supernatural* fast. There are two instances of these. When Moses wrote of his meeting with God on Mount Sinai, he said, "I remained on the mountain forty days and forty nights. I neither ate bread nor drank water" (Deuteronomy 9:9). First Kings 19:8 may be saying that Elijah did the same thing when he went to the site of Moses' miraculous fast: "And he arose and ate and drank, and went in the strength of that food forty days and forty nights to Horeb, the mount of God." These required God's supernatural intervention into the bodily processes and are not repeatable apart from the Lord's specific calling and miraculous provision.[4]

A *private* fast is the one referred to most often in this chapter and what Jesus meant in Matthew 6:16-18 when He said we should fast in a way not to be noticed by others.

Congregational fasts are the type found in Joel 2:15-16: "Blow the trumpet in Zion; consecrate a fast; call a solemn assembly;

gather the people. Consecrate the congregation." At least a part of the congregation of the church at Antioch was fasting together in Acts 13:2, as evidenced by Luke's words: "While they were worshiping the Lord and fasting . . ."

The Bible also speaks of *national* fasts. In response to an invasion, King Jehoshaphat (in 2 Chronicles 20:3) called a national fast: "Then Jehoshaphat was afraid and set his face to seek the Lord, and proclaimed a fast throughout all Judah." All Jews were called to fast in Nehemiah 9:1 and Esther 4:16, and the king of Nineveh proclaimed a fast for all his people in response to the preaching of Jonah (see 3:5-8). Incidentally, during the early days of our nation, Congress proclaimed three national fasts. Presidents John Adams and James Madison each called all Americans to fast, and Abraham Lincoln did so on three separate occasions during the Civil War.[5]

God established one *regular* fast in the Old Covenant. Each year, every Jew was to fast on the Day of Atonement (see Leviticus 16:29-31). While they were in Babylon, the leaders of the Jews instituted four other annual fasts (see Zechariah 8:19). The Pharisee in Luke 18:12 congratulated himself in prayer for keeping the tradition of the Pharisees by saying, "I fast twice a week." Although without biblical warrant, John Wesley would not ordain a man to the Methodist ministry who did not regularly fast every Wednesday and Friday.

Finally, the Bible mentions *occasional* fasts. These occur on special occasions as the need arises. This was the kind of fast Jehoshaphat, as well as Esther, called for in view of their circumstances. This is the kind of fast implied by Jesus in Matthew 9:15: "Can the wedding guests mourn as long as the bridegroom is with them? The days will come when the bridegroom is taken away from them, and then they will fast."

The most common fast among Christians today would probably fall under the categories of normal (abstaining from food but drinking water), private, and occasional.

FASTING IS EXPECTED

To those unfamiliar with fasting, the most surprising part of this chapter may be the discovery that Jesus expected His followers would fast. Notice Jesus' words at the beginning of Matthew 6:16-17: "And *when* you *fast.* . . . But *when* you *fast* . . ." (emphasis added). By giving us instructions on what to do and what not to do when we fast, Jesus assumes that we will fast.

This expectation is even more obvious when we compare these words with His statements in that same passage—Matthew 6:2-3—about giving: "Thus, *when* you *give.* . . . But *when* you *give* . . ." (emphasis added). Compare also His words in the same section—Matthew 6:5-7—about praying: "And *when* you *pray.* . . . But *when* you *pray.* . . . And *when* you *pray* . . ." (emphasis added). No one doubts that we are to give and to pray. In fact, Christians commonly use this passage to teach Jesus' principles on giving and praying. And since there is nothing here or elsewhere in Scripture indicating that we no longer need to fast, and since we know that Christians in the book of Acts fasted (see 9:9; 13:2; 14:23), we may conclude that Jesus still expects His followers to fast today.

Plainer still are Jesus' words in Matthew 9:14-15. Immediately after calling Matthew the tax collector to follow Him, Jesus went to Matthew's house for a meal. The Pharisees came and asked how Jesus could eat with such a sinner. The disciples of John the Baptist had a problem with this too. Like John, they were single-minded men who shared in his ministry of calling people to repentance, and fasting was part of their discipleship. They were to point people to Jesus as John did, but they were confused by the contrast of Jesus feasting here and the fasting John often urged upon them. So they asked Jesus, "'Why do we and the Pharisees fast, but your disciples do not fast?' And Jesus said to them, 'Can the wedding guests mourn as long as the bridegroom is with them? The days will come when the bridegroom is taken away from them, and *then they will fast*'" (emphasis added).

Jesus said the time would come when His disciples "will fast." That time is now. Jesus, the "Bridegroom" of the church, is away in heaven. His people fast as part of their longing for and anticipation of His return. "Christian fasting," wrote John Piper, "at its root, is the hunger of a homesickness for God."[6] Fasting sometimes seems the only way to answer the ache in our hearts for the consummation of all things, for the time when we are at last with God and all things are restored, made new, and made right. Until the Bridegroom returns for His bride, He knows how these yearnings for Him will incline our hearts, with the result that we "will fast."

The only instructions He gave, in addition to those already mentioned, are in Matthew 6:16-18. There Jesus gave us a negative command, a positive command, and a promise. The negative command is first: "And when you fast, do not look gloomy like the hypocrites, for they disfigure their faces that their fasting may be seen by others. Truly, I say to you, they have received their reward" (verse 16). When you fast, don't announce it by the way you look or act. Don't look miserable. Don't talk about how hungry you are. Don't neglect your appearance.

The positive command is next: "But when you fast, anoint your head and wash your face, that your fasting may not be seen by others but by your Father who is in secret" (verses 17-18). Instead of looking like a hungry scavenger, present yourself so well that no one can tell by your appearance that you are fasting. The only Observer of your fast should be the Secret One. No one else should know that you are fasting unless it is absolutely unavoidable or necessary. If you are married, or if someone regularly cooks for you, courtesy may require that you tell your spouse or someone else about your fast. The problem is not whether another person knows or asks about your fast, but whether you *want* him or her to know or ask so you can appear more spiritual. The former case simply provides information that someone needs or requests; the latter reveals hypocrisy and violates the command Jesus gave at the beginning of this very chapter of Matthew—"Beware of practicing your righteousness before other people in order to be seen by them, for then you will have no reward from your Father who is in heaven" (6:1).

Then Jesus gave us a promise about fasting: "And your Father who sees in secret will reward you" (verse 18). He did not say when the Father will reward you, nor how He will reward you, but Jesus promised that "your Father who sees in secret *will* reward you" (emphasis added). As certain as any promise in Scripture is the promise that God will bless you and reward you when you fast according to His Word.

It's interesting that Jesus gave us no command regarding how often or how long we should fast. Like the other Spiritual Disciplines, fasting should never devolve into an empty, legalistic routine. God offers to bless us through fasting as often as we desire.

Since Jesus didn't specifically instruct us on the matter, how long should we fast? In the Bible we find examples of fasts that lasted one day or part of a day (see Judges 20:26; 1 Samuel 7:6; 2 Samuel 1:12; 3:35; Nehemiah 9:1; Jeremiah 36:6), a one-night fast (see Daniel 6:18-24), three-day fasts (see Esther 4:16; Acts 9:9), seven-day fasts (see 1 Samuel 31:13; 2 Samuel 12:16-23), a fourteen-day fast (see Acts 27:33-34), a twenty-one-day fast (see Daniel 10:3-13), forty-day fasts (see Deuteronomy 9:9; 1 Kings 19:8; Matthew 4:2), and fasts of unspecified lengths (see Matthew 9:14; Luke 2:37; Acts 13:2; 14:23). Strictly speaking, abstinence from one meal for spiritual purposes constitutes a fast. So the length of your fast is up to you and the leadership of the Holy Spirit.

FASTING IS TO BE DONE FOR A PURPOSE

There's more to a biblical fast than merely abstaining from food. Without a spiritual purpose for your fast it's just a weight-loss fast. You'll be like the man who told one writer on fasting,

> I've fasted on several occasions; and nothing happened.
> I just got hungry. . . . Several years ago I heard a couple
> of pastors discussing fasting. On their recommendation

I tried my first fast. They said it was commanded in the Bible and should be practiced by every Christian. Being a Christian, I decided to try it. After putting it off for several days, I mustered up enough courage to start. I couldn't go to the breakfast table with my family because I didn't think I would have enough willpower to abstain from eating, so I went on to work. The coffee break was almost unbearable, and I told a little white lie about why I didn't go with the group. All I could think about was how hungry I was. I said to myself, "If I ever get through this day, I'll never try this again." The afternoon was even worse. I tried to concentrate on my work, but all I could hear was the growling of my stomach. My wife prepared a meal for herself and our child, and the aroma of the food was all I could bear. I figured that if I could make it till midnight, I would have fasted all day. I did—but immediately after the striking of the hour of twelve, I dug into food. I don't think that day of fasting helped me one bit.[7]

Of course, he was probably right. This man had no biblical purpose for his fast. Without a purpose, fasting can be a miserable, self-centered experience about willpower and endurance.

Having a biblical purpose for your fast may be the single most important concept to take from this chapter. In real life, here's how it works: As you are fasting and your head aches or your stomach growls and you think, *I'm hungry!* your next thought is likely to be something like, *Oh, right—I'm hungry because I'm fasting today.* Then your next thought *should* be, *And I'm fasting for this purpose:*

_____.

Without a clear biblical purpose, fasting becomes an end in itself. Every hunger pang only makes you calculate the time remaining until you can eat. Such thinking disconnects the experience in your mind and heart from the gospel and descends into the deception that perhaps your suffering will earn God's favor.

Although the physical discomfort is unpleasant—perhaps even painful—it is important to feel some degree of hunger during your fast.[8] Your hunger helps you, serving as a continual reminder of your spiritual purpose. For instance, if your purpose is to pray for your spouse, then every time your stomach growls or your head aches, your hunger reminds you that you're fasting, which in turn reminds you that you're fasting for the purpose of praying for your spouse—and then you pray. So throughout your fast, every time you feel hunger—whether you are working, driving, talking to someone, sitting at the computer, walking, or whatever—you are reminded of your purpose, in this case to pray for your spouse. As a result you will be prompted by your hunger to pray for your spouse far more often than you would have otherwise, which is exactly what you wanted to do.

Scripture sets forth many purposes for fasting. I've condensed them into ten major categories. Notice that *none* of the purposes is to earn God's favor. It is useless to fast as a way to impress God and earn His acceptance. Faith in the work of Jesus Christ makes us acceptable to God, not our efforts, regardless of their intensity or sincerity. Fasting has no eternal benefit for us until we have come to God through repentance and faith. (See Ephesians 2:1-10 and Titus 3:5-7.) Only after we come alive to God through Christ can we engage in Christian fasting. And then, according to Piper, "This is the essence of Christian fasting: We ache and yearn—and fast—to know more and more of all that God is for us in Jesus. But only because he has already laid hold of us and is drawing us ever forward and upward into 'all the fullness of God.'"[9]

As a Christian then, whenever you fast, you should do so for at least one of these biblical purposes.

To Strengthen Prayer

"Whenever men are to pray to God concerning any great matter," wrote John Calvin, "it would be expedient to appoint fasting along with prayer."[10] There's something about fasting that sharpens the edge of our intercessions and deepens the passion of our supplications. So the people of God have frequently utilized fasting when they have felt a special urgency about the concerns they lift before the Father.

When Ezra was about to lead a group of exiles back to Jerusalem, he proclaimed a fast in order for the people to seek the Lord earnestly for safe passage. They were to face many dangers without military protection during their nine-hundred-mile journey. Their vulnerability meant this was no ordinary matter. "So we fasted and implored our God for this," says Ezra 8:23, "and he listened to our entreaty."

The Bible does not teach that fasting is a kind of spiritual hunger strike that compels God to do our bidding. If we ask for something outside of God's will, fasting does not cause Him to reconsider. Fasting does not change God's hearing so much as it changes our praying. One of the ways it changes our praying, as Piper explains, is that fasting "is an intensifier of spiritual desire."[11] In his book *God's Chosen Fast*, Arthur Wallis concurred:

> Fasting is calculated to bring a note of urgency and importunity into our praying, and to give force to our pleading in the court of heaven. The man who prays with fasting is giving heaven notice that he is truly in earnest. . . . Not only so, but he is expressing his earnestness in a divinely-appointed way. He is using a means that God has chosen to make his voice to be heard on high.[12]

Note that biblical fasting is God's idea. When we sense the need to strengthen our prayers, God says in Scripture to apply the force of fasting. Biblical fasting is not derived from man's imagination as a way to persuade God, similar to the efforts of the prophets of Baal who, in their famous confrontation with Elijah on Mount Carmel, cut themselves with swords in a vain attempt to awaken their god (see 1 Kings 18:28). Our Lord is always pleased to hear the prayers of His people. But He is also pleased when we choose to enhance our prayers in a way He Himself has ordained.

Other biblical figures who added fasting to prayer include Nehemiah, who "continued fasting and praying before the God of heaven" (Nehemiah 1:4). Daniel devoted himself to pleading with God "by prayer and pleas for mercy with fasting" (Daniel 9:3). In a direct, divine command through the prophet Joel, Israel was told, "'Yet even now,' declares the LORD, 'return to me with all your heart, with fasting, with weeping, and with mourning'" (Joel 2:12). It wasn't until "after fasting and praying" that the church in Antioch "laid their hands" on Barnabas and Saul of Tarsus and "sent them off" on the first missionary journey (Acts 13:3).

Of all the purposes for fasting found in Scripture, fasting in order to strengthen prayer receives the most emphasis by far. In fact, in one way or another, all the other biblical purposes of fasting relate to prayer. Fasting is one of the best friends we can introduce to our prayer lives. Despite this potential power, however, very few seem willing to enjoy its benefits. To quote Wallis again,

> In giving us the privilege of fasting as well as praying, God has added a powerful weapon to our spiritual armory. In her folly and ignorance the Church has largely looked upon it as obsolete. She has thrown it down in some dark corner to rust, and there it has lain forgotten for centuries. An hour of impending crisis for the Church and the world demands its recovery.[13]

To Seek God's Guidance

A second purpose for fasting is to more clearly discern the will of God. In Judges 20 the other eleven tribes of Israel prepared for war against the tribe of Benjamin. The soldiers gathered at Gibeah because of a shocking sin committed by the men of that Benjamite city. They sought the Lord before going into battle, and even though they outnumbered the Benjamites by fifteen to one, they lost the battle and twenty-two thousand men. The next day they sought the Lord with prayer and tears, but again they lost the battle and suffered thousands of casualties. Confused, the third time they not only sought guidance from the Lord in prayer and with tears, but they also "fasted that day until evening" (verse 26). "Shall we go out once more to battle against our brothers, the people of Benjamin, or shall we cease?" they asked. Then the Lord made His will plain: "Go up, for tomorrow I will give them into your hand" (verse 28). Only after they sought Him with fasting did the Lord give Israel the victory.

According to Acts 14:23, before Paul and Barnabas would appoint elders in the churches they founded, they first prayed with fasting to receive God's guidance.

David Brainerd prayed with fasting to discern the Lord's leadership regarding his entry into ministry. On Monday, April 19, 1742, he recorded in his journal: "I set apart this day for fasting and prayer to God for his grace, especially to prepare me for the work of the ministry, to give me divine aid and direction in my preparations for that great work, and in his own time to send me into his harvest."[14] He said of his experience with fasting that day,

> I felt a power of intercession for precious immortal souls, for the advancement of the kingdom of my dear Lord and Saviour in the world; and withal, a most sweet resignation and even consolation and joy in the thoughts of suffering hardships, distresses, and even death itself, in the promotion of it. . . . My soul was drawn out very much for the world; I grasped for multitudes of souls. I think I had more enlargement for sinners than for the children of God; though I felt as if I could spend my life in cries for both. I enjoyed great sweetness in communion with my dear Saviour. I think I never in my life felt such an entire weanedness from this world and so much resigned to God in everything.[15]

A few weeks later, on June 14, Brainerd again fasted for the purpose of seeking God's guidance regarding the ministry to which he believed God had appointed him: "I set apart this day for secret fasting and prayer, to entreat God to direct and bless me with regard to the great work I have in view, of preaching the gospel."[16] As his body fasted, his soul feasted: "The Lord visited me marvelously in prayer; I think my soul never was in such an agony before: I felt no restraint; for the treasures of divine grace were opened to me: I wrestled for absent friends, for the ingathering of souls, for multitudes of poor souls, and for many that I thought were the children of God, personally, in many distant places."[17]

Fasting does not *ensure* the certainty of receiving such clear guidance from God and confirmation of direction as did Brainerd on this occasion. Rightly practiced, however, it does make us more receptive to the One who loves to guide us.

To Express Grief

Three of the first four references in the Bible to fasting connect it with an expression of grief. As mentioned in Judges 20:26, one of the reasons the Israelites wept and fasted before the Lord was not only to seek His guidance, but to express their grief for the forty thousand brothers they had lost in battle. After the Philistines killed King Saul and his sons in battle, the men of Jabesh Gilead walked all night to recover the bodies. After the burial, 1 Samuel 31:13 says they mourned when they "fasted seven days." Second Samuel gives the response of David and his men when they heard the news: "Then David took hold of his clothes and tore them, and so did all the men who were with him. And they mourned and wept and fasted until evening for Saul and for Jonathan his son and for the people of the LORD and for the house of Israel, because they had fallen by the sword" (1:11-12).

Grief caused by events other than a death also can be expressed through fasting. For instance, Christians have fasted because of grief for their sins. Doing so should not be viewed as an attempt to pay for our sins, because we cannot pay that price and because Christ has already done so once for all (see Hebrews 9:12; 10:10;

1 Peter 3:18). God has promised that "if we confess our sins, he is faithful and just to forgive us our sins and to cleanse us from all unrighteousness" (1 John 1:9). But that does not mean that confession is a light and easy thing, a simple mouthing of words, a verbal ritual. Mere admission is not confession. We dishonor Christ by a frivolous view of confession that fails to appreciate how much our sin cost Him. Although not a spiritual self-flagellation, biblical confession does involve at least some degree of grief for the sin committed. And inasmuch as fasting can be an expression of grief, it is never inappropriate for fasting to be a voluntary, heartfelt part of confession. On a few occasions I felt such a deep grief over my sin that words alone seemed powerless to express to God what I wanted. And though it made me no more worthy of forgiveness, fasting communicated the grief and confession mere words could not.

Fasting also can be a means of expressing grief for the sins of others, such as for the sins of people within your church or for sins by your country. When a jealous King Saul was trying unjustly to kill David, the response of his son Jonathan was that he "ate no food the second day of the month, for he was grieved for David" (1 Samuel 20:34), meaning that he fasted because of his grief over his father's sinful treatment of David.

Caffy and I have a friend who has been a Christian just a few years. When she veered away from her profession of faith, we expressed our grief and prayed for her through a mutual fast of several days. Although we'd confronted her about her situation several times, she said after being restored that knowing we and others in the church had fasted for her was one of the main influences God used to return her to fellowship. In addition, our church has observed some occasional fast days together, partially to express our grief to the Lord over the sins of our nation.

Since fasting, like weeping, is often a means of physically expressing to God the depth of our feelings, it is just as appropriate for grief-stricken prayers to be accompanied by fasting as by tears.

To Seek Deliverance or Protection

One of the most common fasts in biblical times was a fast to seek salvation from enemies or circumstances. After being notified that a vast army was coming against him, King Jehoshaphat "was afraid and set his face to seek the LORD, and proclaimed a fast throughout all Judah. And Judah assembled to seek help from the LORD; from all the cities of Judah they came to seek the LORD" (2 Chronicles 20:3-4).

Earlier we read of the fast called by Ezra when he led a group of exiles back to Jerusalem. There we noticed that they fasted in order to strengthen their prayers. But notice from the larger context of Ezra 8:21-23 that the prayer they wanted to strengthen with fasting was for God's protection:

> Then I proclaimed a fast there, at the river Ahava, that
> we might humble ourselves before our God, to seek from
> him a safe journey for ourselves, our children, and all our
> goods. For I was ashamed to ask the king for a band of
> soldiers and horsemen to protect us against the enemy
> on our way, since we had told the king, "The hand of our
> God is for good on all who seek him, and the power of
> his wrath is against all who forsake him." So we fasted and
> implored our God for this, and he listened to our entreaty.

The best known cooperative fast in Scripture is likely the one in Esther 4:16, and its purpose was to seek God's protection and deliverance. Queen Esther called for the fast in support of her petition to God for protection from the king's wrath. She planned to risk death by entering the court of King Xerxes uninvited in order to appeal to him for the deliverance of the Jews from mass extermination. She said to her cousin Mordecai, "Go, gather all the Jews to be found in Susa, and hold a fast on my behalf, and do not eat or drink for three days, night or day. I and my young women will also fast as you do. Then I will go to the king, though it is against the law, and if I perish, I perish."

When our church has a day of fasting in grief for the sins of our country, we also include prayers asking the Lord to protect and deliver us from enemies that might result from our sins. We realize that He often disciplined Israel. Perhaps we don't think of the reality of national sin as often as we should, and how Christians will experience part of any national judgment that comes, even though we did not contribute directly to the national sin.

But not all fasts that seek deliverance or protection from God are corporate fasts. David wrote Psalm 109 as an appeal for personal relief from a group of enemies and their leader in particular. A private fast was accompanying his prayer, as indicated by verse 24: "My knees are weak through fasting; my body has become gaunt, with no fat." Apparently this was an unusually long fast.

Fasting, rather than fleshly efforts, should be one of our first defenses against "persecution" from family, schoolmates, neighbors, or coworkers because of our faith. Typically we're tempted to strike back with anger, verbal abuse, counteraccusations, or even legal action. But instead of political maneuvering, gossiping, and imitating the worldly tactics of our enemies, we should appeal to God with fasting for protection and deliverance.

To Express Repentance and the Return to God

Fasting for this purpose is similar to fasting for the purpose of expressing grief for sin. But as repentance is a change of mind resulting in a change of action, fasting can represent more than just grief over sin. It also can signal a commitment to obedience and a new direction.

The Israelites expressed repentance through fasting in 1 Samuel 7:6 when they "drew water and poured it out before the LORD and fasted on that day and said there, 'We have sinned against the LORD.'" In Joel 2:12, the Lord specifically commanded His people to signify their repentance and their return to Him by fasting: "'Yet even now,' declares the LORD, 'return to me with all your heart, with fasting, with weeping, and with mourning.'"

Surely the most thorough fast ever recorded is the one in Jonah 3:5-8, and it is a fast to express repentance. After God blessed Jonah's preaching with a great spiritual awakening,

> The people of Nineveh believed God. They called for a fast and put on sackcloth, from the greatest of them to the least of them.
>
> The word reached the king of Nineveh, and he arose from his throne, removed his robe, covered himself with sackcloth, and sat in ashes. And he issued a proclamation and published through Nineveh, "By the decree of the king and his nobles: Let neither man nor beast, herd nor flock, taste anything. Let them not feed or drink water, but let man and beast be covered with sackcloth, and let them call out mightily to God. Let everyone turn from his evil way and from the violence that is in his hands."

Not only can fasting express repentance, it can be in vain *without* repentance. As with all Spiritual Disciplines, fasting is little more than a "dead work" if we have persistently hardened our hearts to God's call to deal with a specific sin in our lives. We must never try to immerse ourselves in a Spiritual Discipline as an attempt to drown out conviction from the Holy Spirit about forsaking a sin. We pervert the very essence of fasting if we try to use it as a counterweight of self-punishment against a sinful part of life we want to continue feeding. A Scottish stalwart of the later Puritan pastor-writers, Thomas Boston, said,

> In vain will ye fast, and pretend to be humbled for our sins, and make confession of them, if our love of sin be not turned into hatred; our liking of it, into loathing; and our cleaving to it, into a longing to be rid of it; with full purpose to resist the motions of it in our heart, and the outbreakings thereof in our life; and if we turn not unto God as our rightful Lord and Master, and return to our duty again.[18]

To Humble Oneself Before God

Fasting, when practiced with the right motives, is a physical expression of humility before God, just as kneeling or prostrating yourself in prayer can reflect humility before Him. And as there are times when you desire to express humility by praying on your knees or on your face before the Lord, so there are times when you may want to express a sense of humility before the Lord in every activity throughout the day by fasting.

Many who are accustomed to expressing humility in prayer by kneeling might ask why we would want to express humility all day by fasting. Conversely, John Calvin asked a better question: Why not? "For since [fasting] is a holy exercise both for the humbling of men and for their confession of humility, why should we use it less than the ancients did in similar need? . . . What reason is there why we should not do the same?"[19]

One of the most wicked men in Jewish history, King Ahab, eventually humbled himself before God and demonstrated his humility by fasting:

> When Ahab heard those words, he tore his clothes and put
> sackcloth on his flesh and fasted and lay in sackcloth and
> went about dejectedly. And the word of the LORD came
> to Elijah the Tishbite, saying, "Have you seen how Ahab
> has humbled himself before me? Because he has humbled
> himself before me, I will not bring the disaster in his days;
> but in his son's days I will bring the disaster upon his
> house." (1 KINGS 21:27-29)

On the other hand, one of Israel's godliest men humbled himself before the Lord in exactly the same way. King David wrote, "I wore sackcloth; I afflicted myself with fasting" (Psalm 35:13).

Remember that fasting itself is not humility before God, but should be an *expression* of humility. There was no humility in the Pharisee of Luke 18:12, who bragged to God in prayer that he fasted twice a week. Author David Smith, in *Fasting: A Neglected Discipline*, reminds us,

By this we must not conclude that the act of fasting has some virtuous power, and that we have made ourselves more humble; there is no virtue in fallen man by which he can make himself more godly; there is, however, virtue in the divinely appointed means of grace. If we, by the power of the Holy Spirit, mortify the deeds of the body (through fasting), we shall grow in grace, but the glory of such change will be God's alone.[20]

To Express Concern for the Work of God

Just as a parent might fast and pray out of concern for the work of God in the life of a child, so Christians may fast and pray because they feel a burden for the work of God on a relatively broad scale. For example, a Christian might feel compelled to fast and pray for the work of God in a place that has experienced tragedy, disappointment, or apparent defeat.

This was the purpose for Nehemiah's fast when he heard that despite the return of many Jewish exiles to Jerusalem, the city still had no wall to defend it:

> They said to me, "The remnant there in the province
> who had survived the exile is in great trouble and shame.
> The wall of Jerusalem is broken down, and its gates are
> destroyed by fire." As soon as I heard these words I sat
> down and wept and mourned for days, and I continued
> fasting and praying before the God of heaven.
> (NEHEMIAH 1:3-4)

After his fast, Nehemiah then set about doing something tangible and public to strengthen the work of God in Jerusalem.

Daniel, too, felt a heavy burden for the return of the Jews from exile and for the restoration of Jerusalem. Also like Nehemiah, he expressed this burden by fasting: "Then I turned my face to the Lord God, seeking him by prayer and pleas for mercy with fasting and sackcloth and ashes" (Daniel 9:3).

John Piper voiced some of the longings in the souls of those who fast out of concern for the work of God:

> My heart is hungry for "all the fullness of God." I long for a deeper work of God in the midst of his people. I yearn for a mighty tide of missionary zeal to spread a passion for the supremacy of Christ in all things for the joy of all peoples. I long to see unmistakable, supernatural new birth taking place week in and week out through the compelling witness of God's transformed people wherever he is named.[21]

Obviously we can't fast continually, but may the Lord at least occasionally give us a concern for His work so great that our normal concern for food will seem secondary in comparison.

To Minister to the Needs of Others

Those who think the Spiritual Disciplines foster tendencies of introspection or independence should consider Isaiah 58. In the most extensive passage in Scripture dealing exclusively with fasting, God emphasizes fasting for the purpose of meeting the needs of others. The people originally addressed in this section had complained to the Lord that they had fasted and humbled themselves before Him, but He had not answered them. The reason He had not heard them was their disobedience. Their lives stood in hypocritical contrast to their fasting and praying. "Behold, in the day of your fast," the Lord said to them in verses 3-4, "you seek your own pleasure, and oppress all your workers. Behold, you fast only to quarrel and to fight and to hit with a wicked fist. Fasting like yours this day will not make your voice to be heard on high." So although they were fasting, they were also arguing, fighting, and mistreating others. But God will not allow us to compartmentalize fasting from the rest of our lives. The Spiritual Disciplines do not stand alone. The Lord will not bless the practice of any Discipline, including fasting, when we disregard His Word regarding relationships with people.

What should we do? How *does* God want us to fast? "Is not

this the fast that I choose," the Lord asked in verses 6-7, "to loose the bonds of wickedness, to undo the straps of the yoke, to let the oppressed go free, and to break every yoke? Is it not to share your bread with the hungry and bring the homeless poor into your house; when you see the naked, to cover him, and not to hide yourself from your own flesh?" In other words, the kind of fasting that pleases God is one that results in concern for others and not just for ourselves.

"But," someone objects, "I'm so busy just meeting my needs and those of my family that I don't have the time to minister to other people." One possible solution is to fast for a meal or for a day and minister to the needs of others during the time you would normally spend eating. That way you've lost none of the time you say you must give to your regular commitments. Several months ago I started scheduling a regular fast each week and devoting one of the mealtimes during that day to meet for counseling or discipling. I've been amazed at how convenient and preferable that late-afternoon period is for many people. The result is that the time that became available because of fasting has developed into my single most productive, need-meeting, one-on-one ministry slot all week.

There are other ways of fasting to meet the needs of others. Some fast so they can take the money they would have spent on food and give it to the poor, or to missions, or to some other ministry. How could you minister to the needs of others with the extra time or money fasting could provide?

To Overcome Temptation and Dedicate Yourself to God

Ask Christians to name a fast by a biblical character and most will probably think first of the lengthy fast of Jesus prior to His temptation in Matthew 4:1-11. Verse two of that familiar passage tells us that Jesus fasted "forty days and forty nights." In the spiritual strength of that prolonged fast He was prepared to overcome a direct onslaught of temptation from Satan himself. This fast was also the time when Jesus privately dedicated Himself to the Father for the public ministry He was about to begin.

Nowhere in Scripture does God ask us to fast for forty days. And the significance of this passage has much more to do with declaring who Jesus is than it does with fasting. But that doesn't mean there is nothing from Jesus' unique experience for us to learn about fasting. One principle we learn from Jesus' example is this: Fasting is a way of overcoming temptation and of freshly dedicating ourselves to the Father.

Sometimes when we struggle with temptation, or when we anticipate grappling with it, we know that we need extra spiritual strength to overcome it. Perhaps we are traveling (or our spouse is traveling) and temptations for mental and sensual unfaithfulness abound. At the start of school or a new job or ministry there may be new temptations, or it may just seem appropriate at that time to dedicate ourselves anew to the Lord. Often we face decisions that place unusual temptations before us. Do we take a new job that will mean much more money but much less time with the family? Do we accept the promotion that includes a transfer that would end a significant ministry in our local church, or when it means going where our families' spiritual growth may suffer? In times of exceptional temptation, exceptional measures are required. One such exceptional measure in your situation might be a Christlike fast for the purpose of overcoming the temptation and of renewing your dedication to God.

To Express Love and Worship to God

By now you may have associated fasting only with dire circumstances and great troubles. But the Bible also says that fasting may be purely an expression of love and devotion to God. In Luke 2 there is an unforgettable woman whose entire eighty-four years flash before us in three brief verses. Her name is Anna. The summary of her life is found in Luke 2:37: "She did not depart from the temple, worshiping with fasting and prayer night and day."

Although Anna's story has its primary significance in the context of Mary and Joseph presenting the newborn Jesus at the temple, how she lived from day to day is what concerns us here. Anna was married for only seven years before being widowed. Assuming she married as a young lady, this godly woman devoted at least half a century, "night and day," to a worship of God characterized by "fasting and prayer."

Fasting can be a testimony—even one directed to yourself—that you find your greatest pleasure and enjoyment in life from God. It's a way of demonstrating to yourself that you love God more than food, that seeking Him is more important to you than eating, that Jesus—the Bread of heaven (see John 6:51)—is more satisfying to you than earthly bread. When you fast you remind yourself that unlike many (see Philippians 3:19), your stomach is not your god. Rather, it is the servant of the true God, because you're willing to sublimate your stomach's desires to those of the Spirit. When Christians fast because of their love for God, they illustrate what Piper said: "What we hunger for most, we worship."[22]

Christians throughout history have fasted for this purpose in preparation for the Lord's Supper. In addition to the elements of repentance and humility before God in this kind of fast, it helps people focus their attention and affections on the Lord of the Supper.

Another way of fasting to express love to God is to spend your mealtime in praise and worship of God instead of eating. A variation is to delay eating a particular meal until you have had your daily time of Bible intake and prayer. Just remember that your fast is a privilege, not an obligation; it's the acceptance of a divine invitation to experience His grace in a special way.

Fasting must always have a spiritual purpose—a God-centered purpose, not a self-centered one—for the Lord to bless our fast. Thoughts of food during a fast must prompt thoughts for God, and remind us of our purpose. Rather than focusing the mind on food, we should use every desire to eat as a reminder to pray and to remember our purpose.

There is no doubt that God has often crowned fasting with extraordinary blessings. Biblical, historical, and contemporary testimonies bear witness to God's delight in providing unusual blessings to those who fast. But we should be careful not to develop what Martyn Lloyd-Jones called a mechanical view of fasting; that is, believing that if we will fast, God is obligated to give us what we ask. We cannot manipulate God to do our bidding by fasting any more than we can by any other means. As with prayer, we fast in hope that by His *grace* God will bless us as we desire. When our fast is rightly motivated, we can be sure God *will* bless us and do so in the way infinite wisdom knows is best, even if it is not in the way we wanted.

Again David Smith has it right:

Any blessing which is bestowed by the Father upon His undeserving children must be considered to be an act of grace. We fail to appreciate the mercy of the Lord if we think that by our *doing something* we have forced (or even coerced) God to grant that blessing which we have asked for. . . . All of our fasting, therefore, must be on this basis; we should use it as a scriptural means whereby we are melted into a more complete realization of the purposes of the Lord in our life, church, community, and nation.[23]

While fasting recently over concern for the work of God in the church I pastor, I began to pray about several critical matters. Suddenly I realized that while I *thought* I was praying in conformity with God's will about these things, it was possible that my understanding of them needed readjusting. So I asked the Lord to show me how to pray according to His will on these matters and to grant me contentment with His providence. This, I think, is what Smith meant by fasting being "a scriptural means whereby we are melted into a more complete realization of the purposes of the Lord." Fasting should always have a purpose, but we must learn to elevate God's purposes over ours.

So in one sense, regardless of the stated purpose of a fast, all fasts are primarily about God. On each occasion, seeking God in the fast should be more important to us than what we seek from God through the fast. John Piper summarizes this in the title of his book on fasting, *A Hunger for God.*[24] Fasting is when we hunger for God—for a fresh encounter with God, for God to answer a prayer, for God to save someone, for God to work powerfully in our church, for God to guide us or protect us—more than we hunger for the food God made us to live on.

God once rebuked the Jews, not for their failure to fast, but for fasting without a God-centered hunger. A delegation was sent from Bethel to Jerusalem to inquire of the Lord. At issue was whether to continue two fasts the Jews had held to commemorate the destruction of the temple. For seventy years they had kept these fasts in the fifth and seventh months, but now they wondered if God wanted them to continue the fasts since they had been restored to their land and were building a new temple. The Lord's response to them was, "Say to all the people of the land and the priests, When you fasted and mourned in the fifth month and in the seventh, for these seventy years, was it for me that you fasted?" (Zechariah 7:5). These fasts had become empty rituals, not God-centered experiences. Matthew Henry's comments on this passage are instructive for our own fasting.

> Let them all take notice that, whereas they thought they had made God very much their Debtor by these fasts, they were much mistaken, for they were not acceptable to Him, unless they had been observed in a better manner, and to better purpose. . . . They were not chargeable with omission or neglect of the duty, . . . but they had not managed [it] aright. . . . They had not an eye to God in their fasting. . . . When this was wanting, every fast was but a jest. To fast, and not to fast to God, was to mock Him and provoke Him, and could not be pleasing to Him. . . . If

the solemnities of our fasting, though frequent, long, and severe, do not serve to put an edge upon devout affections, to quicken prayer, to increase Godly sorrow, and to alter the temper of our minds, and the course of our lives, for the better, they do not at all answer the intention, and God will not accept them as performed to Him.[25]

Before we fast we must have a purpose, a biblical, God-centered purpose. But even in our best fasts we do not deserve what we desire, nor can we force God's hand. Having said that, however, let's balance that truth with the incontestable promise of Jesus in Matthew 6:17-18: "But when you fast, anoint your head and wash your face, that your fasting may not be seen by others but by your Father who is in secret. And your Father who sees in secret will reward you." God *will* bless a biblical fast by any of His children. And whether or not you receive the specific blessing you seek, one thing is sure: If you knew what God knew, you would give yourself the identical blessing that He does. And none of His rewards are worthless.

MORE APPLICATION

Will you confess and repent of any fear of fasting? There's something about saying, "I'm not going to eat today," that causes anxiety in many Christians. It seems that most believers would rather give an offering of money than give up food for a day. Do you have a mild case of fasting-phobia? It's silly when you put it in perspective. We think about missing a meal or two for the sake of seeking God and becoming more like Jesus, and we get anxious. And yet we willingly miss meals sometimes while shopping, working, recreating, or otherwise occupying our time. Whenever we believe another activity is at that moment more important, we will go without food fearlessly and without complaint. We need to learn that there are times when it is not only more important, but much more rewarding to abstain from food for the purpose of more richly feasting on God (see Matthew 4:4). Do not fear the blessings of fasting.

Will you fast as the Holy Spirit directs? Are you willing to obey God when He prompts you to fast? Because Jesus expected that His followers would fast, I believe it is very likely that from time to time His Spirit will direct you to fast. Will you determine in advance to obey Him?

One of the ways the Holy Spirit prompts us to fast is through a need in our lives. If you need stronger prayer about a matter, that may be an invitation from the Lord to fast. If you need God's guidance, maybe that's an encouragement to fast. If you need deliverance or protection, perhaps it's a call to fast. Will you do it? Or will you miss the unique opportunities for grace that He extends to you through fasting?

Don't wait for a special day when everything is perfect for a fast; such a day probably won't come. For many, a regular workday can be a fast day, unless your job requires an unusual amount of physical exertion. The best day for most might be the Lord's Day. Typically it's less demanding physically than weekdays and may even provide the opportunity for an afternoon rest. In addition, it may afford extended time not available on other days for seeking and enjoying God through other Spiritual Disciplines.

A word of warning: Do not spiritualize a sinful neglect of food and call it fasting. Many sin by eating too much. That's the sin of gluttony. But as with most sins, there's a contrasting sin in the opposite direction, meaning that a person may also sin by willfully eating too little. Usually this is rooted in vanity. But the will of God for all of us almost every day of our lives is to eat. He made us as creatures who survive by eating. He made the world to work in such a way that it provides food for us to eat. In fact, in 1 Timothy 4:3 the Bible describes those who deny this and actually "require abstinence from foods that God created to be received with thanksgiving by those who believe and know the truth" as those who "depart from the faith" (4:1). Those who eat too much and those who intentionally eat too little are looking for satisfaction in something other than God.

Remember to get medical counsel where necessary. If you're planning an extended fast, or if you are expecting, nursing, diabetic, get migraines, or have a physical condition that depends on a regular diet, talk to your doctor before starting your fast. And if you've never fasted before, start with a one-, two-, or at most three-meal fast. But start somewhere. Don't search for loopholes to avoid it. Look instead for ways to experience God's grace through fasting. Remember that God considered fasting such a good thing for His people that He commanded every Israelite to fast for one whole day each year on the Day of Atonement.

Like all the Spiritual Disciplines, fasting hoists the sails of the soul in hopes of experiencing the gracious wind of God's Spirit. But fasting also adds a unique dimension to your spiritual life and helps you grow in Christlikeness in ways that are unavailable through any other means. If this were not so, and if the blessings of fasting could be experienced by other means, Jesus would not have taught and modeled fasting.

Will you plan a fast of dedication now as an expression of your willingness to fast from now on? Before you go any further, why not schedule a time of fasting soon that will express your hunger for God and your willingness to discipline yourself to fast in the future? There's no need to make it complicated. It's a simple discipline. Piper's words bear repeating: "This is the essence of Christian fasting: We ache and yearn—and fast—to know more and more of all that God is for us in Jesus. But only because he has already laid hold of us and is drawing us ever forward and upward into 'all the fullness of God.'"[26]

CHAPTER 10

SILENCE AND SOLITUDE . . .
FOR THE PURPOSE OF GODLINESS

The word discipline has disappeared from our minds,
our mouths, our pulpits, and our culture. We hardly know
what discipline means in modern American society.
And yet, there is no other way to attain godliness;
discipline is the path to godliness.

JAY ADAMS

My favorite short story is "The Bet," by Anton Chekhov, a Russian writer of the last half of the nineteenth century. The plot involves a wager between two educated men regarding solitary confinement. A wealthy, middle-aged banker believed that the death penalty was a more humane penalty than solitary confinement because "an executioner kills at once, solitary confinement kills gradually." One of his guests at a party, a young lawyer of twenty-five, disagreed, saying, "To live under any conditions is better than not to live at all."

Angered, the banker impulsively responded with a bet of two million rubles that the younger man could not last five years in solitary confinement. Convinced of his endurance, the lawyer announced he would stay fifteen years alone instead of only five.

They agreed on the arrangements, and the young man moved into a separate building on the grounds of the banker's large estate. He was allowed no visitors or newspapers. He could write letters but receive none. Guards watched to ensure he never violated the agreement, but were stationed so that he could not see them or any other human being from his windows. He received his food in silence through a small opening where he could not see the one who served him. Everything else he wanted—books, certain foods, musical instruments—was granted by special written request.

The story develops with a description of the things the lawyer asked for through the years and the observations of the guards who occasionally stole a glance through a window. During the first year the piano could be heard at almost any hour, and he asked for many books, mostly novels and other light reading. The next year the music ceased and the works of various classical authors were requested. In the sixth year of his isolation he began to study languages and soon had mastered six. After the tenth year of his confinement, the prisoner sat motionless at the table and read the New Testament. After more than a year's saturation of the Bible, he began to study the history of religion and works on theology. During the last two years his reading broadened to cover many subjects in addition to theology.

The second half of the story focuses on the night before the noon deadline when the lawyer would win the bet. The banker was now at the end of his career. His risky speculations and impetuosity had gradually undermined his business. The once self-confident millionaire was now a second-rate banker, and paying off the wager would destroy him. Angry at his foolishness and jealous of the soon-to-be-wealthy man who was now only forty, the old banker determined to kill his opponent and frame the guard with the murder. Slipping into the man's room, he found him asleep at the table and noticed a letter the lawyer had written to him. He picked it up and read the following:

> Tomorrow at twelve o'clock I shall be free, . . . but before leaving this room, . . . I find it necessary to say a few words to you. With a clear conscience, and before God, who sees me, I declare to you that I despise . . . all that your books

call the joys of this world. For fifteen years I have studied
attentively the life of this world. It is true that I neither saw
the earth nor its peoples, but in your books I lived. . . . I
sang songs, I hunted the deer and the wild boar in the forests. . . . In your books I climbed to the summit of Elburz
and Mont Blanc, and I saw from those heights the sun
rise in the morning, and at night it shed its purple glow
over the sky and the ocean and the mountain-tops. I saw
beneath me the flashing lightning cut through the clouds.
I saw green fields, forests, rivers, lakes and towns. I heard
the song of the sirens and the music of the shepherd's reed-
pipes. I felt the touch of the wings of beautiful [angels] who
had flown to me. . . . Your books gave me wisdom. All that
had been achieved by the untiring brain of man during
long centuries is stored in my brain in a small compressed
mass. . . . I know I am wiser than you all. . . . And I despise
all your books, I despise all earthly . . . wisdom. All is
worthless and false, hollow and deceiving like the mirage.
You may be proud, wise and beautiful, but death will wipe
you away from the face of the earth, as it does the mice that
live beneath your floor; and your heirs, your history, your
immortal geniuses will freeze or burn with the destruction
of the earth. You have gone mad and are not following the
right path. You take falsehood for truth, and deformity for
beauty. To prove to you how I despise all that you value I
renounce the two millions on which I looked, at one time,
as the opening of paradise for me, and which I now scorn.
To deprive myself of the right to receive them, I will leave
my prison five hours before the appointed time, and by so
doing break the terms of our compact.

The banker read these lines, replaced the paper on the table,
kissed the strange, sleeping man, and with tears in his eyes quietly left the house. Chekhov writes, "Never before, not even after

sustaining serious losses . . . , had he despised himself as he did at that moment." His tears kept him awake the rest of the night. And at seven the next morning the watchmen ran in to say that they had seen the man crawl through a window, go to the gate, and then disappear.[1]

I don't advocate isolating ourselves in this way, and I do not think the Bible does, either. But my point in presenting the story is this: I believe Chekhov looks into a room where every Christian dreams of living—sometimes.

There is something both appealing and transforming about silence and solitude. And there are moments in our pressure-cooker lives when years of escape to some hidden place sounds wistfully compelling.

When we consider it in the light of Scripture, we realize that it would be neither right nor desirable to be cloistered from our God-given privileges and responsibilities involving other people. Biblical reality calls us to family, fellowship, evangelism, ministry, and other aspects of life together in the local church for the sake of Christ and His kingdom. And yet, sometimes our souls crave separation from noise and crowds into silence and solitude. Just as we must engage with others for some of the Disciplines of the Christian life,[2] so there are times when we must temporarily withdraw into the Disciplines of silence and solitude. In this chapter, we will explore what these twin Disciplines are, find biblical reasons for practicing them, and conclude with some sensible suggestions for starting.

EXPLANATION OF SILENCE AND SOLITUDE

The Discipline of silence is the voluntary and temporary abstention from speaking so that certain spiritual goals might be sought. Sometimes silence is observed in order to read the Bible, meditate on Scripture, pray, journal, and so on. Though there is no outward speaking, there may be intentional, biblical self-talk or prayer to God. At other times you might choose not to talk at all, but simply to focus your mind upon God and to "set your minds on things that are above" (Colossians 3:2), resting your soul in the love He displayed through Christ.

Solitude is the Spiritual Discipline of voluntarily and temporarily withdrawing to privacy for spiritual purposes. The period of solitude may last only a few minutes or for days. As with silence, solitude may be sought in order to participate without interruption in other Spiritual Disciplines, or just to be alone with God and think.

Three brief thoughts before proceeding in depth. First, think of silence and solitude as complementary Disciplines to fellowship. By fellowship I do not mean socializing, that is, talking about news, weather, sports, work, and family. In its broad, God-given place in life, socializing is a great blessing and enjoying it is part of what it means to be human. Biblical fellowship, however, involves talking about God and the things of God. Perhaps we do much less of that than we think, even at church. The emphasis here, though, is that fellowship requires interaction with other people, whereas silence and solitude do not. It seems that each of us is inclined a little more in one direction than the other. That is, we enjoy meaningful conversation with other Christians more than solitude or vice versa. But both have a place in the life of a biblically consistent believer. Without silence and solitude we can be active, but shallow. Without fellowship we can be deep, but stagnant. Christlikeness requires both sides of the equation.

Second, silence and solitude are usually found together. Though they can be distinguished (as seen in the definitions above), in this chapter we will think of them as a pair.

Third, recognize that culture conditions us to be comfortable with noise and crowds, not with silence and solitude, and to feel more at home in a mall than at a park. In her book *Finding Focus in a Whirlwind World*, Jean Fleming observed, "We live in a noisy, busy world. Silence and solitude . . . fit the era of Victorian lace, high-button shoes, and kerosene lamps better than our age of television, video arcades, and joggers wired with earphones. We have become a people with an aversion to quiet and an uneasiness with being alone."[3] This is confirmed by the inability of many to ever be at home or in a car by themselves without turning on some "background noise." Unlike previous generations, technology now makes it possible for us to enjoy the benefits of news, music, educational content, and more whenever we want and wherever we are. But the downside is that the appeal and accessibility of these things means the elimination of almost all quiet spaces in our lives. More than any generation in history we must *discipline* ourselves to enjoy the blessings of silence and solitude. Therefore, be careful not to let the world prejudice you against the biblical witness on the importance of these matters.

VALUABLE REASONS FOR SILENCE AND SOLITUDE

There are many biblical reasons for making priorities of the Disciplines of silence and solitude.

To Follow Jesus' Example

The Scriptures teach that Jesus engaged in periods of silence and solitude, some for only a few minutes or hours, and at least one for several days. Note these four references:

1. Matthew 4:1: "Then Jesus was led up by the Spirit into the wilderness to be tempted by the devil." The primary purpose of this event was for Jesus to receive and conquer Satan's temptations. Still, we note that the Holy Spirit led Jesus to experience this encounter during a lengthy period of fasting and solitude.

2. Matthew 14:23: "After he had dismissed the crowds, he went up on the mountain by himself to pray. When evening came, he was there alone." He sent both the seeking multitudes and His disciples away so He could be alone with the Father.

3. Mark 1:35: "Rising very early in the morning, while it was still dark, he departed and went out to a desolate place, and there he prayed." The previous verses tell us that after dark "the whole city" gathered at the door of the house where Jesus was staying. There He healed many people and cast out demons. But before it was daylight again, He went to spend time alone in prayer. Jesus knew that had He waited until after sunrise, He would have been surrounded again by the curious eyes and urgent voices of the whole city.

4. Luke 4:42: "When it was day, he departed and went into a desolate place. And the people sought him and came to him, and would have kept him from leaving them." Put yourself in Jesus' sandals for a moment. People are clamoring for your help and have many real needs, and you are able to meet all those needs. Can you ever feel justified in pulling away to be alone? Jesus did. We love to feel wanted. We savor the sense of importance/power/indispensability (pick one) that comes from doing something no one else can do. But Jesus did not allow those desires to determine His course of action. Despite the interminable cries of people pressing forward with needs He had the power to meet (indeed, on some occasions He "healed them all"—Matthew 12:15; Luke 6:19), Jesus knew the importance of disciplining Himself to have some time alone with the Father.

By now the point should be obvious: To be more like Jesus we must discipline ourselves to find times of silence and solitude. Then through these Disciplines we can pursue many of the blessings Jesus experienced through them.

To Minimize Distractions in Prayer

One of the more obvious reasons for getting away from the sounds and surroundings that divert our attention is to better focus the mind in prayer. In addition to the examples of Jesus in the previous section, other biblical examples of this might include Elijah going to "Horeb, the mount of God" (1 Kings 19:8) where he heard the "low whisper" of God (see 19:11-13), Habakkuk entering a guard post and keeping watch to hear from and answer to God (see Habakkuk 2:1), and possibly the apostle Paul going away to Arabia after his conversion where he was presumably alone with God (see Galatians 1:17).

Of course, it isn't absolutely necessary to get far away from noises and people in order to pray, otherwise we'd rarely be able to pray in the course of everyday life or in a prayer meeting. But there are times when it helps to eliminate the voices of the world in order to lift our voices without distraction to the God of heaven.

According to Jonathan Edwards, this desire to be alone with God was part of what attracted him to Sarah Pierpont. In his first record of her, penned while his future wife was still a teenager, he wrote, "She hardly cares for anything, except to meditate on Him. . . . She loves to be alone, walking in the fields and groves, and seems to have someone invisible always conversing with her."[4] Where Sarah had "fields and groves," we may have to walk in the park, around the block, or find another place for regular solitude. Wherever it is, it's good to have a place where we can withdraw and speak uninterrupted with Him whose presence is unseen yet more real than any other.

Many of us need to realize the addiction we have to noise. It's one thing to listen to the television or another device while doing housework or chores, but it's another to be unable to stay in a room for a while without it. Even worse is the requirement of background noise during Bible intake or prayer. Sometimes ambient music can mask other, unwanted sounds and increase concentration. But I'm referring to a dependence upon music, an inability to function in silence and solitude. As I've mentioned, the portability and accessibility of technology is a mixed blessing. While we should be grateful for its massive benefits, we should also recognize its invasive, distracting tendencies. The more we use audio and video technology, the more we need to learn the Disciplines of silence and solitude.

To Express Worship to God

The worship of God does not always require words, sounds, or actions. Sometimes worship consists of a God-focused stillness and hush. Scriptural precedent for this includes texts like Habakkuk 2:20, "But the LORD is in his holy temple; let all the earth keep silence before him"; Zephaniah 1:7, "Be silent before the Lord GOD"; and Zechariah 2:13, "Be silent, all flesh, before the LORD." Notice that it's not just a silence that's enjoined, but a silence "before him," "before the Lord GOD," and "before the LORD." That's not merely silence; it's a worshipful silence. There are times to speak to God, and there are times simply to behold and adore Him in silence.

Recorded in the journals of the great evangelist George Whitefield is an incident of silent worship that he once had in the solitude of his home. He wrote that in the May 9, 1739, experience, "God was pleased to pour into my soul a great spirit of supplication, and a sense of His free, distinguishing mercies so filled me with love, humility, and joy and holy confusion that I could at last only pour out my heart before Him in an awful silence. I was so full that I could not well speak. Oh, the happiness of communion with God."[5]

Worshiping God in silence may occur because your heart, like Whitefield's, is so full that words cannot express your love for Him. At other times you may feel just the opposite, so passionless that any words seem hypocritical. Regardless of the state of your emotions, there is always a place for wordless worship, a God-centered silence based upon what God has revealed of Himself in His Word.

To Express Faith in God

The simple act of silence before the Lord, as opposed to coming to Him in a wordy fret, can be a demonstration of faith in Him. Twice in Psalm 62 David displayed this kind of faith. In verses 1-2 he affirmed, "For God alone my soul waits in silence; from him comes my salvation. He alone is my rock and my salvation, my fortress; I shall not be greatly shaken." Then in verses 5-6, he said again, "For God alone, O my soul, wait in silence, for my hope is from him. He only is my rock and my salvation, my fortress; I shall not be shaken." Verbalized prayers can sometimes be filled more with fear and doubt than faith; silence before the Lord can sometimes express more faith and submission to God's providence than words.

A favorite verse of many, Isaiah 30:15, connects silence before God with faith in Him: "Thus said the Lord GOD, the Holy One of Israel, 'In returning and rest you shall be saved; in *quietness* and in *trust* shall be your strength'" (emphasis added). Trust in the Lord God is frequently expressed through prayer. But sometimes it is better exhibited through a wordlessness before the Lord that, by its quiet absence of anxiety, communicates trust in His sovereign control.

I discovered a daily-life illustration of this in the journal of the early American missionary to the Indians, David Brainerd. On Wednesday, April 28, 1742, he wrote,

> Withdrew to my usual place of retirement in great peace
> and tranquility, and spent about two hours in secret duties.
> I felt much as I did yesterday morning, only weaker and
> more overcome. I seemed to hang and depend wholly upon
> my dear Lord; wholly weaned from all other dependences.
> *I knew not what to say to my God, but only lean on his
> bosom,* as it were, and breathe out my desires after a perfect
> conformity to him in all things. Thirsting desires and insatiable longings possessed my soul after perfect holiness:
> God was so precious to my soul that the world with all its
> enjoyments was infinitely vile: I had no more value for the
> favor of men than for pebbles. The Lord was my all; and he
> overruled all; which greatly delighted me. *I think my faith
> and dependence upon God scarce ever rose so high. I saw*

him such a fountain of goodness, that it seemed impossible I should distrust him again, or be any way anxious about anything that should happen to me.[6]

We may not be able to express ourselves in a journal as well as Brainerd, but we can, in seasons where we intersperse supplication with silence, express our faith to God in ways He deems equally precious.

To Seek the Salvation of the Lord

Times of silence and solitude to seek the salvation of the Lord can refer either to a non-Christian seeking salvation from sin and guilt in Christ or to a believer seeking God's salvation from certain circumstances. The words of Jeremiah in Lamentations 3:25-28 are appropriate in either case: "The LORD is good to those who wait for him, to the soul who seeks him. It is good that one should wait quietly for the salvation of the LORD. It is good for a man that he bear the yoke in his youth. Let him sit *alone* in *silence* when it is laid on him" (emphasis added).

In a sermon on this text, C. H. Spurgeon said:

I commend solitude to any of you who are seeking salvation, first, that you may study well your case as in the sight of God. Few men truly know themselves as they really are. Most people have seen themselves in a looking-glass, but there is another looking-glass, which gives true reflections, into which few men look. To study one's self in the light of God's Word, and carefully to go over one's condition, examining both the inward and the outward sins, and using all the tests which are given us in the Scriptures, would be a very healthy exercise; but how very few care to go through it![7]

As Spurgeon later did on this and all occasions when he was in the pulpit, and as we find throughout the New Testament narratives, whenever the Bible is publicly preached we too should call people to seek salvation in "Jesus Christ and him crucified" (1 Corinthians 2:2) without delay. But in addition to such a call to hearers among the crowds, we shouldn't minimize the value of urging seclusion to help avoid distractions when considering the state of one's soul. Solitude and silence can help us come to grips with the realities of our sin, death, judgment, and so on—solemn themes that are frequently drowned out of our consciousness by the audio track of everyday life. Given the ubiquity of the sights and sounds conveyed by personal technology, how often do you think an unconverted person sits alone, attention undiverted, and considers himself or herself in light of the gospel? In my estimation, the incidence per one million people is extremely rare. We should never reduce the emphasis on coming to Christ immediately, but we also need to encourage people more to "sit alone in silence" and, in Spurgeon's words, "to study one's self in the light of God's Word."

To Be Physically and Spiritually Restored

Everyone has a regular need for restoring the resources of both the inward and outward person. It was true even for those who lived most closely with Jesus. After spending themselves in several days of physical and spiritual output, notice the means of replenishment Jesus prescribed for His disciples: "Come away by yourselves to a desolate place and rest a while" (Mark 6:31). Doesn't that sound good?

Like the twelve disciples, we all need times to unstring the bow of our routine stresses and enjoy the restoration that retreat can provide for our bodies and souls.

One evening I saw a news report about the life of pianist Glenn Gould. He was described as a miraculous instrumentalist when he burst onto the music scene as a teenager during the 1950s. He toured the world and amazed listeners with his skills. But in 1964 he quit playing in public. From then on, even though he was one of the world's greatest pianists, Gould played only in private and for recording. Even his recording sessions were accomplished in complete privacy. He was convinced that *isolation* was the only way to create. Anyone who likewise has to "create" music, lessons, papers, reports, sermons, art, presentations, and so on knows that it can't be done well in five-minute snatches between digital or personal interruptions. Gould's musical monkishness is not a practice most can or should imitate. But as he found that isolation helped him to create, discover for yourself how silence and solitude help to physically and spiritually *re*-create you in ways that are deeply therapeutic.

To Regain a Spiritual Perspective

One of the best ways to step back and get a more balanced, less worldly perspective on matters is through the Disciplines of silence and solitude.

When Zechariah was told by the angel Gabriel that he and his elderly wife would miraculously have a son, he doubted. In response Gabriel said, "And behold, you will be silent and unable to speak until the day that these things take place, because you did not believe my words, which will be fulfilled in their time" (Luke 1:20). And what happened to Zechariah's perspective about these things during this time of enforced silence? When the baby was born, Luke 1:63-64 says, "He asked for a writing tablet and wrote, 'His name is John.' And they all wondered. And immediately his mouth was opened and his tongue loosed, and he spoke, blessing God." A negative illustration perhaps, but it shows how closing our mouths can sometimes help us open our minds to see things God's way.

One of the most famous and life-changing events in the life of Billy Graham happened in August 1949, immediately preceding the Los Angeles crusade that thrust him into national prominence. For a short period prior to Graham, the unofficial title of North America's best-known evangelist applied to a man named Chuck Templeton. However, by 1949 Templeton was crumbling spiritually under the influence of men who doubted the inspiration of

Scripture, and this eventually led to his complete denial of the faith. He began to share with Graham the books and ideas that were shaping him. And only days before Graham drove to California, Templeton told him that by continuing to believe the Bible the young evangelist was committing intellectual suicide.

While speaking at a youth conference in the San Bernardino Mountains, Graham knew he had to get God's perspective on the matter, and he found it through solitude. Here's how he described that night: "I went back alone to the cottage and read in my Bible for a while, and then I decided to take a walk in the forest." There he recalled that phrases such as "the Word of the Lord came" and "thus saith the Lord" were used more than two thousand times in Scripture. He meditated on the attitude of Christ, who fulfilled the Law and the Prophets, who quoted from them constantly and never indicated that they might be wrong. As he walked he said, "Lord, what shall I do? What shall be the direction of my life?" He saw that intellect alone couldn't resolve the question of the Bible's inspiration and authority. Beyond that it ultimately became an issue of faith. He thought of the faith he had in many everyday things that he did not thoroughly understand, such as airplanes and cars, and asked himself why it was only in regard to the things of the Spirit that such faith was considered wrong.

"So I went back and got my Bible," he continued, "and I went out in the moonlight. And I got to a stump and put the Bible on the stump, and I knelt down, and I said, 'Oh, God; I cannot prove certain things. I cannot answer some of the questions Chuck is raising and some of the other people are raising, but I accept this Book by faith as the Word of God.'"[8] And through that time of solitude and the spiritual perspective he gained that night, Billy Graham was further shaped into the man the world has known since.

Graham's experience demonstrates what the prolific Puritan theologian John Owen said of our solitudes: "What we are in them, that we are indeed, and no more. They are either the best or the worst of our times, wherein the principle that is predominant in us will show and act itself."[9] In other words, what we are when we are alone is what we really are. If we habitually seek God and His perspective through His Word when we are alone—and not just at church or when with other Christians—then we may be hopeful that we do know God.

To Seek the Will of God

Perhaps one of the most common reasons believers pursue God in silence and solitude is to discern His will about a matter. Jesus did this in Luke 6:12-13 when deciding among all His disciples those who would travel with Him: "In these days he went out to the mountain to pray, and all night he continued in prayer to God. And when day came, he called his disciples and chose from them twelve, whom he named apostles."

Christian history is rich with memorable stories of men and women who secluded themselves from all others in order to seek the will of Him who matters most. A favorite of these stories involves Hudson Taylor, a young, exhausted missionary to China. In 1865, while back in England to rest and continue some medical studies, he struggled with a decision. He sensed that God might be leading him to start a daring and unprecedented mission work—taking the gospel to the unreached millions in the vast interior of China. For decades, almost all missionaries worked only in the coastal cities, rarely going inland. But Taylor was fearful of leading such a great enterprise, knowing that the burden of enlisting missionaries, as well as finding and maintaining their financial support, would rest on his shoulders.

By the quiet summer Sunday of June 25, Hudson Taylor could stand the uncertainty no longer. Worn out and ill, he had gone to rest with friends at Brighton. But instead of enjoying their constant company, he also sought refuge in silence and solitude, and he wandered out along the sands left by the receding tide. Although the scene was peaceful, he was in agony. A decision had to be made. He must know God's will. As he walked, the thought came,

Why, if we are obeying the Lord, the responsibility rests *with Him*, not with us! *Thou*, Lord, *Thou* shalt have all the burden! At Thy bidding, as Thy servant I go forward, leaving results with Thee.

How restfully I turned away from the sands. . . . The conflict ended, all was joy and peace. I felt as if I could fly up the hill to Mr. Pearse's house. And how I did sleep that night! My dear wife thought Brighton had done wonders for me, and so it had.[10]

And so, on the hinge of seeking His will through silence and solitude, God opened the door for the China Inland Mission. That same work continues with the blessing of God and has grown into the Overseas Missionary Fellowship, one of the world's great missionary endeavors.

God often makes His will clear to us in public, but there are times when He discloses it only in private. To discover it requires the Disciplines of silence and solitude.

To Learn Control of the Tongue

Learning to keep silent for short periods of time can help us better control our tongue all the time.

There's no doubt that learning control of the tongue is critical to Christlikeness. The Bible says that the religion of the person with no tongue control is worthless (see James 1:26). Proverbs 17:27-28 relates the Christlike qualities of godly knowledge, understanding, wisdom, and discernment to the power to rein in words: "Whoever restrains his words has knowledge, and he who has a cool spirit is a man of understanding. Even a fool who keeps silent is considered wise; when he closes his lips, he is deemed intelligent."

Ecclesiastes 3:7 refers to control of the tongue in a twofold sense, that is, the ability to restrain it as well as to use it, for it says there is both "a time to keep silence, and a time to speak." Godliness, therefore, involves learning when you shouldn't talk as well as when you should.

In the New Testament, James 1:19 also describes power over the tongue in terms of the ability to keep it in check: "Know this, my beloved brothers: let every person be quick to hear, slow to speak, slow to anger." This applies to our online "speaking" as well as that done with our lips.

How do the Disciplines of silence and solitude help with Christlike tongue control? On a long fast you discover that some of the food you normally eat isn't really necessary. When you practice silence and solitude, you find that you don't need to say some things you previously thought necessary. In silence we learn to rely more on God's control in matters where we would normally feel compelled to speak, or to speak too much. We find out that He is able to manage situations in which we once thought our input was indispensable. The skills of observation and listening are also sharpened in those who practice silence and solitude; when they do speak there's more of a freshness and depth to their words.

One reason why the dual Disciplines of silence and solitude can be so thoroughly transforming is because of how they help connect us with the other Spiritual Disciplines.[11] They should normally be the context, for example, where we engage in personal Bible intake and prayer. They are also a necessary component of private worship. In silence and solitude we can maximize time for Disciplines such as learning and journaling. It's also common to practice fasting during times of silence and solitude. But more than anything else, the Disciplines of silence and solitude can be so transfiguring because they provide time to think about life and to seek God. The plain fact is that most of us don't do that enough. Not many generations ago, most of our forebears would have spent their days working in the fields or in the home where the only other sounds were those of God's creation or human voices. Without electrified motors and media, there were fewer artificial distractions from the voice of conscience and the work of the Holy Spirit in our souls. This is not to glamorize the supposed "good old days" (a sinful practice; see Ecclesiastes 7:10) or to suggest we try to return to them. I'm simply reaffirming what we've said from the beginning of this chapter: One of the costs of technological advancement is a greater temptation to avoid quietness. While we have broadened our intake of news and information of all kinds, these advantages may come at the expense of our spiritual depth if we do not practice silence and solitude.

Remember that the great purpose for engaging in these Disciplines is godliness, that we may be like Jesus, that we may be more holy. In *The Still Hour*, Austin Phelps wrote, "It has been said that no great work in literature or in science was ever wrought by a man who did not love solitude. We may lay it down as an elemental principle of religion, that no large growth in holiness was ever gained by one who did not *take* time to be often long *alone with God*."[12]

SUGGESTIONS FOR SILENCE AND SOLITUDE

Some people enjoy the Disciplines of silence and solitude like they enjoy reading or watching some great adventure. Instead of developing these practices for themselves, they enter into them only vicariously and admire them from afar. They dream about these Disciplines, but they don't do them. Here are some practical helps for making silence and solitude less a mere longing and more a reality and a habit.

"Minute Retreats"

A Christian radio station in my area used to air a thirty-second spot emphasizing the benefits of silence. Then it provided ten silent seconds to make its point. As simple as it sounds, the impact of that unexpected quiet moment was remarkable.

It's possible to provide that same kind of brief refreshment on occasion throughout your day. A moment at a traffic light, in an elevator, or in line at a drive-through can become a "minute retreat" when you consecrate it as a time of silence and solitude. You can use the time of prayer at a meal for a spiritual pause.

I can't provide suggestions for every person's circumstances. But

I can encourage you to find ways to turn the routine into the holy, to "improve" (as the Puritans used to say) a stray minute here or there even in the busiest of days, by repurposing it as a minute retreat.

Of course, the key is not just taking a breath and relaxing for a moment, as helpful as that is. What I'm advocating is looking to Christ more intentionally during that moment and resting by faith in Him. It's practicing what we sing in the hymn, "Take my *moments* and my days, let them flow in ceaseless praise."[13] Seize these unexpected opportunities given you by the Lord and concentrate exclusively on Him and life in the Spirit. Even if you are provided with only a few seconds, even if you are not in an absolutely quiet or completely solitary place, enjoy the restoration found in the knowledge of Jesus Christ.

A Goal of Daily Silence and Solitude

Without exception, the men and women I have known who've made the most rapid, consistent, and evident growth in Christlikeness have been those who develop a daily time of being alone with God. This time of silence is devoted to Bible intake and prayer, and in this solitude they enjoy an occasion of private worship.

Many battle to develop this daily devotional habit because they lead such busy lives and face such a determined Enemy who's aware of the stakes involved. Missionary martyr Jim Elliot knew of the struggle: "I think the devil has made it his business to monopolize on three elements: noise, hurry, crowds. . . . Satan is quite aware of the power of silence."[14] Our days are usually filled with more than enough noise, plenty of hurry, and equally busy people. Unless we *plan* for daily times of solitary silence before God, these other things will rush in to fill our time like water into the *Titanic*.

These daily times are the lifeblood of the Disciplines of silence and solitude. Those who practice silence and solitude well on an everyday basis are more likely to discipline themselves to enjoy them on an occasional basis, such as on "minute retreats," the Lord's Day, and on extended periods. The person who rarely exercises struggles with both a brief climb up the stairs and a mile run. The one who jogs every day has no trouble with either. In the same way, the person who has a time of daily spiritual exercises is the one who most enjoys both "minute retreats" and extended periods of silence and solitude.

Getting Away for Solitude and Silence

"Getting away" for an extended time of silence and solitude may be nothing more than finding an empty room in your church in which to spend a few hours, an evening, or a Saturday. Or it may involve spending a night or a weekend at a retreat center, lodge, or cabin.

On some of these getaways you may want to take nothing but your Bible and a notebook. On others you might want to devour a book you believe will help you develop as a disciple of Jesus. Such retreats are also a good time for planning, goal-setting, and evaluation.

If you've never spent an entire evening, half a day, or longer in silence and solitude, you may be wondering what you would do with all that time. I would advise you to prepare a schedule either in advance or first thing upon arrival, because you'll be surprised at how quickly the time will pass if you remain busy, and how it will drag if you don't have a plan. Don't feel as though you must stick slavishly to your schedule. Even if it's not an overnight event, sleep if you need to. But a plan can help you use your time for the intended purposes rather than inadvertently misspending it.[15]

Although overnight getaways at distant places are wonderful, don't wait for times when you can go like Elijah to Mount Horeb for forty days before you start practicing silence and solitude. Remember that, generally speaking, all the Spiritual Disciplines, including these two, are intended for common practice in the places where we live our daily lives.

Special Places

Locate special places that can be used for silence and solitude. Find them within the home, within walking distance, within a few minutes' drive, and within a reasonable distance for overnight or longer retreats.

If you have children at home, finding a secluded spot there to meet with God may be difficult. You may need the creativity (or desperation!) of A. W. Tozer, who for a while could find the necessary privacy only in the furnace room.[16] Or you might repurpose a closet.[17] Godly Susanna Wesley, mother of John (the founder of the Methodist movement) and Charles (the prolific hymn writer), raised a very large family and for many years found it virtually impossible to experience physical isolation. But almost as well known as being the mother of two influential sons was her habit, when she needed silence and solitude, to bring her apron up over her head and read her Bible and pray underneath it. Obviously that did not block out much noise, but it was a sign to her children for those minutes that she was not to be bothered and that the older ones were to care for the younger.

Perhaps you can find sufficient solitude outdoors. Jonathan Edwards found seclusion in an open field. While traveling on the Connecticut River he recorded, "At Saybrook we went ashore to lodge on Saturday, and there kept the Sabbath; where I had a sweet and refreshing season, walking alone in the fields."[18] More commonly he retreated to the woods for silence and solitude with God: "I rode out into the woods for my health, . . . having alighted from my horse in a retired place, as my manner commonly has been, to walk for divine contemplation and prayer."[19] You may not live near fields or woods, but there may be a park not far away that could provide a place to walk and think and pray with few distractions. A pharmacist in my church frequently stops at a park two blocks from his house for a few minutes of silence and solitude before going home in the evening to his wife and four young children. For years my favorite spot was the Morton Arboretum near where I lived; now it's a quiet, leafy lane where I can stroll alone.

Dawson Trotman routinely walked to a knoll at the end of his street. "Here he spent precious hours alone, praying aloud, singing praise to the Lord, quoting Scriptures of promise and challenge that flooded his mind—now wrestling in urgent prayer, now pacing the hillside in silence."[20] One of my good friends takes index cards containing his prayer concerns and walks for blocks in his neighborhood while silently pouring out his heart before God.

As already noted, the building where your church meets might be an ideal location for a few hours of isolation. Most church buildings have a lot of unoccupied space during the week. It may be relatively close to you (if not, another church willing to accommodate you probably is), and would be free, safe, available on short notice, and provide a number of conveniences.

The prophetic Welsh preacher Howell Harris, a friend of George Whitefield, had a special place for silence and solitude in a church building. Writing about the time prior to the Welshman's evangelistic ministry, Arnold Dallimore says,

> Harris's knowledge of Divine things during these days was small. He simply knew he loved the Lord and wanted to love Him more, and in this pursuit he sought out quiet places where he could be secluded with Him in prayer. One of his favourite retreats was the church at Llangasty—the village in which he then taught school—and on one occasion shortly after his conversion he climbed into its tower to be more alone with the Lord. There, as he remained in intercession for some hours, he experienced an overwhelming sense of the presence and power of God. That lonely church tower became to him a holy of holies, and afterwards he wrote, "I felt suddenly my heart melting within me, like wax before the fire, with love to God my Saviour; and also felt, not only love and peace, but a longing to be dissolved with Christ. There was a cry in my inmost soul which I was totally unacquainted with before, 'Abba, Father!' . . . I knew I was His child, and that He loved and heard me. My soul being filled and satiated,

cried, 'It is enough! I am satisfied! Give me strength and I will follow Thee through fire and water.'"[21]

Like Susanna Wesley's apron, your regular place may not be ideal, and you may have to change locations from time to time, but do your best to locate some singular spot for you to pursue godliness through silence and solitude.

Trade Off Daily Responsibilities

Arrange a trade-off system of daily responsibilities with your spouse or a friend when necessary in order to have the freedom for extended times of silence and solitude.

Your initial response to the suggestion of extended times in these Disciplines may have been, "You don't know my situation! I have a family to feed and children to take care of. I can't just go off by myself for hours at a time." Most people, including those who practice silence and solitude, have similar obligations that can't be neglected. The most practical, inexpensive method of overcoming this problem is to ask your spouse or a friend to temporarily assume your responsibilities in order to give you time alone. Then return the favor by providing the same or another service. Mothers of young children tell me this is the best, most workable way they've found for getting extended time for these Disciplines. So, for example, your spouse or a friend might keep the kids (at home or at, say, your church) during the morning while you meet with God alone. Afterward you have lunch together, and then trade off in the afternoon. Perhaps you could organize a group to serve as do some in one church I know where they provide child care for a couple of hours one morning per week so that moms can enjoy some time alone with God elsewhere in the building.

One word of warning: Reality can hit especially hard when you come home again. A mother of five told me she cushions the shock by preparing a meal in advance for the microwave or in a slow-cooker. If things are disorderly around the home when she returns, she can make her adjustment without having to worry about cooking right away. As tough as it is sometimes to come back, the rigors of reality only prove how much we need the refreshment of silence and solitude.

MORE APPLICATION

Will you seek daily times of silence and solitude? When Solomon's temple was erected, "neither hammer nor axe nor any tool of iron was heard in the house while it was being built" (1 Kings 6:7). In like manner, our personal "temple of the Holy Spirit" (1 Corinthians 6:19) needs to be built up with interludes of silence and solitude. Schedule such a retreat for every day. The busier you are and the more hectic your world, the more you need to plan daily spaces of silence and solitude.

A. W. Tozer expanded on this by saying,

> Retire from the world each day to some private spot, even if it be only the bedroom (for a while I retreated to the furnace room for want of a better place). Stay in the secret place till the surrounding noises begin to fade out of your heart. . . . Give yourself to God and then be what and who you are without regard to what others think. . . . Learn to pray inwardly every moment. . . . Call home your roving thoughts. Gaze on Christ with the eyes of your soul. . . . All the above is contingent upon a right relation to God through Christ and daily meditation on the Scriptures. Lacking these, nothing will help us; granted these, the discipline recommended will go far to neutralize the evil effects of externalism and to make us acquainted with God and our own souls.[22]

As daily sleep and rest refresh the body, so daily silence and solitude refresh the soul. These Disciplines have a way of airing out the mind and ironing out the wrinkles of the soul. Plan to come to the quiet every day to meet God in His Word and through prayer.

Will you seek extended times of silence and solitude? Plan for them. Put them on the calendar. The routine and responsibilities of daily living will expand to fill all your time and keep you from spending protracted periods alone with God unless you act decisively.

You may need an extended time of silence and solitude to settle your doubts or reestablish your spiritual moorings. That's what the late Francis Schaeffer did during a critical period of his life in 1951. He came to a crisis that had two parts. He described his struggle this way:

> First, it seemed to me that among many of those who held the orthodox position [that is, biblically orthodox doctrine] one saw little reality in the things that the Bible so clearly said should be the result of Christianity. Second, it gradually grew on me that my own reality was less than it had been in the early days after I had become a Christian. I realized that in honesty I had to go back and rethink my whole position.[23]

This was a crisis important enough to warrant extended times of silence and solitude. Of this period of many days he said, "I walked in the mountains when it was clear and when it was rainy I walked back and forward in the hayloft of the old chalet where we lived. I walked, prayed, and thought through what the Scriptures taught as well as reviewing my own reasons for being a Christian."[24] Gradually he began to see that his problem was a lack of understanding what the Bible says about the meaning of the finished work of Christ for our present lives. And little by little, in his soul the sun came out again and the song came back. Those days of silence and solitude were a major turning point in Schaeffer's life and the foundation upon which the rest of his unique and now-famous ministry, L'Abri, in Switzerland, was built.

Perhaps you need to get alone with God and deal with some issues and questions. Maybe you have come to a crisis of faith that needs time for prayer, meditation on Scripture, deep thinking, and much soul searching. There's too much at stake to neglect the matter or to deal with it superficially. If your body had an emergency, you would take the necessary time to deal with it. Don't do any less for an emergency of the soul.

But don't think of extended periods of silence and solitude as times only for dealing with crises or for spiritual urgent care. The memoir of the first missionary from America, Adoniram Judson, tells this story:

> Once, when worn out with translations, and really needing rest, he went over the hills into the thick jungle, far beyond all human habitation. . . . To this place he brought his Bible, and sat down under the wild jungle trees to read, and meditate, and pray, and at night returned to the "hermitage" [a bamboo house he'd built at the edge of the jungle].[25]

Judson spent an incredible forty days like this in the dangerous jungle of Burma. But of this lifestyle, we are told, "He only adopted it *for a time.*" Why would he break his routine for this prolonged period of silence and solitude? His biographer says it was "as a means of moral improvement by which the whole of his future life might be rendered more in harmony with the perfect example of the Saviour whom he worshipped."[26] Judson engaged in this extended time of withdrawal for purposes of rest, his future usefulness, and "for the purpose of godliness." Shouldn't you seek to do the same (even though something closer to forty hours may be more realistic for you than forty days)?

Will you start now? The time for silence and solitude will rarely be easy to chisel out of your schedule. The world, the flesh, and the Enemy of your soul will see to that. But if you discipline yourself to do it, your only regret will be that you didn't start sooner.

Don't expect each occasion to have the same effect on your life as some of those quoted here from Christian history. Dramatic results or intense emotions may rarely occur. However, as with all the Spiritual Disciplines, silence and solitude are profitable even though you often conclude them feeling "normal." Still, there is a delight that comes from meeting alone with God that, while not always remarkable, is almost always refreshing.

These words from Jonathan Edwards are an appropriate concluding reminder:

> Some are greatly affected from time to time, when in company; but have nothing that bears any manner of proportion to it, in secret, in close meditation, secret prayer, and conversing with God, when alone, and separated from all the world. . . . A true Christian doubtless delights in religious fellowship, and Christian conversation, and finds much to affect his heart in it: but he also delights at times to retire from all mankind, to converse with God in solitary places. And this also has its peculiar advantages for fixing his heart, and engaging its affections. True religion disposes persons to be much alone in solitary places, for holy meditation and prayer. . . . It is the nature of true grace, that however it loves Christian society in its place, yet it in a peculiar manner delights in retirement, and secret converse with God.[27]

Have you experienced this "true grace," the work of God in your soul that causes you not only to delight in fellowship with God's people, but also compels you "to converse with God in solitary places"? God created us for rich communion with Himself, but in the Garden of Eden that communion was broken by sin. Since then, "All we like sheep have gone astray; we have turned—every one—to his own way" (Isaiah 53:6). We "all have sinned and fall short of the glory of God" (Romans 3:23), so we turn to our own way and show little interest in knowing the way to God and drawing close to Him. But just as God came seeking Adam in the garden after he had sinned, so God came seeking us when He sent His Son, Jesus, "to seek and to save the lost" (Luke 19:10). In order to remove the barrier of our rebellion against God and restore our fellowship with the Father, Jesus offered Himself on the cross as a substitute to God and received the judgment we deserve for our sins. As the apostle Peter put it, "Christ also suffered once for sins, the righteous for the unrighteous, that he might bring us to God" (1 Peter 3:18). God showed His acceptance of Jesus' death on behalf of others by raising Jesus from the dead. And God shows His willingness for Jesus to bring us to Him by inviting us to come to Him in Jesus' name. All who will turn from going their own way, and who will place their faith in Jesus to make them acceptable to God, are eternally welcome. Those who come to the Father through Jesus receive the Holy Spirit, who makes them alive to God and causes them to cry, "Abba! Father!" (Romans 8:15). And thus those who know God feel a Spirit-ignited heart-cry for Him, longing to worship Him with His people, seeking to talk about the things of God in "religious fellowship" with others, and delighting in "secret converse with God."

Will you commit yourself to the Disciplines of silence and solitude? If you've experienced God's saving grace, then silence and solitude will be, in the words of Edwards, a "delight," a faithful fountain of refreshment, joy, and transformation. If I had them, I would almost bet you two million rubles on it.

CHAPTER 11

JOURNALING . . .
FOR THE PURPOSE OF GODLINESS

The present benefit of spiritual discipline is a fulfilled,
God-blessed, fruitful, and useful life. If you get involved
in spiritual gymnastics, the blessings of godliness will carry
on into eternity. Although many people spend far more
time exercising their bodies than their souls, the excellent
servant of Jesus Christ realizes that spiritual
discipline is a priority.

JOHN MACARTHUR JR.

More than almost any other Discipline, journaling has a fascinating appeal for nearly all who hear about it. One reason is the way journaling blends the Bible and daily living, like the confluence of two great rivers into one. And since each believer's adventure down life's river involves bends and hazards previously unexplored by him or her on the way to the Celestial City, something about journaling this journey appeals to the adventuresome spirit of Christian growth.

EXPLANATION OF JOURNALING

A *journal* (a word usually synonymous with *diary*[1]) is a place (tangible or digital) in which a person records information important to him or her personally for preservation or consideration. As a Christian, your journal is a place to document the works and ways of God in your life. Your journal also can include an account of daily events, a record of personal relationships, a notebook of insights into Scripture, and/or a list of prayer requests. Spontaneous

devotional thoughts or lengthy theological musings can be preserved there. A journal is one of the best places for charting your
progress in the other Spiritual Disciplines and for holding yourself
accountable to your goals.

Woven throughout this fabric of entries and events are the col-
orful strands of your reflections and feelings about them. How you
respond to these matters, and how you interpret them from your
own spiritual perspective, also express the heart of journaling.

Does a Christian have to keep a journal in order to grow more like
Jesus Christ? No, nothing in Scripture obligates the followers of Jesus
to keep a journal. In fact, I have never read or heard anyone make
such a claim. Many of the most Christlike people in history have kept
journals, and many equally godly men and women have not.

Can we say, then, that there is any biblical basis for journaling?

On the one hand, unlike prayer, the practice of journaling certainly isn't a direct outgrowth of the gospel. Scripture would support the fact that all those who come to know God through the
gospel will pray, for the Spirit causes them to cry, "Abba! Father!"
(Romans 8:15). Salvation through the gospel of Christ also causes
all converted people to hunger for the Word of God. But it can't be
said that the gospel always produces disciples of Jesus who keep
spiritual journals. Such a preposterous claim would necessarily
imply that throughout history no lifelong illiterate people have ever
been converted, for they were unable to produce journals.

On the other hand, something very similar to what has historically been called journaling is found by example in Scripture.
King David poured out his soul to God in the scrolls of the Psalms,
repeatedly writing things such as, "Incline Your ear, O LORD, and
answer me; For I am afflicted and needy" (Psalm 86:1, NASB). Cries
like these are not unlike a believer today writing a very similar
heartfelt plea to the Lord in a journal. When the prophet Jeremiah
expressed to God the depth of his grief about the fall of Jerusalem
in his Lamentations, he was doing something not very different
from the contemporary Christian who types his or her Godward

feelings into a word processor file named "Journal." Of course, unlike the words of David and Jeremiah in Scripture, no believer's writings today are divinely inspired. But the example of these men in writing their prayers, meditations, questions, and so on provides scriptural validation for encouraging Christians today to consider the value of doing the same in a journal.

As long as people have been able to write, they have written about what is most important to them. And thus the people of God, of course, have recorded their thoughts about the things of God, and they have done so in something akin to what is today referred to as a journal. The fourth-century theologian Augustine opened his heart in the pages of his famous *Confessions*. Jonathan Edwards found the practice so useful for sharpening his thinking and deepening his devotion that he kept several different kinds of journals and notebooks (such as his "Miscellanies" and "Notes on Scripture") concurrently. Whether in something called a *journal, diary, commonplace book, notebook*, or something else, Christians have been irrepressible chroniclers of their spiritual lives.

Let's make clear that Jesus did not live and die for sinners to turn us into journal-keepers. He came to make us right with God. But once we are right with God through repentance and faith in who Jesus is and what He has done, a journal can be, as millions of those right with God throughout history have found, a great tool for thinking about and applying the life and death of Jesus. Specifically, your journal is a place to reflect upon God's Word and the riches of God's grace to us in the gospel of Jesus Christ, and how we move forward in enjoying those riches.

As you read this chapter, consider the biblical and historical reasons for joining those of God's people who have taken up the Discipline of journaling[2] "for the purpose of godliness." Remember, the goal of becoming more like Jesus should be the main reason for beginning any Spiritual Discipline, including this one. With that fresh in mind, consider the words of the United Kingdom's Maurice Roberts about journaling.

The logic of this practice is inevitable once men have felt the urge to become molded in heart and life to the pattern of Christ. No one will keep a record of his inward groans, fears, sins, experiences, providences and aspirations unless he is convinced of the value of the practice for his own spiritual progress. It was this very conviction which made it a commonplace practice in earlier times. We suggest the practice should be revived and something needs to be said in its defense.[3]

VALUE OF JOURNALING

Keeping a journal not only promotes spiritual growth by means of its own virtues, but it's a valuable aid to many other aspects of the spiritual life as well.

Help in Self-Understanding and Evaluation

In Romans 12:3, each Christian is exhorted "not to think of himself more highly than he ought to think, but to think with sober judgment." Keeping a journal certainly does not guarantee protection against either conceit or self-abasement. But the simple discipline of recording significant events in my life and noting my reactions to them does cause me to examine myself in light of Scripture much more thoroughly than I would without such a pause.

This is no minor point or small need in our lives. A more God-centered theologian never lived than John Calvin, yet even he wrote on the first page of his monumental *Institutes*: "Without knowledge of self there is no knowledge of God."[4] Through the knowledge of ourselves and our condition, he explained, we are aroused to seek God. A journal can be the means by which the Holy Spirit shows us areas of sin or weakness, the emptiness of a path we have chosen, insight into our motives, or other things that can transform the journal page into an altar of seeking God.

At an 1803 meeting of the "Eclectic Society," where evangelical ministers of London gathered each week to sharpen their minds and deepen their fellowship by discussing theological issues, Josiah Pratt noted the value of a journal in self-examination.

> The practice of keeping a diary would promote vigilance. The lives of many are spent at a sort of hazard. They fall into certain religious habits: and are perhaps under no strong temptations. They are regular at church and sacrament, and in [family worship]. They read the Bible and pray daily in secret. But here it ends. They know little of the progress or decline of the inner man. They are Christians, therefore, of very low attainments. The workings of sin are not noticed, as they should be, and therefore grace is not sought against them: and the genial emotions of grace are not noticed, and therefore not fostered and cultivated. Now, a diary would have a tendency to raise the standard to such persons by exciting vigilance.[5]

One of the ways the "progress or decline of the inner man" can be noted through journaling is by the observation of previously undetected patterns in your life. When I review my journal entries for a month, six months, or a year, I usually see myself and events more objectively. I can analyze my thoughts and actions apart from the feelings I had at the time. From that perspective it's easier to observe whether I've made spiritual progress or have backslidden in a particular area.

Journaling is not a time for navel gazing, however. Nor is it an excuse for becoming self-centered at the expense of a needy world. Writing on the Puritans and their relationship to society, Edmund S. Morgan cites an entry from the journal of a godly young man during an illness from which he died in the late 1600s. In it the young man evaluated whether he had shown sufficient love to others. Then says Morgan,

> The fact that many Puritans kept diaries of this kind helps to explain their pursuit of social virtue: diaries were the

reckoning books in which they checked the assets and liabilities of their souls in faith. When they opened these books, they set down lapses of morality with appropriate expressions of repentance and balanced them against the evidences of faith. Cotton Mather made a point of having at least one good action to set down in his diary on every day of the week.[6]

Used appropriately, instead of drawing us more into ourselves, a journal can actually become a means of propelling us into action for others.

The journal can be a mirror in which we see more clearly our attitudes, thoughts, words, and actions. Since we will be held accountable for each of these at the Judgment, evaluating them by *any* means is wisdom.

Help in Meditation

As I mentioned in chapter 3, I believe meditation on Scripture is the single greatest devotional need of most Christians (compare Joshua 1:8; Psalm 1:1-3; 2 Timothy 2:7). However, meaningful meditation requires a concentration not often developed in our fast-paced, media-distracted society. Perhaps the most valuable contribution the Discipline of journaling makes to the pursuit of godliness is how it facilitates meditation on Scripture, especially the ability to intensify attention on the text.

I read the tale of a New England man convinced that nowhere in the world was fog any thicker than at his coastal home. Once while roofing his house, he claimed to be in a cloud so dense that he unknowingly continued on past the edge of the roof, "shingling off into the fog." Without pen in hand or fingers on the keyboard, I can get so distracted in meditation that I begin tacking one unrelated thought to another until I'm shingling off into the fog of daydreams instead of thinking in the light of Scripture. The discipline of writing down my meditations in my journal helps me concentrate.

Sitting with pen and paper or fingers floating above the keys also heightens my sense of expectation as I think on God and His words in the passage before me. I always listened better in school when I was taking notes. I'm the same way with hearing a sermon; I listen more attentively when I'm writing down the more significant thoughts of the message. The same principle transfers to journaling. When I record in a journal my meditations on a passage of Scripture, I simply focus on the text better and find meditation more fruitful.

Help in Expressing Thoughts and Feelings to the Lord

No matter how close the friendship or how intimate the marriage, we can't always tell others what we think. And yet sometimes our feelings are so strong and our thoughts so dominant that we must find some way to give them expression. Our Father is always available and willing to listen. "Pour out your heart before him," says Psalm 62:8. A journal is a place where we can give expression to the fountain of our heart, where we can unreservedly pour out our passion before the Lord.

Since human thoughts and emotions range between the extremes of exhilaration and despondency, we can expect to find both within the pages of our journal. That's true in all the well-known journals of church history. Notice the depths in which David Brainerd found himself in this entry:

> Lord's Day, December 16, 1744. Was so overwhelmed with dejection that I knew not how to live. I longed for death exceedingly; my soul was sunk into deep waters and the floods were ready to drown me. I was so much oppressed that my soul was in a kind of horror. I could not keep my thoughts fixed in prayer for the space of one minute, without fluttering and distraction. It made me exceedingly ashamed that I did not live to God. I had no distressing doubt about my own state, but I would have cheerfully ventured (as far as I could possibly know) into eternity.

While I was going to preach to the Indians, my soul was in anguish. I was so overborne with discouragement that I despaired of doing any good, and was driven to my wit's end. I knew nothing what to say, nor what course to take.[7]

Conversely, a short time later, Brainerd's journal reveals this profound expression of joy:

Lord's Day, February 17, 1745. I think, I was scarce ever enabled to offer the free grace of God to perishing sinners with more freedom and plainness in my life. Afterwards, I was enabled earnestly to invite the children of God to come renewedly and drink of this fountain of water of life, from whence they have heretofore derived unspeakable satisfaction. It was a very comfortable time to me. There were many tears in the assembly and I doubt not but that the Spirit of God was there, convincing poor sinners of their need of Christ. In the evening I felt composed and comfortable, though much tired. I had some sweet sense of the excellency and glory of God; and my soul rejoiced that He was "God over all, blessed forever"; but was too much crowded with company and conversation and longed to be more alone with God. Oh, that I could forever bless God for the mercy of this day, who "answered me in the joy of my heart."[8]

Perhaps you read Brainerd's words with the same sense of distance from your own experience as I do. Was he odd? Did he live on some higher spiritual plane inaccessible to Christians like me? Can the difference between his experiences with God and mine be explained exclusively by the difference in our times? Because I am unable to express in writing the kinds of emotions toward God that he did, am I the one who is strange?

I think every child of God can indeed experience more of what Brainerd expresses here, and a journal can help with the pursuit. Maurice Roberts explains,

A spiritual diary will tend to deepen and sanctify the emotional life of a child of God. There is great value to us of becoming more deeply emotional over the great issues of our faith. Our age is not deep enough in feelings. Biblical men are depicted as weeping copious tears, as sighing and groaning, as on occasion rejoicing with ecstasy. They were ravished by the very idea of God. They had a passion for Jesus Christ—His person, offices, names, titles, words and works. It is our shame to be so cold, unfeeling and unemotional in spite of all that God has done to us and for us in Christ. . . . The keeping of a diary might help to put us right in this respect also.[9]

We tend to *feel* most deeply about what we *think* most deeply about. By slowing us down and prompting us to think more deeply about the things of God, journaling helps us feel more deeply about them. Writing in a journal provides an opportunity for the intangible grays of mind-work and heart-work to distill clearly into black and white. Then we're better able to express those thoughts and feelings to the Lord.

Help in Remembering the Lord's Works

Many people think God has not blessed them with much until they have to move it all to a new address. In the same way, we tend to forget just how many times God has answered specific prayers, made timely provision, and done marvelous things in our lives. But having a place to collect all these memories prevents their being forgotten.

A journal helps us to be like Asaph in Psalm 77:11-12, who said, "I will remember the deeds of the LORD; yes, I will remember your wonders of old. I will ponder all your work, and meditate on your mighty deeds." Even the kings of Israel were required by the Lord to write for themselves a copy of the Law of Moses to help them remember what God had said and done in the lives of the patriarchs (see Deuteronomy 17:18).[10]

The testimony of Luci Shaw, widow of Christian publisher Harold Shaw, illustrates how a journal is not only helpful but *essential* for remembering the works of God's providence in your life.

> All my life long I've thought I should keep a journal. But I never did until a few years ago, when the discovery that my husband, Harold, had cancer suddenly plunged us into the middle of an intense learning experience, facing things we'd never faced before. Confronted with agonizing decisions, we would cry out to the Lord, "Where are you in the middle of this?" It suddenly occurred to me that unless I made a record of what was going on, I would forget. The events, details, and people of those painful days could easily become a blur. So I started to write it all down.[11]

Francis Bacon put it bluntly, "If a man write little, he had need have a great memory."[12]

One of the greatest benefits of keeping a record of the works of the Lord is the encouragement it can be to faith and prayer. C. H. Spurgeon, the lionhearted British Baptist preacher in the last half of the 1800s, said, "I have sometimes said, when I have become the prey of doubting thoughts, 'Well, now, I dare not doubt whether there be a God, for I can look back in my Diary, and say, On such a day, in the depths of trouble, I bent my knee to God, and or ever I had risen from my knees, the answer was given me.'"[13]

"How worthy it is to remember former benefits," said Stephen Charnock, author of the classic *The Existence and Attributes of God*, "when we come to beg for new."[14] A journal is one of the best ways to keep fresh the memory of the Lord's "former benefits."

Help in Creating and Preserving a Spiritual Heritage

Journaling is an effective way of teaching the things of God to our children and grandchildren, and of transmitting our faith into the future (compare Deuteronomy 6:4-7; 2 Timothy 1:5).

There could be an unimaginable future spiritual impact in

something we write today. My dad died suddenly on August 20, 1985. He was the manager of a small-town radio station. Each morning he hosted a folksy, thirty-minute program of music and local news. On his desk I found the devotional material he had used to begin his final broadcast. He had read the words to William Cowper's hymn, "God Moves in a Mysterious Way." Finding his initials and "8/19/85" written beside these lines of faith provided me with more comfort and spiritual strength than anything said to me by anyone else. After his death his old guitar became one of my most cherished possessions. His early days as a radio announcer came during the time when much of the programming was broadcast live. He had a popular show of his own in which he played this guitar and sang. On my first Thanksgiving Day without a dad I was rummaging around in the guitar case. In it I found more than a dozen old letters postmarked within a few days after my birth. All were from his listeners who had written to rejoice with him that my mother and I had survived a difficult birth. They noted that it was obvious he was very proud of me and many referred to remarks he had made on the air about his gratitude to the Lord for my safe arrival. I sat on the floor by the open case with these scraps of my heritage and wept tears of thanksgiving to the Lord for this remnant of his life. How precious it would be if only more of his walk with God were recorded for me in some written form.

For how many of your eight great-grandparents do you know the first and last names? I've asked this question of several hundred people, and in my experience only about one in ten knows the names of as many as three of his or her great-grandparents. One hundred years ago—just 1,200 months ago—they were probably as alive and active as you are right now. And yet, despite a lifetime of labor and acquiring things, not even their direct descendants—the people most likely to have an interest in them—know their names, much less anything else about them. Well, one hundred years from now, that's you. What trace of your life will remain? Except for the pictures you take and the things you write, nothing except legal records and the like may remain of your decades on the earth. And because of the changes in technology, it's questionable whether your descendants will even be able to access your photographs. So what you write, in places like a journal, may be the most enduring legacy of your walk on the earth.

Moreover, the most significant impact you make on your children and future generations spiritually may occur through something like a journal. For instance, is the story of your conversion recorded anywhere? How about dramatic answers to prayer or the major spiritual turning points in your life? These stories of God's grace in the life of your family should be preserved. You may have children or grandchildren who are far from God at present and have no interest in your witness, who yet might be turned to the Lord by means of reading your journal someday. God may be pleased to use the Christ-centered testimony of your salvation, or your meditations on Jesus and the Scriptures, to bring to Himself grandchildren or great-grandchildren you may never hold and who may have parents who do not teach them the things of God—all through their interest in reading some family history. I know that this happens.

Never underestimate the power of a written record of faith acting as a spiritual time capsule. The writer of Psalm 102:18 recognized it when he said of his experience with God: "Let this be recorded for a generation to come, so that a people yet to be created may praise the LORD."

Help in Clarifying and Articulating Insights

An old adage says that thoughts disentangle themselves when passed through the lips and across the fingertips. While reading makes a full man, and dialogue a ready man, according to Francis Bacon, *writing* makes an *exact* man. I've discovered that if I write down the meditations of my quiet time with the Lord they stay with me much longer. Without journaling, by day's end I usually can remember little from my devotional time.

The great champion of prayer and faith, George Müller, used

his journal to articulate insights into Scripture and thoughts about God:

> July 22, 1838. This evening I was walking in our little garden, meditating on Hebrews 13:8, "Jesus Christ is the same yesterday and today, and forever." Whilst meditating on His unchangeable love, power and wisdom, and turning all as I went into prayer respecting myself; and whilst applying also His unchangeable love, power, and wisdom both to my present spiritual and temporal circumstances—all at once the present need of the orphan houses was brought to my mind. Immediately I was led to say to myself, "Jesus in His love and power has hitherto supplied me with what I have needed for the orphans, and in the same unchangeable love and power He will provide me with what I may need for the future." A flow of joy came into my soul whilst realising thus the unchangeableness of our adorable Lord. About one minute after, a letter was brought me enclosing a cheque for twenty pounds. In it was written: "Will you apply the amount of the enclosed cheque to the objects of your Scriptural Knowledge Society, or of your Orphan Establishment, or in the work and cause of our Master in any way that He Himself, on your application to Him, may point out to you. It is not a great sum, but it is a sufficient provision for the exigency of today; and it is for today's exigencies that ordinarily the Lord provides. Tomorrow, as it brings its demands, will find its supply."[15]

When insights from my quiet time are clearly fixed in my mind through journaling, I've also found them ready to use later in conversation, counseling, encouraging, and witnessing (see 1 Peter 3:15).

Help in Monitoring Goals and Priorities

A journal is a good way to keep before us the things we want to do and emphasize. Some put a list of goals and priorities in their journal and review it every day. For many years (until I began to use digital reminders), I would draw a small rectangle at the beginning of each journal entry. With one horizontal line and two vertical ones I divided the box into six tiny squares. Each square represented a particular spiritual goal I wanted to accomplish every day, such as encouraging at least one person. Before I made a journal entry for a day, I turned to the entry for the previous day and colored in the appropriate squares for the daily goals I accomplished. This isn't legalism, for I had no internal or external requirement to do those things. I wanted to develop these habits and character qualities as part of pressing on toward the goal of Christlikeness (see Philippians 3:12-16), and I utilized reminders in my journal to help me.

The resolutions made by young Jonathan Edwards are still well known to many Christians today. They included the resolve of his soul concerning the use of time, temperance in eating, growth in grace, self-denial, and other matters dealt with in seventy resolutions.[16] These were much more than today's halfhearted New Year's resolutions. They became Edwards' lifelong spiritual goals and priorities. What isn't so well known is how he evaluated his conduct daily by these resolutions and recorded the results in his journal. On Christmas Eve, 1722, he wrote, "Higher thoughts than usual of the excellency of Christ and his kingdom. Concluded to observe, at the end of every month, the number of breaches of resolutions, to see whether they increase or diminish, to begin from this day, and to compute from that the weekly account my monthly increase, and out of the whole, my yearly increase, beginning from new-year days."[17] Another example of this use of his journal is found in the entry of the following January 5: "A little redeemed from a long dreadful dullness, about reading the Scriptures. This week, have been unhappily low in the weekly account: and what are the reasons of it? abundance of listlessness and sloth; and, if this should continue much longer, I perceive that other sins will begin to discover themselves."[18] Years later, Edwards came to believe that he was too self-reliant in some of his efforts to keep his resolutions. That awareness did not cause him to change his mind about keeping them, nor did he forsake any Disciplines related to them, especially those involving his pen. As award-winning Edwards biographer George Marsden put it, "The mature Edwards looked back on this rigor as involving 'too great a dependence on my own strength; which afterward proved a great damage to me.' Yet he never abandoned his belief in the value of strict spiritual disciplines, as his later *Life of Brainerd* would reveal."[19] The change Edwards did make was to seek and rely more on the power of the Holy Spirit upon his practice of the Disciplines to bring about greater conformity to Christ.

The ocean-hopping evangelist of the First Great Awakening, George Whitefield, is best remembered for his inimitable, passionate preaching. Like his contemporary Edwards, Whitefield's *Diary* reveals that his spirituality was at least as deep as his influence was wide. The book begins with a list of criteria that he used each night as a basis of self-examination.

Have I,

1. Been fervent in prayer?
2. Used stated hours of prayer?
3. Used ejaculatory prayer each hour?
4. After or before every deliberate conversation or action, considered how it might tend to God's glory?
5. After any pleasure, immediately given thanks?
6. Planned business for the day?
7. Been simple and recollected in everything?
8. Been zealous in undertaking and active in doing what good I could?
9. Been meek, cheerful, affable in everything I said or did?
10. Been proud, vain, unchaste, or enviable of others?
11. Recollected in eating and drinking? Thankful? Temperate in sleep?

12. Taken time for giving thanks according to (William) Law's rules?
13. Been diligent in studies?
14. Thought or spoken unkindly of anyone?
15. Confessed all sins?[20]

Each day's entry in Whitefield's *Diary* is in two parts, one page per part. On the first page he listed the specific activities of his day, then he evaluated each on the basis of his fifteen questions. On the second page, according to his biographer, Arnold Dallimore, "He records any unusual activity throughout the day, but above all, gives expression to his inner self. The longings of his soul, a searching of his motives, severe self-reproach for the slightest wrong and bursts of praise to God, are all recorded without inhibition."[21]

How did men like Edwards and Whitefield become so unusually conformed to the image of Christ? Part of their secret was their use of the Spiritual Discipline of journaling to maintain self-accountability for their spiritual goals and priorities. Before we give all the reasons why we cannot be as godly as they were, let us first try doing what they did.

Help in Maintaining the Other Spiritual Disciplines

My journal is the place where I record my progress with all the Spiritual Disciplines. For instance, I also used some of the small squares mentioned above to keep myself accountable with Disciplines like Scripture memory. It's very easy for me to become lazy and slip away from memorizing God's Word, which the Bible says is so helpful to holiness (see Psalm 119:11). Whenever I return to the habit of *not* memorizing Scripture, momentum keeps me there. However, when I have a daily prompter such as my journal, where I find a reminder to "discipline myself for the purpose of godliness," I can more easily reverse the negative momentum.

The flesh, our natural inclination toward sin, does not contribute to our spiritual growth. Unless "by the Spirit" we *labor* to "put to death the deeds of the body" (Romans 8:13), our progress in godliness will be very slow. Unless we find *practical* ways to fight against our congenital tendency toward spiritual sloth, and pray for the Holy Spirit's power upon those practical ways, we will not build ourselves up in the faith (see Jude 20); we will drift toward spiritual entropy instead.

This fact was affirmed by Maurice Roberts in an article, "Where Have the Saints Gone?"

> There will be no marked growth in Christian holiness if we do not labor to overcome our natural disinclination towards secret spiritual exercises. Our forefathers kept honest diaries where the soul's battles were recorded. Thomas Shepherd, Pilgrim Father and founder of Harvard, wrote in his private papers, "It is sometimes so with me that I will rather die than pray." So is it with us all. But this honesty is not commonplace. Such men climbed high only as they labored with sweat and tears to cultivate the soul. We, too, must "exercise ourselves unto godliness" (1 TIMOTHY 4:7).[22]

Missionary Jim Elliot used his now-famous journal to irrigate the practice of the Disciplines in his life when the tide of zeal for them ran low. On November 20, 1955, less than two months before he was killed by Auca Indians in Ecuador, he wrote,

> Also read parts of *Behind the Ranges* and am resolute to do something about it in my private devotional and prayer life. In studying Spanish I left off English Bible reading, and my devotional reading pattern was broken. I have never restored it. Translation and preparation for daily Bible lessons is not sufficient to empower my soul. Prayer as a single man was difficult, I remember, because my mind always reverted to Betty. Now it's too hard to get out of bed in the morning. I have made resolutions on this

score before now but not followed them up. Tomorrow it's to be—dressed by 6:00 a.m. and study in the Epistles before breakfast. So help me, God.[23]

Apparently the desire to revitalize his devotional life had surged through Elliot's mind and emotions many times before. Transferring that desire to paper, however, seemed to channel it like water into a turbine, so that what was once mere fluid desire, by God's help, began producing power.

Recording the joys and freedom I experience through the Spiritual Disciplines is another way journaling helps maintain my involvement with them. When I review my journal and read in my own handwriting of my inexpressible delight in sharing the gospel with elderly people in the bush of Kenya who have never heard of Jesus, or of preaching and seeing Brazilian teenagers repent of involvement in spiritism, I am resolved to maintain the Discipline of evangelism in overseas missions projects regardless of the cost. Reviewing the sense of victory I recorded during a day of fasting creates in me a hunger for another such day of spiritual feasting.

The Christian life is, by definition, a living thing. If we can think of the Discipline of Bible intake as its food and prayer as its breath, many Christians have made journaling its heart. For them it pumps life-maintaining blood into every Discipline connected with it.

WAYS OF JOURNALING

How is it done? "Your way of keeping a journal is the right way.... There are no rules for keeping a journal!"[24] In other words, the method you find most edifying and useful in your pursuit of godliness is the way you should keep a journal. This goes for content, format, length, and frequency. So whereas one Christian usually journals on a computer two or three times per week, entering only brief meditations on Scripture, and another disciple of Jesus typically writes prayers at great length and does so with a fountain pen in a leather-bound volume almost every day, both are valid insofar as they help the person draw closer to God and conform biblically to Christlikeness.

Today I was in a local Christian bookstore and noticed at least a dozen books to be used as journals. There were cloth-covered volumes and paperbacks. Some posted devotional thoughts or inspirational quotes on each page. Others simply provided blank pages with headings like "Prayer Requests" and "Insights from Scripture" at the top. Many mainstream bookstores sell beautifully bound, gilt-edged books of empty pages, as well as nontraditional, edgier styles, all of which work well as journals.

Many Christians find that the most practical approach is to use an everyday notebook or common printer paper. While some prefer a spiral-bound notebook, I find loose-leaf pages more workable. Besides being less expensive, using plain paper also does not force you to confine your entries to the designated space of a professionally bound journal. On the other hand, some find that writing in an attractive book gives their journaling a special appeal that stimulates their faithfulness in the Discipline. (This motivation backfires on some people when they begin to feel as though their entries are rather mundane for such a fine depository. They start writing less frequently and soon stop altogether.)

Another reason I prefer the loose-leaf format is convenience. Although it is handy to carry around a book or spiral-bound notebook, it's even handier to carry only a few pages of paper. My journal pages are 8½" x 5½"[25] and fit easily into my Bible, briefcase, a book, or almost anything I take with me. Such convenient access means I can immediately record any sudden flash of insight, important thought, conversation, quotation, and so on. This leads to another advantage over the bound volume or spiral notebook method: I can more easily go back and insert new pages, photocopies, printouts, and more. Besides, the loose-leaf approach permits the flexibility of typing my entries and printing hard copies if desired. But having said that, I return to this maxim: "Your way of keeping a journal is the right way." Use the method that works best for you.

The means you use to actually put the words on paper will also affect the format you choose. I like to make my journal entries on a word processor. That's because I can type faster than I can write, and also because it's easier to read when it's printed. Frequently, however, my journaling time occurs when I cannot or prefer not to use a digital device, and so I'll enjoy writing by hand with a good fountain pen and ink from a bottle.[26] Some feel strongly about journaling only by hand, that it's more spontaneous and expressive. While I'm a big fan of fountain pens and use one every day, I find that the speed and other advantages of a digital method normally tip the scale for me to journal by that means more often than not.

The ever-increasing development of technology will certainly see a corresponding increase in the use of its capabilities for journaling. Already the Internet and personal technologies provide countless resources for journal-keeping. If you find that some of them can help you grow in grace and godliness, use them. If they don't appeal to you, feel no pressure to conform. Regardless of the pace or number of technological advances related to this Discipline, there will always be a place for journaling with the simplest of tools—pen and paper.

As a starting entry for each day, try listing the one verse or idea from your Bible reading that impressed you most. Meditate on that for a few minutes, then record your thoughts and insights. From there consider adding recent events in your life and your feelings and responses to them, brief prayers, joys, successes, failures, quotations, and so on.

Don't think that "official journaling" (there is no such thing!) means you have to write a certain number of lines every day or a certain number of days per week. Whenever I fall into needlessly long lapses between entries, I discipline myself to write at least one sentence per day. Inevitably, that one sentence turns willingly into a paragraph or a page, for my biggest problem is just getting started. Once I do that, I'm glad I'm there and usually experience no problem in writing a few additional lines, if not many more.

Don't worry about trying to get "caught up." Major life events—the kinds of experiences we always want to journal about—often require an unreasonable amount of time to record in a journal. The events last so long or consist of so many details that trying to journal about them can feel burdensome. The Discipline of journaling is not a burden from God to document your entire life; rather it is meant to bless you and be a means to joy and godliness.

MORE APPLICATION

As with all the Disciplines, journaling can be fruitful at any level of involvement. Journaling is profitable regardless of how well you think you write, compose, or spell. Whether or not you write every day, whether you write little or much, whether your soul soars like a psalmist's or plods from thought to thought, journaling can help you grow in grace.

As with all the Disciplines, journaling requires persistence through the dry times. The novelty of journaling soon wears off. There will be days when you will have a spiritual version of "writer's block." At other times you just won't have any insights from either the Scriptures or your experience with God that seem noteworthy. While it's okay to write little or nothing on a given day or during a longer stretch of time, remember that you must eventually push through this barrier in order to enjoy the long-term benefits of journaling. In other words, don't quit the Discipline entirely just because the excitement of the first day eventually erodes. That will happen. Plan on it. But also plan for persistence.[27]

As with all the Disciplines, you must start journaling before you can experience its value. Irishman Thomas Houston was pastor of a Presbyterian church in Knockbracken, County Down (near modern Belfast), for fifty-four years during the 1800s. At the beginning of his ministry there he began keeping a journal, which he called "A Diary of God's Dealings and Providences with a Most Unworthy Sinner." In his entry for April 8, 1828, he revealed the inward struggle that ultimately resulted in the birth of his Spiritual Discipline of journaling:

For a considerable period I have been resolved on keeping
a register of the dealings and providences of my Heavenly
Father towards me, but, what through want of what I considered a fit opportunity, and through what was, I fear, a
greater cause, spiritual sloth, I have hitherto neglected it.
When I first began to think of this subject, various objections appeared to me to lie against diary writing altogether.
It would give room for spiritual pride; it led persons to
measure themselves by themselves; and as it is not easy to
determine between the motions of the spirit and the natural outworkings of the unrenewed conscience or the arti-
fices of the Deceiver, there is a danger of forming incorrect
judgments. These and other reasons kept me a length of
time from determining for the thing. Of late I have got over
these objections entirely, and am now of the opinion that
such a record may be of much service to an individual to
furnish him with matter for prayer and self-examination,
and to be a monument to God's faithfulness.[28]

Perhaps you can identify with Houston's struggle. As millions
want to begin walking, jogging, biking, or some other form of exercise but never do, so there are many who have wanted to begin the
spiritual exercise of journaling but have never done so. It sounds
interesting, and you are convinced of its value, but the words never
find their way onto paper or the computer screen. There just never
seems to be the time, a "fit opportunity" as Houston called it. But
in our heart of hearts we know that the "greater cause" is probably
the same "spiritual sloth" that clung drowsily to the will of this Irish
pastor. Consider journaling, not only as a way to raise up a "monument to God's faithfulness" in your life, but more importantly "for
the purpose of godliness."

CHAPTER 12

LEARNING . . .
FOR THE PURPOSE OF GODLINESS

*We must face the fact that many today are notoriously
careless in their living. This attitude finds its way into
the church. We have liberty, we have money, we live in
comparative luxury. As a result, discipline practically
has disappeared. What would a violin solo sound like if
the strings on the musician's instrument were all hanging
loose, not stretched tight, not "disciplined"?*

A. W. TOZER

Years ago I pastored a church near a county seat town with two
small universities. One school was the main educational institution
of the largest evangelical denomination in the state. Known for producing students zealous for Christ's kingdom, this university often
led the dozens of other schools in its denomination in numbers
of alumni on the mission field. One complaint I frequently heard
from students in the religion department, however, related to the
apparent lack of spiritual zeal among some of the professors. To
many students, these men paired enlarged theological brains with
pygmy-like, passionless hearts. We've all heard teachers or preach-
ers who could anchor a theological Mensa Club but whose lack of
zeal made their Christianity seem as dry and stale as the inside of
a basketball. But that just doesn't sound like the Lord Jesus, or even
the apostle Paul, does it?

In this same pastorate a man who was a deacon in his church
once said to me, "I never liked school, and I don't want to learn

anything when I come to church." Somehow there's something un-like Jesus in that attitude as well, isn't there?

Why do we seem to think we must choose between the two? Why do many Christians live as though they've been told, "Choose you this day whom you will serve: scholarship or devotion"? I maintain that the more Christlike we grow, the more we will pursue both a full head and a full heart, and the more we will radiate both spiritual light and heat.

If absolutely forced to allow one to predominate over the other, we must choose the burning heart. If people have the truth in their heads but not in their hearts (that is, they know the truth but do not believe it and experience its power) then they are not right with God. Like the Pharisees, apart from faith an awareness of the truth will only magnify our guilt before God at the Judgment. But if we have understood and properly responded to the gospel from the heart, in the end we shall be saved even though the rest of our doctrinal understanding is shallow or muddy. Not only would I choose the latter option for myself, but I would also prefer that for those to whom I minister. It's much harder to get a ship out of the harbor than to correct one on the sea that has drifted off course.

But let us be both out of the harbor *and* on course. Christians must realize that just as a fire cannot blaze without fuel, so burning hearts are not kindled by brainless heads. We must not content ourselves to be like those the Bible condemns as having "a zeal for God, but not according to knowledge" (Romans 10:2).

Does this mean we must be brilliant to be Christians? Absolutely not. But it does mean that to be like Jesus we must be learners, even as He was at only age twelve, "sitting among the teachers, listening to them and asking them questions. And all who heard him were amazed at his understanding and his answers" (Luke 2:46-47). Does this mean we must have several diplomas hanging on the wall to be first-rate Christians? It certainly does not. But it does mean we should discipline ourselves to be intentional learners like Jesus. He learned the Scriptures so well on His own apart from the formal training of the rabbis that He caused His adversaries to marvel, "How is it that this man has learning, when he has never studied?" (John 7:15).

An examination of the New Testament word *disciple* reveals that it means to be not only "a follower" of Christ but also "a learner." Are you a disciple of Jesus? To follow Christ and become more like Him, we must engage in the Spiritual Discipline of learning.

LEARNING CHARACTERIZES THE WISE PERSON

According to a book of the Bible written specifically to give us practical wisdom, one of the characteristics of a wise man or woman is a desire for learning. We read in Proverbs 9:9, "Give instruction to a wise man, and he will be still wiser; teach a righteous man, and he will increase in learning." Wise and righteous people can never get enough wisdom or knowledge. Unteachable people or those prideful about their learning only expose how shallow they really are. The truly wise are humble because they know they still have so much to learn. And according to this verse, wise and righteous people remain teachable. They can learn from anybody, regardless of age or background. Give one of them instruction, and "he will be still wiser . . . and he will increase in learning." The biblically wise are always looking to learn.

In Proverbs 10:14, we're told, "The wise lay up knowledge." The Hebrew word here means "to store up like a treasure." Wise men and women love to learn because they realize that knowledge is like a precious treasure.

I met a man who treasured knowledge despite living in a place where it was scarce as diamonds. During the mission trip to Kenya I mentioned in chapter 2, my interpreter was a schoolteacher in his early thirties named Bernard. He lived in the back of a store that was one of four buildings in the Kilema community. He walked several miles even farther into the bush country each day to the mud-brick elementary school where he taught. He returned home to his "cube," an eight-foot-by-eight-foot-by-eight-foot room where he lived with his wife and infant son. A twin bed was against the back wall with a sheet hanging from the ceiling to separate the "bedroom" from the rest of the cube. Only a small table with one chair occupied the front half. What interested me most was on the cement walls. Taped on every wall were several pages from long-outdated magazines or pictures from old calendars. They were all Bernard had to read. Though he'd been a Christian for many years, he was too poor even to own a Bible. The only books that ever came into his hands were a few secondhand textbooks kept at the school. So as he paced with his son in his arms, trying to get him to sleep, he read the words on the magazines for the umpteenth time. While he ate at his table or lay on his bed, he looked at the pictures of far-off people and places and pondered them.

As I stood in that concrete cube, looking at a couple of dozen faded pictures and yellowing pages, I realized that before me stood a wise man. Bernard understood that knowledge really is like a rare treasure. Though it is more scarce than gold, he had stored up all he could. That's the attitude all who are wise will have, for "the wise lay up knowledge." (Incidentally, some people in our church sent Bernard boxes of books and subscribed to a couple of magazines for him.)

Notice Proverbs 18:15: "An intelligent heart acquires knowledge, and the ear of the wise seeks knowledge." A wise person not only "acquires" knowledge, he or she "seeks" it. Wise ones desire to learn and will discipline themselves to seek opportunities for learning.

One other verse in Proverbs deserves our attention. In 23:12 we're commanded, "Apply your heart to instruction and your ear to words of knowledge." No matter how much previous instruction you have received or how extensive your knowledge—especially about God, Christ, the Bible, and the Christian life—and regardless of how intelligent or slow you consider yourself, you still need to apply your heart and ears to learn, for you haven't learned it all.

Learning is a lifelong Discipline, a Spiritual Discipline that characterizes the wise person. Samuel Hopkins, one of the early biographers of Jonathan Edwards, said that when he met Edwards he was impressed by the fact that a man already twenty years in the ministry still had "an uncommon thirst for knowledge, in the pursuit of which he spared no cost nor pains. He read all the books, especially books of divinity, that he could come at, from which he could hope to get any help in his pursuit of knowledge."[1] Edwards had an undeniably superior mind, but he never stopped applying it to learn. It was that, blended with an equally strong devotional zeal, that made him wise and great in the kingdom of God.

A durable yearning for learning characterizes all those who are truly wise.

FULFILLING THE GREATEST COMMANDMENT

Part of God's greatest commandment, said Jesus, is "Love the Lord your God . . . with all your mind" (Mark 12:30). What God wants most from you is your love. And one of the ways He wants you to show love and obedience to Him is by godly learning. God is glorified when we use the mind He made to learn of Him, His Word, His ways, and His world.

Lamentably, many Christians do not associate learning with loving God. In fact, we live in a very anti-intellectual age. That may sound strange in light of the infinite storehouse of information accessible through the Internet; the widespread availability and growth of online education; the almost daily, dazzling advances in technology; and the fact that there are more advanced academic degrees being awarded today than ever before. Perhaps it is precisely because of such things that people—including Christian people—are more averse to things intellectual. Kids who are smart may be unpopular just because they are smart. They're dismissed as "nerds," and the social attention goes to the "underachievers." Our culture glorifies the physical much more than the mental. Nobody sells posters of the top software engineers or architects, much less the leading theologians. Instead we sell posters of athletes, some of whom can do everything with a ball except autograph it and read its label. Some political candidates are described as too intellectual to be electable, as though we don't want thinkers running the government. In the church, everything must be "relevant," and we tend to disregard doctrine and theology as very irrelevant.

There is an intellectual*ism* that is wrong, but it is also wrong to be anti-intellectual. We should love God just as much with our mind as with our heart and soul and strength. How can it all fit together? As contemporary Christian thinker R. C. Sproul wrote, "God has made us with a harmony of heart and head, of thought and action. . . . The more we know Him the more we are able to love Him. The more we love Him the more we seek to know Him. To be central in our hearts He must be foremost in our minds. Religious thought is the prerequisite to religious affection and obedient action."[2]

Unless we love God with a growing mind, we will be Christian versions of the Samaritans to whom Jesus said, "You worship what you do not know" (John 4:22).

LEARNING—ESSENTIAL FOR INCREASED GODLINESS

The Christian life begins with learning—learning the gospel. No one is made right with the God about whom he knows nothing. No one is made right with God unless he or she learns about Him and His message to the world, a message of good news called the gospel. To know God, people must learn that there is a God (see Hebrews 11:6), that they have broken His law, and that they need to be reconciled to Him. They must learn that Jesus, God's Son, came to accomplish that reconciliation, and that He did so by means of His sinless life and His death on the cross as a substitute for sinners. They must learn of His bodily resurrection and their need to repent of their sin, and to believe in Jesus and what He has done. For apart from people learning these things, "how are they to believe in him of whom they have never heard?" (Romans 10:14).

No one believes in Jesus unless he or she has heard the story of Jesus and has at least a minimal understanding of it. No one loves Jesus unless he or she knows about Jesus. And just as we cannot *believe* and *love* Him about whom we've *learned nothing*, so we cannot *grow* in our faith and love of Him unless we *learn more* about Him. We will not *grow* much in godliness if we do not *know* much of what it means to be godly. We will not grow more like Christ if we don't know more about Christ.

The twentieth-century London preacher Martyn Lloyd-Jones reminded us, "Let us never forget that the message of the Bible is addressed primarily to the mind, to the understanding."[3] God's truth must be understood before it can be applied. The Word of God must first go through your head if it's going to change your heart and your life. That's why the apostle Paul said, "Do not be conformed to this world, but be *transformed* by the renewal of your *mind*" (Romans 12:2, emphasis added). Christlike transformation of the heart and life—growth in godliness—involves a mental renewal that cannot happen without learning.

Suppose someone gave you a book about prayer and said, "This will change your life!" But when you looked, you realized that the book was written in a language you could not read. You might be holding the best book on prayer ever written, but if you could not understand the contents it would do you no good. Without the knowledge of that language, you couldn't learn about prayer and grow in Christlikeness from that book. There's little difference, however, between failing to grow in godliness because you *can't* read a book on prayer and failing to grow because you *don't* read one. Without a disciplined commitment to learning, the lack of growth is the same in both cases.

No one will grow into and enjoy the blessings of any teaching of Scripture if he or she hasn't learned it. Jonathan Edwards said it plainly: "It is impossible that anyone should see the truth or excellency of any doctrine of the gospel, who knows not what that doctrine is. A man cannot see the wonderful excellency and love of

Christ in doing such and such things for sinners, unless his understanding be first informed."[4]

People may attend church worship faithfully, serve the Lord in and through the church eagerly, give to the work of Christ's kingdom generously, and desire to live Christianly in every aspect of their lives—and yet, year after year, demonstrate little evident growth in godliness. How can this be for people who love Jesus Christ and are indwelled by the Holy Spirit of God? In many cases it's because they devote so little mental energy to the most important kind of learning—learning about God and the things of God. No one grows into Christlikeness without learning about it—what Christlikeness looks like, how they should cultivate it, why it's necessary, where it leads, and more. No one experiences the sweetness of growing closer to and more like Christ unless he or she is first introduced to such things. Edwards is concise and clear: "He cannot have a taste of the sweetness and divine excellency of such and such things contained in divinity, unless he first have a notion that there are such and such things."[5]

If you know little *about* godliness, you will grow little *in* godliness. To know it requires the Discipline of learning.

LEARNING IS MOSTLY BY DISCIPLINE, NOT BY ACCIDENT

As every dust ball gets bigger the longer it rolls around under the bed, so every mind picks up at least a little knowledge the longer it rolls around on the earth. But we must not assume that we have learned true wisdom just by growing older. The observation found in Job 32:9 is, "The abundant in years may not be wise" (NASB). Haven't you heard of an "old fool"? Age and experience by themselves don't increase your spiritual maturity. Becoming like Jesus doesn't happen incidentally or automatically with the passing of birthdays. Godliness, as 1 Timothy 4:7 says, requires a deliberate discipline.

Those who are not *trying* to learn will only get spiritual and biblical knowledge by accident or convenience. Occasionally they will hear a biblical fact or principle from someone else and profit from it. Once in a while they will display a brief burst of interest in a subject. But this is not the way to godliness. The Discipline of learning transforms accidental learners into *intentional* learners.

Of course, it's a lot easier to be an accidental learner and a convenience learner than an intentional learner. We're born that way. And television spoon-feeds that inclination in megadoses. Watching TV or video is so much easier than choosing a good book, reading words, creating your own mental images, and relating it to your life. Television decides for you what will be presented, speaks the words to you, shows you its own images, and tells you what impact it wants to have on your life, if any. Compared to that, books often appear too demanding for the contemporary mind. Alas, it takes *discipline* to become an intentional learner.

Without the discipline of an intentional learner, not only will we fail to learn the things that promote godliness, but what we will learn by accident will be of little or no real benefit. For instance, without discipline no one will learn the books of the Bible. Sure, most who have been in church for a while can name quite a few, but those only randomly. So most churchgoers couldn't even list the names of the books God inspired, much less say anything about the contents of them. On the other hand, they—and their children— likely could name as many brands of beer, wine, and whiskey as they could books of the Bible. Is it because they tried to learn them? Probably not. Many Christians, without ever having had a single drink of any of these products, could not only name lots of them, but could also recall where some are manufactured or other details about them. How? Merely by accident, because advertising made it convenient to learn them. If you doubt this, try it on your small group at church. Try it with your young children, who presumably have never had a drink. How would *you* do? Learning that's mostly by accident does not lead to godliness. We must become disciplined, intentional learners if we're going to become like Jesus.

Speaking of children, in *What Every Christian Should Know:*

Combating the Erosion of Christian Knowledge in our Generation, Jo
Lewis and Gordon Palmer show that the reason young people are
not intentional learners is because their parents aren't.

> Young people are not readers. This is not surprising since
> their parents rarely prize reading. At one Christian college,
> a fifth of the students said their parents had never read to
> them. The lack of reading is partly the result of the strong
> vocational orientation of Americans: Parents don't read
> because it doesn't seem practical. They are more concerned
> with "Can my kid operate computers and get a job?" It fits
> the American obsession with the bottom line. These par-
> ents have never learned for the sake of learning, so neither
> have their children. In this way the value of education has
> become attenuated and relativized by the marketplace. So
> it follows that young people who read little of anything do
> not read their Bibles. One researcher found that "in the
> liveliest evangelical churches, people strongly feel they
> should read their Bible daily, but only around fifteen per-
> cent do so." Adults, we should also point out, are affected
> by many of the same pressures as the youth. If they watch
> television, listen to pop radio, and go to popular movies,
> they will imbibe these values that are targeted at teens. The
> result is that many younger adults in their twenties and
> thirties are, like their younger counterparts, to some extent
> dulled in their ability to read and understand the Bible.[6]

The Bible says, "Brothers, do not be children in your thinking.
Be infants in evil, but in your thinking be mature" (1 Corinthians
14:20). For this to occur, accidental and convenience learners must
become disciplined, intentional learners.

LEARNING IN A VARIETY OF WAYS

Since some people have legitimate difficulties with reading, here's a
list of some other methods of learning, methods that learners who

do thrive on reading will enjoy also. First, I strongly commend listening to recorded books. It's so easy to listen while getting ready for the day, commuting, driving around town, traveling long-distance, exercising, or working around the house. Much the same is true for audio and video recordings via the Internet as well as Bible teaching programs on Christian radio. Just make sure you're listening to a reputable ministry, not just to someone whose speaking style you enjoy. Don't forget the use of study guides. These are available from your Christian book sources and can direct you into an investigation of any book of the Bible, many doctrinal and practical topics, or help you go deeper into a book by a Christian author.[7]

One of my favorite ways of learning is to plan for meaningful dialogue with, and ask prepared questions of, spiritually mature Christians. Twice in recent weeks I had the privilege of an all-day car ride with some godly and experienced men whom I admired. In anticipation of each trip I prepared a list of questions to discuss. On both excursions I learned some valuable lessons and felt confident that I was "making the best use of the time" (Ephesians 5:16). With me always are several lists of questions to which I am frequently adding. This includes lists of questions for use when meeting new people, as well as when talking with fellow church members, children, youth, the elderly, students, and more. These questions have served me well in both anticipated and serendipitous conversations, and minimized the number of times when afterward I feel like I squandered an opportunity.[8]

While this is a book on *personal* spiritual disciplines, I can't neglect to mention the multiple opportunities for learning likely available to you by means of *inter*personal spiritual disciplines in your local church, especially through classes and small groups. If this chapter stimulates you to further discipline yourself in intentional learning, be sure to speak with your pastor about the role your church could play in helping you learn "for the purpose of godliness."

Having said all that, I still want to return to the emphasis on learning by reading. I've always found it true that growing Christians are reading Christians. For some it's a habit they find hard to develop. Others love to read, but because of the demands of their jobs or because they have small children in perpetual motion, they can't seem to find the time for it. But let me encourage you to make time to read, even if it's no more than *one page per day*.[9] Jean Fleming, author of *Finding Focus in a Whirlwind World* and mother of three adult children and several grandchildren, told me she has observed that women who don't make at least some space in their lives for devotional disciplines—including reading—when they have young children, rarely develop them once they do have more time.[10] I can think of four women I have pastored who had at least four small children each and who were readers. One of them determined to read at least one page per day, and though it took several weeks, finished a major book on Christlike living with much profit to her pursuit of godliness. Another read a two-volume, nine-hundred-page Christian biography in a matter of months. A third read a steady stream of worthy books every year and even wrote a manual for our vacation Bible school workers on sharing the gospel with children in a God-centered way. When you consider that each woman made the time-consuming commitment to homeschool her children, you realize that with the necessary discipline almost anyone can make spiritual progress through reading.

Yet increasingly, with the lure of ubiquitous entertainment and video, fewer people are book readers, regardless of the format. I have a theory why this is the case for many people. For them, "reading" always conjures up memories of being forced to read poorly written textbooks about subjects that did not interest them. In other words, for them the definition of "reading" involves forcing yourself to pore over dull or difficult material that has no real appeal to you. When that's what "reading" means, it's no wonder many have no appetite for it. How would you like to have to read your seventh-grade science textbook again? For many, such is the image that always comes to mind when people speak of reading, and they believe some people enjoy that sort of thing and others—like themselves—do not. This means, of course, that they've never enjoyed the pleasure of what readers call a "page-turner." They've never read a book that's (1) well written and (2) about a subject that fascinates them. The starting place with these folks is to help them find that page-turner about a subject they love to discuss, including sports, hobbies, and other special interests. As they begin to discover the pleasure of reading, help them get as soon as possible to well-written books more closely connected with the Word of God and the Christian life. Another effective approach is to adapt something I've seen at one church that has interested hundreds in reading Christian books. They gather in small groups to read through books aloud together, stopping after each paragraph to discuss it. You have too much to lose by not reading, and too much to gain by disciplined reading.

Discipline yourself to learn by reading, and choose your books well. You will be able to read relatively few books in your lifetime, so read the best books. Suppose you were to read ten books every year between now and when you died. If you lived to be eighty, how many books would you read? Even if you read a few more or a few less than that, it still doesn't amount to very many, especially when you consider that hundreds of books are published in America every day. In other words, many times more books are published every single day in the United States than you're likely to read before you die. So don't waste your time on books you'll regret reading when you look back upon them from the perspective of eternity. I believe in recreational reading. Not every volume must be didactic or even theological. Some books are just for relaxation and refreshment. But even these should be edifying and help you in some sense to love God with your mind.

MORE APPLICATION

Will you discipline yourself to become an intentional learner? I read a short account of the famous Greek mathematician Euclid,

author of a formidable thirteen-volume text for the study of geometry. "But Ptolemy I, King of Egypt, wished to learn the subject
without laboring through so many books. As a king, he was accustomed to having his way made easy by servants, so he asked if there
was a shortcut to mastering geometry. Euclid's reply to the throne
was terse: 'There is no royal road to learning.'"[11]

The same is true with godliness. It requires discipline, the discipline of an intentional learner. Are you willing to pray for the grace
and to make the effort necessary to break the habits of an accidental
and convenience learner?

Where will you start? How will you begin to "apply your heart
to instruction" and to store up knowledge? What habit will you
stop and what habit will you begin? Is there a place in your life
for a method of learning you have previously overlooked? What
about your reading? Is there something you should *stop* reading
because it doesn't build up your life or because it doesn't deserve
a place on your life's reading list? Do you need to make the "one
page per day" commitment so that you don't lose the Discipline
of learning?

When will you start? When does your plan begin? Let's apply
the principle of Proverbs 13:4 here: "The soul of the sluggard craves
and gets nothing, while the soul of the diligent is richly supplied."
This says that all people crave something, but only the souls of
the diligent are satisfied because they discipline themselves to do
something while sluggards do not. There is a sense in which everybody "craves" to learn something and every Christian wants to be
more like Jesus. But only those who diligently discipline themselves
to learn will satisfy those desires.

Above all, remember that learning has a goal. The goal is
Christlikeness. Jesus said in Matthew 11:28-29, "Come to me, all
who labor and are heavy laden, and I will give you rest. Take my
yoke upon you, and *learn* from *me*" (emphasis added). There is
a false or superficial knowledge that "puffs up" (1 Corinthians
8:1), but godly learning leads to godly living. John Milton, the

Englishman who penned the classic poem *Paradise Lost*, wrote, "The end of learning is to know God, and out of that knowledge to love Him and to imitate Him."[12] May God give us an unquenchable desire for the knowledge that leads us to love Him more and that makes us more like Jesus Christ.

CHAPTER 13

PERSEVERANCE IN THE DISCIPLINES . . . FOR THE PURPOSE OF GODLINESS

*We must discipline our lives, but we must do so
all the year round, and not merely at stated periods.
I must discipline myself at all times.*

MARTYN LLOYD-JONES

As usual, the workweek begins early on Monday. Very little flex time is built into the schedule of showering, dressing, eating, getting the kids ready, and heading out the door. From then on, you sprint through most of the day. You take the kids to school, run errands, and work around the house until the very minute you have to pick up the kids. Or else you battle the traffic to work where you make it just at starting time and plug away relentlessly until deep in the day, when you merge wearily into the traffic again.

Once home, often after a hasty but necessary stop or two on the way, you find it's more and more common to shove a meal in the microwave while you hurriedly change clothes for your evening responsibilities. One or two nights a week it's a school-related function with the kids. Another evening might find the entire family at a midweek event at church. Still another night holds a committee responsibility for someone. Next, throw in an occasional evening of working late or doing work at home, work-related travel, or work around the house. Don't forget the nights of helping with home-work, getting involved in the community, taking classes, shopping, and socializing.

Complicating all this may come the pressures of single-parenting, family conflict, illness, job stress, a second job, financial tension, and so on.

Sound familiar? Is your life a testimony to the surveys that tell us—despite all our labor-saving devices and technological advance-ments—that our enjoyment of leisure has decreased dramatically in the last generation?

Then you read this book, which encourages you to practice all these Spiritual Disciplines. And it makes you feel like an exhausted, staggering juggler on a high wire, trying to keep a dozen heirloom crystal goblets in the air with someone else wanting to throw you a half dozen more.

For starters, it should relieve some anxiety to realize that most of the Disciplines advocated in this book can be practiced in the same devotional episode. For example, while you are alone with God (silence and solitude), you can enjoy one or more forms of Bible intake, as well as prayer and worship. On this same occasion you might write in a journal and read in a Christian book. And all this might occur during a time of fasting and represent a good steward-ship of time. The only categories of personal Spiritual Disciplines expounded in this book *not* being practiced in this single event are evangelism and serving.

I've come to the conclusion that, with rare exceptions, the godly person is a busy person. The godly person is devoted to God and to people, and that leads to a full life. Though never frantic in pace, Jesus was a busy man. Read Mark's gospel, and notice how often the word *immediately* describes the transition from one event in Jesus' life to the next. We read of Him sometimes ministering all day and even after dark, then getting up before dawn to pray and travel to the next ministry venue. The Gospels tell of occasional nights when He did not sleep at all. They tell us He got tired, so tired that He could sleep in the stern of a storm-tossed ship. Crowds of people pressed upon Him almost daily. Everyone wanted time with Jesus and clamored for His attention. None of us knows job-related stress like the kind He continually experienced. If Jesus' life, as well as that of Paul, were measured against the "balanced life" envisioned by many Christians today, the Savior and the apostle would be considered workaholics who sinfully neglected their bodies. Scripture confirms what observation perceives: Laziness never leads to godliness.

All this is to say that God makes Christlike people out of busy people, and He does so through the biblical Spiritual Disciplines. These Disciplines are not intended only for Christians with lots of spare time on their hands (where are they?). Rather they are *the* God-given means by which busy believers become like Christ. God offers His life-changing grace to taxi-driving, errand-running moms; to hardworking, overcommitted dads; to homework-heavy, extracurricular-busy students; to schedule-packed singles; to responsibility-overloaded single parents—in short, to every believer—*through* the Spiritual Disciplines.

But how can we maintain the pace? For one thing, conflicting priorities often clarify while we practice the Spiritual Disciplines. The older you grow, the more you tend to accumulate responsibilities like barnacles. The addition and growth of children requires an increase in attention to their lives in church, school, sports, lessons, and transportation. Job advancement brings with it more commitments as well as opportunities. The accumulation of goods and property over the years tends to escalate the time required for their maintenance. Consequently, your life will periodically call for an evaluation of priorities. Perhaps through the Discipline of Bible intake, or prayer, or worship, or silence, or solitude, or journaling, the Holy Spirit might identify which activities are "barnacles" to cut away. Instead of adding additional weight, the Spiritual Disciplines are actually one of the ways God lightens your load and gives you smoother sailing.

Even with the consistent evaluation of priorities, the godly person will remain a busy person. And the busy person is also the one most severely tempted to lapse in the practice of the Disciplines that lead to godliness. Without practicing the Spiritual Disciplines we will not be godly; but neither will we be godly without *perseverance* in practicing the Disciplines. Even the "tortoise" of a slow, plodding perseverance in the Spiritual Disciplines makes progress better than the "hare" of a sometimes spectacular, but generally inconsistent practice.

How can we persevere more faithfully in the Disciplines of godliness? When the emotions that usually accompany the beginning of a Spiritual Discipline have ebbed, how can we stay faithful? There are three matters referenced briefly until now that are indispensable in helping you persevere in the practice of the Spiritual Disciplines: the role of the Holy Spirit, the role of fellowship, and the role of struggle in Christian living.

THE ROLE OF THE HOLY SPIRIT

We must perpetually remind ourselves that despite the most fervent diligence to our responsibility to discipline ourselves "for the purpose of godliness," we cannot make ourselves more like Jesus. The Holy Spirit does that, working through the Disciplines to bring us closer to Jesus and making us more like Him. Any emphasis on the Spiritual Disciplines runs the risk of overlooking this important fact. As D. A. Carson warns, "What is universally presupposed by the expression 'spiritual discipline' is that such disciplines are intended to increase our spirituality. From a Christian perspective, however, it is simply not possible to increase one's spirituality without possessing the Holy Spirit and submitting to his transforming instruction and power."[1]

In *The Discipline of Grace*, Jerry Bridges concurs:

A major temptation in the self-discipline approach to holiness, however, is to rely on a regiment of spiritual disciplines instead of on the Holy Spirit. I believe in spiritual disciplines. I seek to practice them. . . . But those disciplines are not the source of our spiritual strength. The Lord Jesus Christ is, and it is the ministry of the Holy Spirit to apply His strength to our lives.[2]

Wherever the Holy Spirit dwells, His holy presence creates a hunger for holiness. His primary task is to magnify Christ (see John 16:14-15), and it is He who gives the believer a desire to be like Christ. In our natural condition we have no such passion. But in the Christian, the Spirit of God begins to carry out the will of God to make the child of God like the Son of God (see Romans 8:29). And He who began this good work in the life of the believer "will bring it to completion at the day of Jesus Christ" (Philippians 1:6).

So it is the role of the Holy Spirit to produce within us the desire and the power for the Disciplines that lead to godliness. That He develops this in every believer is evident from 2 Timothy 1:7: "For God has not given us a spirit of timidity, but of power and love and discipline" (NASB). Therefore, whether or not your natural temperament or personality inclines toward orderly and disciplined habits, the supernatural presence of the Holy Spirit equips you with enough of a supernatural "spirit of . . . discipline" for you to obey the command to "discipline yourself for the purpose of godliness."

That's why on the days when you are tempted to quit Christianity altogether, or to give up on the people of God, or to abandon the Spiritual Disciplines as a waste of time, you just can't allow yourself to do it. Ultimately, that's not simply the result of your spiritual grit or determination; that's the work of the Holy Spirit causing you to persevere. In those times when laziness overtakes you and you feel no enthusiasm for any Spiritual Discipline, or when you consistently fail to practice a once-habitual Discipline, it is the Holy Spirit who prompts you to pick it up in spite of your feelings. Left to yourself you would have forsaken these means of God's sustaining grace long ago, but the Holy Spirit preserves you in faithfulness by giving you the grace to persevere in them.

Self-control, according to Galatians 5:23, is a direct product, or "fruit," of the Spirit's control in the believer's life. And when the Christian expresses this Spirit-produced self-control by practicing the Spiritual Disciplines, the result is progress in godliness.

To illustrate the role of the Holy Spirit in helping the child of God to persevere in the Disciplines of godliness, one contemporary writer tells of his struggle and success with the Discipline of prayer.

> Recently I read again of a woman who simply decided one day to make such a commitment to pray, and my conscience was pricked. But I knew myself well enough to know that something other than resolve was being called for. I began to pray about praying. I expressed to God my frustrated longings, my jaded sense of caution about trying again, my sense of failure over working at being more disciplined and regular. I discovered something surprising happening from such simple praying: I was drawn into the presence of One who had, far more than I did, the power to keep me close. I found my focus subtly shifting away from my efforts to God's, from rigor to grace, from rigidity to relationship. I soon realized that this was happening regularly. I was praying much more. I became less worried about the mechanics and methods, and in turn I was more motivated. And God so cares for us, I realized anew, that He Himself helps us pray. When we "do not know what we ought to pray for . . . the Spirit Himself intercedes for us with groans that words cannot express" (Rom. 8:26).[3]

The Bible doesn't explain the mechanics of the mystery of the Spirit's ministry to us. How prayer (or the practice of any other Spiritual Discipline) is prompted and produced by Him on the one hand, and yet on the other hand is our responsibility, is unfathomable. But these two things are clear: (1) the Holy Spirit will be ever faithful to help each of God's elect to persevere to the end in those things that will make us like Christ, and (2) we must not harden our hearts, but instead respond to His promptings if we would be godly.

THE ROLE OF FELLOWSHIP

No one should read of these Disciplines and imagine that by practicing them in isolation from other believers he or she can be as Christlike—perhaps even more so—than Christians who are active members of a local body of Christ. Thinking of the Spiritual Disciplines as a part of the Christian life unrelated to the fellowship of believers is unbiblical thinking.

Anyone who measures progress in Christlikeness only in terms of growth in his or her fellowship with God takes an incomplete measurement. Spiritual maturity also includes growth in fellowship with the children of God. The apostle John juxtaposed these two in 1 John 1:3: "That which we have seen and heard we proclaim also to you, so that you too may have fellowship with us; and indeed our fellowship is with the Father and with his Son Jesus Christ." New Testament fellowship is with both the triune God and with His people. Just as the human maturity of Jesus included growth in favor with both God and man (see Luke 2:52), so will the spiritual maturity of those who seek to be like Jesus.

One obvious reason we can't take the Spiritual Disciplines and become spiritual recluses is that many biblical Disciplines—public worship, united prayer, participation in the Lord's Supper, serving other disciples, and more—cannot be practiced without other Christians. Furthermore, one of God's purposes of fellowship is to complement the personal Spiritual Disciplines and to stimulate our growth in godliness through them. For example, as studying the Word alone is one God-given Discipline for growing in grace, so is studying the Word with other believers. The Spiritual Disciplines definitely have some nonpublic applications, but they were never meant to be practiced apart from fellowship[4] in the New Covenant community.

One reason for our susceptibility to mentally disconnect our practice of the Disciplines from life in the local church is the common Christian failure to distinguish between socializing and fellowship. Although socializing is both a part of and the context of fellowship, it is possible to socialize without having fellowship. Socializing involves the sharing of human and earthly life in ways common to both believers and unbelievers. Christian fellowship— New Testament *koinonia*[5]—involves talking about God, the things of God, and life from a uniquely Christian perspective. Don't misunderstand: Socializing is a gift of God, a valuable asset to the church, and necessary for a healthy spiritual life. But it's my observation that we engage in true fellowship far less than we believe we do—even at church. Far too often socializing becomes a *substitute* for fellowship. When this happens, our practice of the Spiritual Disciplines suffers and our growth in grace is stunted.

It looks like this: Two or more Christians can sit together for hours, talking only of the news, weather, sports, work, and family (that is, socializing) while completely neglecting any discussion of expressly spiritual matters. I'm not saying that every conversation between Christians must include references to Bible verses, recent answers to prayer, or insights from today's devotional time. But I've observed that many otherwise committed Christians are so independent in their practice of the Spiritual Disciplines that they almost never talk about such things with other believers. And without personal interaction about the mutual interests, problems, and aspirations of discipleship, our spiritual lives are impoverished. Then at the end of the conversation, having merely socialized, we say we've had good fellowship. Only those indwelled by the Spirit of God can have the rich banquet of *koinonia*, but too often we settle for little more than the fast-food kind of socializing that even the world can experience.

Just as we should practice the Discipline of modeling Christ and talking of Him with *un*believers, so we should engage in a similar Discipline with *believers*. Unlike the Discipline of evangelism, where sharing the life of Christ is unidirectional, fellowship involves a bidirectional communication of spiritual life. J. I. Packer defines fellowship as "a seeking to share in what God has made known of Himself to others, as a means to finding strength, refreshment, and instruction for one's own soul."[6] We can enjoy these fruits of fellowship in any context where Christians gather—worshiping, serving, eating, recreating, shopping, commuting, praying, and so on. As we live like Christ when together, we encourage each other in Christian living. As we talk like Christ and about spiritual matters, we also stimulate each other toward godliness.

This mutual edification is described in Ephesians 4:16, which speaks of "the whole body, joined and held together by every joint with which it is equipped, when each part is working properly, makes the body grow so that it builds itself up in love." As we grow in grace we can properly contribute to "each part . . . working properly." As the body of believers "builds itself up in love," each individual Christian is built up in godliness as well. Put directly, as each believer disciplines himself "for the purpose of godliness," his or her individual spiritual growth helps to build up the local body of believers—but only insofar as that believer is in fellowship with them. As that body of Christians is built up collectively, the increased strength of this fellowship also contributes to the spiritual growth of the individual and encourages his or her pursuit of godliness through the Spiritual Disciplines. Practicing the personal Spiritual Disciplines biblically will strengthen the fellowship of believers. Biblical fellowship will strengthen the practice of the personal Spiritual Disciplines.

But without true fellowship, even the Christian who is ardently practicing the personal Spiritual Disciplines will not develop in a biblically proportioned way. The writer of Hebrews 3:13 warned, "But exhort one another every day, as long as it is called 'today,' that none of you may be hardened by the deceitfulness of sin." Fellowship is required to "exhort one another." When we withdraw from the spiritual protection God provides for us within fellowship, we are more easily deceived by sin. Some of the most sin-deceived people rigidly practice many of the personal Disciplines. I've known people who studied the Bible and prayed so much on their own that they believed they didn't need any of the "unspiritual" people in the church. Without the tempering influence of believers with differing gifts, insights, and experiences, these isolationists confidently asserted twisted views of Scripture, delivered "words from God" for everybody, and attempted to justify even gross sin because of their supposed spirituality. Obviously, these are extreme cases, but they illustrate how even those most rigorously exercised in the personal Spiritual Disciplines need the grace God intends for them to receive only through local church life.

"Associate with sanctified persons" was the recommendation of the Puritan Thomas Watson. "They may, by their counsel, prayers, and holy example, be a means to make you holy."[7]

THE ROLE OF STRUGGLE

Although "trust" and "rest" are core values of the Christian life, so are "discipline" and "struggle." Many forces combat the spiritual progress of those still on this side of heaven. Now, the way of Christ is not always an inner struggle or every moment a battle, but neither is it without lifelong opposition. Therefore, don't be misled into thinking that if you drink of the grace God offers through the Spiritual Disciplines then living the Christian life will be easy.

Strange as it may sound, I want to alert you to the reality of struggle in the Christian life in order to encourage you, especially when it's difficult for you to practice the Spiritual Disciplines. While writing the previous paragraph I received a call from a young woman who has been a Christian for about three years. She expressed frustration over a recent spiritual failure and wondered if others at church who appeared so spiritually mature fought any of the battles that had bloodied her. A fresh and timely reminder that *all* Christians struggle in most of the same ways she does brought both comfort and hope. May this chapter do the same for you.

So avoid those who teach that if you follow certain steps or have a particular experience, you can be freed from all struggle against the sins that hinder your holiness. Such promises are a spiritual carrot-on-a-stick, always leading you on but never giving fulfillment.

Instead, we can see in the theme verse for this book that practicing the Spiritual Disciplines and progressing in godliness will be accompanied by struggle. Referring to the godliness mentioned in 1 Timothy 4:7-8, the apostle Paul wrote in verse 10, "For to this end we toil and strive." The words *toil and strive* tell us that becoming like Christ involves something different than "let go and let God," as some claim. The Greek word translated *toil* means "to work until one is weary." We get our English word *agonize* from the term rendered here as *strive*. It literally means "to struggle." Does this sound like a theology of works instead of grace? Am I saying that though we begin the Christian life by the Spirit we must become holy by works of the flesh (see Galatians 3:3)? Nonsense! This is the same equilibrium found throughout the New Testament's teaching on spiritual growth. Advance in the Christian life comes not by the work of the Holy Spirit alone, nor by our work alone, but by our responding to the grace the Holy Spirit initiates and sustains. As mentioned in chapter 1, our experience in Christlike development will happen as it did with Paul, who said, "I toil, struggling with all his energy that he powerfully works within me" (Colossians 1:29). It was Paul who toiled, but his "struggling" was according to the power of the Holy Spirit working (literally, "agonizing") within him. The first part of this chapter dealt with the role of the Holy Spirit keeping us faithful in the Disciplines and producing Christ's character in us through them. But we must keep this truth in tension with the reality of struggle that a forgiven, yet sin-tainted man or woman will experience in becoming like Jesus Christ.

This is trenchant New Testament teaching. It warns us of the world, the flesh, and the Devil and how they constantly war against us. The Bible says that because of this triumvirate of opposition we will experience a struggle to overcome sin as long as we live in this body.

While we live in it, the *world* will put its unending pressure on us. Jesus reminded us that the world hated Him, and it will hate us if we discipline ourselves to follow Him (see John 15:18-19). John further exhorted us, "Do not love the world" (1 John 2:15). Then he proceeded to warn about the lust of the flesh, the lust of the eyes, and the boastful pride of life as part of the world. And there is no experience that can provide a lasting escape from all these worldly temptations except the experience of leaving the world.

One of the more obvious New Testament passages on the reality of spiritual struggle relates to our war against the *flesh*, that indwelling tendency we feel toward sin. The stark reality of Galatians 5:17 is that "the desires of the flesh are against the Spirit, and the desires of the Spirit are against the flesh, for these are opposed to each other, to keep you from doing the things you want to do." Sometimes it's no problem at all to obey God. There are moments when your greatest joy is to get into the Word of God. Occasionally you have experiences in prayer that you wish would never end. Still, many times it's a battle to engage in any Spiritual Discipline. The Spirit will prompt you toward Christlikeness and to practice the Disciplines, and your flesh will rise in defiance. That's because "these are opposed to each other." But even though disciplining yourself is often difficult and involves struggle, self-discipline is not self-punishment. It is instead an attempt to do what, prompted by the Spirit, you actually want to do. The struggle comes when "the desires of the flesh are against the Spirit . . . to keep you from doing the things you want to do." But rather than thinking of entering this battle as a form of self-punishment, it is more scriptural to see the practice of the Spiritual Disciplines as one way of "[sowing] to the Spirit" as Galatians 6:8 encourages. But the biblical fact that the flesh does hurl its desire against the Spirit affirms the reality that while in this body no spiritual experience will permanently free you from the tension of flesh versus Spirit.

In addition to the world and the flesh, you also have a personal Enemy committed to your failure in the Disciplines—the *Devil*.

The apostle Peter reminded us, "Be sober-minded; be watchful. Your adversary the devil prowls around like a roaring lion, seeking someone to devour" (1 Peter 5:8). If we can have an experience whereby we can permanently avoid all spiritual warfare, why didn't Peter tell us about it rather than exhorting us to be alert? Why did Paul command us in Ephesians 6 to put on the armor of God? It's because we are in a battle, a conflict, a struggle. And there is no vacation from the struggle.

Where, then, is the victory? The victory over the world, the flesh, and the Devil was long ago decisively and eternally won by Jesus Christ in His death and resurrection. That victory is mediated to us by the Holy Spirit. For His part, He preserves us in the grace of God. But as previously noted, part of this preservation includes granting us the grace to be faithful. For our part, we take up the struggle of our cross and follow Christ, pursuing Christlikeness by means of the Spiritual Disciplines. The victory that we actually experience in daily life over the forces opposing our progress in the Disciplines comes *through the practice of the Disciplines*. In other words, through *perseverance in* the Spiritual Disciplines we will most consistently experience victory over the *enemies of* the practice of the Disciplines. If we surrender to these enemies of our souls and forsake the Disciplines, victory will never come. But if we will utilize these spiritual weapons, God will give the grace and strength to conquer even more. One day, all struggle will end, all the promises will be fulfilled, and the Spiritual Disciplines will no longer be necessary, for at last "we shall be like him, because we shall see him as he is" (1 John 3:2). Therefore let us face this struggle with Spirit-ignited resolve, for it will be for us as it was for the Puritans whose motto was "*Vincit qui patitur*—he who suffers conquers."[8]

"So we need to remember," advises J. I. Packer, "that any idea of getting beyond conflict, outward or inward, in our pursuit of holiness in this world is an escapist dream that can only have disillusioning and demoralizing effects on us as waking experience daily disproves it. What we must realize, rather, is that any real holiness in us will be under hostile fire all the time, just as our Lord's was."[9]

The Holy Spirit, true fellowship, and the recognition of the ongoing struggle in the Christian life will help you persevere in the practice of the Spiritual Disciplines. Apart from such perseverance, the Disciplines are incomplete and ineffective. Notice in 2 Peter 1:6 how perseverance connects discipline, or self-control, with godliness: "in your self-control, perseverance, and in your perseverance, godliness" (NASB). Without perseverance between the two, the relationship between the self-controlled practice of the Spiritual Disciplines and godliness is like a battery full of power poorly connected to a lightbulb. The light flickers inconsistently and without full benefit. But with a persevering connection between the two, the light shines brightly. In the same way, the light of the life of Christ will shine more steadily through you the more you persevere in the practice of the Spiritual Disciplines.

MORE APPLICATION

Would you be godly? Then practice the Spiritual Disciplines in light of eternity. I read of a man who would pray: "Oh, God, stamp eternity on my eyeballs!" Imagine how differently we would spend our time and make choices in life if we saw everything from the perspective of eternity. So much that seems critical would suddenly become trivial. And many things relegated to the "when I have more time" column of our priority list would take on a dramatic new importance. The practice of the Spiritual Disciplines, when seen through eyes stamped with eternity, becomes a priceless priority because of its intimate connection with godliness.

Practicing the Spiritual Disciplines with eternity in view has always been God's plan. The words of 1 Timothy 4:7 upon which this book has been based, "Discipline yourself for the purpose of godliness," are followed in verse 8 by these: "For bodily discipline is only of little profit, but godliness is profitable for all things, since

it holds promise for the present life and also for the life to come"
(NASB). To see the Spiritual Disciplines only from the pragmatic
and temporal perspective is shortsighted. We need larger thoughts
about the Disciplines than to ask only what they can do for us today
or even in this life. Discipline-cultivated godliness "holds promise"
worth pursuing in "the present life" to be sure. But the value of
godliness, and the practice of its attendant Spiritual Disciplines, is
best seen in the blazing light of eternity.

Whether you realize it or not, everything you do is for eternity.
Nothing has an impact in this life only. Scripture makes this evident
by teaching that we must finally give an account before God of how
we spend our lives (see Romans 14:12) and will suffer reward or
loss based upon each of our works in this life (see 1 Corinthians
3:10-15). Since the weight of all eternity, in the words of the Puritan
Thomas Brooks, hangs upon the thin wire of time, let us use our
time in ways that are profitable not only in this life, but that will
best prepare us for eternity as well. Nothing provides a better preparation for living on this earth and the new one to come like the
faithful practice of the Spiritual Disciplines.

*Would you be godly? There's no other way but through the
Spiritual Disciplines.* The scriptural path to godliness has been
made plain. Would you be godly? Then, said the Lord in 1 Timothy
4:7, "Discipline yourself for the purpose of godliness" (NASB). That
is the way and there is no other.

There are no shortcuts to godliness. But the flesh broods for an
easier way than through the Spiritual Disciplines. It protests, "Why
can't the Christian life be more extemporaneous and unstudied?
All this talk of disciplining myself sounds legalistic and regimented
and harder than I thought being like Christ should be. I just want
to be *spontaneous*!"

John Guest responds well to this temptation:

"Discipline" has become a dirty word in our culture. . . .
I know I am speaking heresy in many circles, but spontaneity

is greatly overvalued. The "spontaneous" person who shrugs off the need for discipline is like the farmer who went out to gather the eggs. As he walked across the farmyard toward the hen house, he noticed the pump was leaking. So he stopped to fix it. It needed a new washer, so he set off to the barn to get one. But on the way he saw that the hayloft needed straightening, so he went to fetch the pitchfork. Hanging next to the pitchfork was a broom with a broken handle. "I must make a note to myself to buy a broom handle the next time I get to town," he thought. . . .

By now it is clear that the farmer is not going to get his eggs gathered, nor is he likely to accomplish anything else he sets out to do. He is utterly, gloriously spontaneous, but he is hardly free. He is, if anything, a prisoner to his unbridled spontaneity.

The fact of the matter is that discipline is the only way to freedom; it is the necessary context for spontaneity.[10]

Does the farmer's day remind you of your spiritual life—spontaneous but sporadic? Do you flitter from one thing to another with apparently little effect or growth in grace? Certainly we want spontaneity, but spontaneity without discipline is superficial. I have several friends who can improvise beautiful melodies on a keyboard or a guitar. But the reason they can play so "spontaneously" is because they spent years devoted to the disciplines of playing musical scales and other fundamental exercises. Jesus could be so spiritually "spontaneous" because He had been the most spiritually disciplined man who ever lived. Do nothing and you will live spontaneously. But if you desire *effective* spontaneity in the Christian life, you must cultivate it with a spiritually disciplined faith.

For many—perhaps most—believers the failure to practice the Spiritual Disciplines is not so much due to the desire for spontaneity as it is a struggle with finding time. But if you desire to be godly, you must face the fact that you will always be busy. To do what God wants most, that is, to love Him with all your heart, soul, mind, and strength, and to love your neighbor as you love yourself (see Mark 12:29-31), can't be done in your spare time. Loving God and others in word and in deed will result in a busy life. This is not to say that God wants us to live hectic lives, but rather to affirm that godly people are never lazy people.

So if you're telling yourself you will practice the Spiritual Disciplines when you have more time, you never will. In a card to my wife and me, Jean Fleming wrote, "I find myself thinking, 'When life settles down, I'll . . .' But I should have learned by now that life *never* settles down for long. Whatever I want to accomplish, I must do with life unsettled." That's a marvelous insight to the mundane. Because life never really settles down, and since we will always feel as though we have more to do than time to do it, if we are ever going to make progress in godliness through the Spiritual Disciplines we must do so when life is like it is now.

During my junior high and high school years, anyone with an interest in basketball wanted to be like Pete Maravich. "Pistol Pete," as he was known, scored more points than anyone in college history and was the most electrifying basketball player of his time. Before his day, dribbling between the legs and making behind-the-back passes were considered just for show. Maravich made them commonplace. After his pro career he was inducted into the Naismith Memorial Basketball Hall of Fame, where he was called "perhaps the greatest creative offensive talent in history."[11] He became a Christian in his midthirties, and suddenly died in January 1988 of a heart attack at only age forty.

A year before he died, Maravich said in an interview,

> The key to my ability was repetition. I practiced and practiced and practiced again. I gave the sport my total commitment. I tried everything I could in every way I could to perfect my skills. It was like an obsession. It paid off for me as a player. I'm not so sure in life. If I had given

that same devotion then to my faith, which is what I do now, I'd have been a better person in the long run.[12]

By disciplining himself to practice shooting, passing, and dribbling, Pete Maravich became one of the greatest basketball players ever. Despite all the money and fame brought to him by the sport, he ultimately regretted giving such productive discipline to anything besides his faith in Christ. Are you willing to discipline yourself in the way Maravich wished he had done? Are you willing to "discipline yourself for the purpose of godliness" as much as he was willing to discipline himself for the purpose of basketball? Does godliness mean as much to you as basketball once meant to Pete Maravich?

Discipline earned Maravich a place in the Hall of Fame, but no amount of discipline will earn anyone a place in heaven. Only Jesus lived a life worthy of that. Because He was willing to receive on the cross what our lives deserve—God's judgment for sin—we can receive the heaven that His life deserved. All the joy, all the forgiveness, all the freedom, all the light, all the love, all of *God* in heaven is promised to those who abandon hope of disciplining themselves into heaven and cling to Christ by faith.

One of the surest signs that someone does cling to Christ is his or her ever-deepening desire to know Him better and to become as much like Him as possible. This is what godliness is, and genuine disciples of Jesus passionately pursue it. And just as the only way to God is through Christ, so the only way to godliness is through the Christ-centered practice of the Spiritual Disciplines. Will you "discipline yourself for the purpose of godliness"? Where and when will you begin?

NOTES

Chapter 1: The Spiritual Disciplines . . . for the Purpose of Godliness

1. I capitalize "Spiritual Disciplines" in these pages to call attention to the term as the subject of the book and to help the reader think of these biblical practices as a group.
2. My book-length treatment of the interpersonal Spiritual Disciplines is *Spiritual Disciplines Within the Church: Participating Fully in the Body of Christ* (Chicago: Moody, 1996).
3. D. A. Carson, "What Is the Gospel?—Revisited," in *For the Fame of God's Name: Essays in Honor of John Piper* (Wheaton, IL: Crossway, 2010), 164–165.
4. Emphasis added.
5. Tom Landry, as quoted by Ray Stedman in *Preaching Today* (Carol Stream, IL: Christianity Today, n.d.), recording number 25.
6. Indeed, the New American Standard Bible translates the verse as "For God has not given us a spirit of timidity, but of power and love and *discipline*" (emphasis added).
7. The famous English poet Samuel Taylor Coleridge (1772–1834) is best known for his poems "The Rime of the Ancient Mariner" and "Kubla Khan."
8. William Barclay, *The Gospel of Matthew* (Philadelphia, PA: Westminster, 1958), vol. 1, 284.
9. "The 10,000-Hour Rule" is a chapter in Malcolm Gladwell's best-selling book *Outliers: The Story of Success* (New York: Little, Brown, 2008, 35–67), which popularized research by Dr. K. Anders Ericsson, professor of psychology at Florida State University.
10. Elisabeth Elliot, as quoted in *Christianity Today*, November 4, 1988, 33, emphasis added.

Chapter 2: Bible Intake (Part 1) . . . for the Purpose of Godliness

1. Although shortwave radio is common overseas, most Americans don't have one and rarely think of the medium. But many of the best Bible teachers on the Internet or on traditional radio stations in the United States also can be heard practically anywhere in the world (including the United States) on the powerful, if lesser quality signal, shortwave stations.

2. Jeremiah Burroughs, *Gospel Worship* (1648; reprint, Ligonier, PA: Soli Deo Gloria Publications, 1990), 200.

3. George Gallup, *100 Questions and Answers: Religion in America* (Princeton Religious Research Center, 1989), cited in *USA Today*, February 1, 1990.

4. *Bookstore Journal*, as quoted in *Discipleship Journal*, issue 52, 10.

5. John Blanchard, *How to Enjoy Your Bible* (Colchester, England: Evangelical Press, 1984), 104.

6. An Internet search for "how much time watching tv," noting especially time use surveys provided by the United States Bureau of Labor Statistics, will reveal a variety of research efforts confirming this claim.

7. Robert L. Sumner, *The Wonder of the Word of God* (Murfreesboro, TN: Biblical Evangelism Press, 1963), 12.

8. Jerry Bridges, *The Practice of Godliness* (Colorado Springs, CO: NavPress, 1983), 51.

9. R. C. Sproul, *Knowing Scripture* (Downers Grove, IL: InterVarsity, 1977), 17.

10. If you are unsure of what cross-references are or how to use them, ask your pastor or another mature Christian.

11. Geoffrey Thomas, *Reading the Bible* (Edinburgh, Scotland: The Banner of Truth Trust, 1980), 22.

Chapter 3: Bible Intake (Part 2) . . . for the Purpose of Godliness

1. Jerry Bridges, *The Discipline of Grace: God's Role and Our Role in the Pursuit of Holiness* (Colorado Springs, CO: NavPress, 1994), 175.

2. Thomas Watson, "How We May Read the Scriptures with Most Spiritual Profit," in *Puritan Sermons* (1674; reprint, Wheaton, IL: Richard Owen Roberts, 1981), vol. 2, 62.

3. Thomas Brooks, as quoted in *The Banner of Truth*, February 1989, 26.

4. Roger Steer, ed., *Spiritual Secrets of George Müller* (Wheaton, IL: Harold Shaw Publishers; and Robesonia, PA: OMF Books, 1985), 62–63.

5. Elisabeth D. Dodds, *Marriage to a Difficult Man: The "Uncommon Union" of Jonathan and Sarah Edwards* (Philadelphia, PA: Westminster, 1971), 67–68.

6. The Bible refers to three general objects of meditation. The one mentioned much more often than any other is meditation on the content of Scripture itself. A second object of meditation is God's works, which could broadly include His creation and His providence. Even though we don't have to have a Bible in our hands to dwell on the glory of God in a sunset or His creative skill in a sunflower, our meditation on creation should always be informed by Scripture. God's providence can be perceived to some degree in circumstances, but our limited understanding of His ways must be guided by His Word. Third, the Bible speaks of meditation on God's attributes. And while we may attempt to interpret them somewhat through God's works, they are revealed infallibly only in Scripture. My point in this is to show that the Bible doesn't limit the scope of meditation to the Bible itself. However, all meditation should focus either on what is revealed in Scripture or be

informed by Scripture. The following chart displays all the Bible verses that explicitly refer to the objects of meditation:

God's Word:	Joshua 1:8, "on it" Psalm 1:2, "on his law" Psalm 119:15, "on your precepts" Psalm 119:15, "on your ways" Psalm 119:23, "on your statutes" Psalm 119:48, "on your statutes" Psalm 119:78, "on your precepts" Psalm 119:97, "your law" Psalm 119:99, "your testimonies" Psalm 119:148, "on your promise"
God's Works:	Psalm 77:12, on "all your work" Psalm 77:12, "on your mighty deeds" Psalm 119:27, "on your wondrous works" Psalm 143:5, "on all that you have done" Psalm 145:5, "on your wondrous works"
God's Attributes:	Psalm 63:6, "on you" Psalm 145:5, "on the glorious splendor of your majesty"

7. Some sections of Scripture, such as much of the book of Proverbs, where an individual verse is often a self-contained concept and not part of a paragraph, make this approach more difficult. When in such sections, you must rely on one of the other methods mentioned to select your text for meditation.

8. Donald S. Whitney, *Simplify Your Spiritual Life: Spiritual Disciplines for the Overwhelmed* (Colorado Springs, CO: NavPress, 2003), 163–164.

9. This is not to imply that this is an exhaustive list of methods of meditation on Scripture.

10. For more on praying through a passage of Scripture, see "Praying Scripture" in Whitney, *Simplify Your Spiritual Life: Spiritual Disciplines for the Overwhelmed*, 80–81.

11. Dr. Andrew Davis, *An Approach to Extended Memorization of Scripture* (Durham, NC: First Baptist Church, n.d.), 2.

12. Jonathan Edwards, "Personal Narrative," in *Letters and Personal Writings*, vol. 16 of *The Works of Jonathan Edwards*, ed. George S. Claghorn (New Haven, CT: Yale University Press, 1998), 794. Available at Edwards.yale.edu.

13. There are many good resources available for mind mapping, but the classic is probably Tony Buzan and Barry Buzan's *The Mind Map Book: How to Use Radiant Thinking to Maximize Your Brain's Untapped Potential* (New York: Plume, 1996).

14. Maurice Roberts, "O the Depth!" *The Banner of Truth*, July 1990, 2.

15. Edwards, "Personal Narrative," 798.

16. Charles Spurgeon, "Memoir of Thomas Watson," in Thomas Watson, *A Body of Divinity* (Edinburgh, Scotland: The Banner of Truth Trust, 1692, reprint, 1993), vii.

17. Watson, 65.
18. William Bridge, *The Works of the Reverend William Bridge* (reprint, 1845; reprint, Beaver Falls, PA: Soli Deo Gloria, 1989), vol. 3, 126.
19. Bridge, 152.
20. Bridge, 135.
21. Richard Baxter, *The Practical Works of Richard Baxter: Select Treatises* (Grand Rapids, MI: Baker, 1981), 90.
22. J. I. Packer, foreword to R. C. Sproul, *Knowing Scripture* (Downers Grove, IL: InterVarsity, 1979), 9–10.

Chapter 4: Prayer . . . for the Purpose of Godliness
 1. I would heartily recommend at this point—especially for mothers of young children—the two pages on "Do What You Can" in Donald S. Whitney, *Simplify Your Spiritual Life: Spiritual Disciplines for the Overwhelmed* (Colorado Springs, CO: NavPress, 2003), 157–158.
 2. John Blanchard, comp., *Gathered Gold: A Treasury of Quotations for Christians* (Welwyn, Hertfordshire, England: Evangelical Press, 1984), 227.
 3. John Piper, *Desiring God: Meditations of a Christian Hedonist* (Portland, OR: Multnomah, 1986), 147.
 4. Andrew Murray (1828–1917) was a devout Christian who authored some 240 publications, mostly related to the devotional life and holy living. Many of these reflected the perspective of what became known as Keswick theology, with which I would have some disagreement. But there is much good in *With Christ in the School of Prayer*, which is quoted here and is one of Murray's best-known works.
 5. Andrew Murray, as quoted in *Christianity Today*, February 5, 1990, 38.
 6. When I speak of responding to what God has said, I'm referring not to some mystical sense of God speaking nor to some words we might imagine God saying, but rather to the Bible.
 7. This is another way of presenting "Meditation Method #9: Pray Through the Text" that I introduced in the previous chapter on page 61. Having engaged in this simple, biblical method of prayer almost daily for nearly thirty years, I can testify that nothing more quickly and consistently kindles my cold heart in prayer than this combination of the fire of God's Word (see Jeremiah 23:29) and prayer.
 8. Richard Baxter, *The Practical Works of Richard Baxter: Select Treatises* (Grand Rapids, MI: Baker, 1981), 103.
 9. John Owen, as quoted in *The Banner of Truth*, August–September 1986, 58.
10. Matthew Henry, *Matthew Henry's Commentary on the Whole Bible* (Old Tappan, NJ: Revell, n.d.), vol. 3, 255.
11. Thomas Manton, *The Complete Works of Thomas Manton* (reprint, Worthington, PA: Maranatha Publications, n.d.), 272–273.
12. W. Farmer, "Memoir of the Author," in William Bates, *The Whole Works of the Rev. W. Bates*, arr. and rev. W. Farmer (reprint, Harrisburg, PA: Sprinkle, 1990), vol. 1, viii.

13. William Bates, *The Whole Works of the Rev. W. Bates*, arr. and rev. W. Farmer (reprint, Harrisburg, PA: Sprinkle, 1990), vol. 3, 130.
14. William Bridge, *The Works of the Reverend William Bridge* (reprint, 1845; reprint, Beaver Falls, PA: Soli Deo Gloria, 1989), vol. 3, 132, 154.
15. Peter Toon, *From Mind to Heart: Christian Meditation Today* (Grand Rapids, MI: Baker, 1987), 93.
16. Today the equivalent term would be "experiential."
17. Roger Steer, ed., *Spiritual Secrets of George Müller* (Wheaton, IL: Harold Shaw Publishers; and Robesonia, PA: OMF Books, 1985), 60–62, emphasis added.
18. Andrew Murray, *With Christ in the School of Prayer* (Old Tappan, NJ: Spire Books, 1975), 33.
19. C. H. Spurgeon, "Thought-Reading Extraordinary," *Metropolitan Tabernacle Pulpit* (London: Passmore and Alabaster, 1885; reprint, Pasadena, TX: Pilgrim Publications, 1973), vol. 30, 539–540.
20. Piper, 150–151, used by permission.
21. Roger Steer, *George Müller: Delighted in God!* (Wheaton, IL: Harold Shaw Publishers, 1975), 310.
22. C. H. Spurgeon, "Prayer—The Forerunner of Mercy," in *New Park Street Pulpit* (London: Passmore and Alabaster, 1858; reprint, Pasadena, TX: Pilgrim Publications, 1981), vol. 3, 251.
23. J. C. Ryle, *A Call to Prayer* (Grand Rapids, MI: Baker, 1979), 35.

Chapter 5: Worship . . . for the Purpose of Godliness
1. In this chapter I will address only public and private worship, with emphasis on the latter. For a brief biblical, historical, and practical discussion of the subject of family worship, see Donald S. Whitney, *Family Worship: In the Bible, In History, and In Your Home* (Shepherdsville, KY: The Center for Biblical Spirituality, 2005).
2. In accordance with Ephesians 5:19 and Colossians 3:16, we should sing "psalms and hymns and spiritual songs."
3. Do not let the significance of this escape you. One way to evaluate whether your worship is according to the truth of Scripture is to evaluate every item in your worship and ask, "Where in the Bible does God tell us to do this in worship?"
4. John Piper, *Desiring God: Meditations of a Christian Hedonist* (Portland, OR: Multnomah, 1986), 70.
5. Piper, 72–73, used by permission.
6. David Clarkson, *The Works of David Clarkson* (London: James Nichol, 1864; reprint, Edinburgh, Scotland: The Banner of Truth Trust, 1988), vol. 3, 193–194.
7. John Blanchard, comp., *Gathered Gold: A Treasury of Quotations for Christians* (Welwyn, Hertfordshire, England: Evangelical Press, 1984), 342.
8. Geoffrey Thomas, "Worship in Spirit," *The Banner of Truth*, August–September 1987, 8.

9. John Blanchard, comp., *More Gathered Gold: A Treasury of Quotations for Christians* (Welwyn, Hertfordshire, England: Evangelical Press, 1986), 344.
10. Clarkson, 209.

Chapter 6: Evangelism . . . for the Purpose of Godliness
1. J. I. Packer, *Evangelism and the Sovereignty of God* (Downers Grove, IL: InterVarsity, 1979), 37–57.
2. George Barna, as quoted in *Discipleship Journal*, issue 49, 40.
3. C. H. Spurgeon, "Tearful Sowing and Joyful Reaping," in *Metropolitan Tabernacle Pulpit* (London: Passmore and Alabaster, 1869; reprint, Pasadena, TX: Pilgrim Publications, 1970), vol. 15, 237.
4. Joseph Clark, as quoted in Ernest C. Reisinger, *Today's Evangelism: Its Message and Methods* (Phillipsburg, NJ: Craig Press, 1982), 142–143.

Chapter 7: Serving . . . for the Purpose of Godliness
1. Christopher Corbett, *Orphans Preferred* (New York, NY: Broadway Books, 2004), 84.
2. Dietrich Bonhoeffer, *The Cost of Discipleship,* trans. R. H. Fuller (1937; New York: Macmillan, 1963), 99.
3. E. M. Bounds, *The Essentials of Prayer* (Grand Rapids, MI: Baker, 1979), 19.
4. C. H. Spurgeon, "Serving the Lord with Gladness," in *Metropolitan Tabernacle Pulpit* (London: Passmore and Alabaster, 1868; reprint, Pasadena, TX: Pilgrim Publications, 1989), vol. 13, 495–496.
5. John Blanchard, comp., *More Gathered Gold: A Treasury of Quotations for Christians* (Welwyn, Hertfordshire, England: Evangelical Press, 1986), 291.
6. Jerry White, *Choosing Plan A in a Plan B World: Living Out the Lordship of Christ* (Colorado Springs, CO: NavPress, 1986), 97.
7. A. W. Tozer, *Signposts: A Collection of Sayings from A. W. Tozer,* comp. Harry Verploegh (Wheaton, IL: Victor, 1988), 183.
8. Tozer, 183.

Chapter 8: Stewardship . . . for the Purpose of Godliness
1. Jonathan Edwards, "The Preciousness of Time and the Importance of Redeeming It," in *Sermons and Discourses, 1743–1758,* vol. 25 of *The Works of Jonathan Edwards,* ed. Wilson H. Kimnach (New Haven, CT: Yale University Press, 2006), 243–260. Available at Edwards.yale.edu.
2. Herbert Lockyer, *Last Words of Saints and Sinners* (Grand Rapids, MI: Kregel, 1969), 133.
3. Lockyer, 132.
4. Jonathan Edwards, "Resolutions," in *Letters and Personal Writings,* vol. 16 of *The Works of Jonathan Edwards,* ed. George S. Claghorn (New Haven, CT: Yale University Press, 2006), 755. Available at Edwards.yale.edu.
5. Richard Baxter, *The Practical Works of Richard Baxter in Four Volumes,*

A Christian Directory (1673; reprint, Ligonier, PA: Soli Deo Gloria Publications, 1990), vol. 1, 237.

6. Wayne Watts, *The Gift of Giving* (Colorado Springs, CO: NavPress, 1982), 35–36.

7. In this edition of the book, unlike the first, I have usually refrained from including recent statistical information supportive of general statements. What is published as "recent" data soon loses its freshness. And in most cases, a quick search on the Internet can provide the latest information on the matter at hand.

8. Robert Rodenmeyer, as quoted in John Blanchard, comp., *Gathered Gold: A Treasury of Quotations for Christians* (Welwyn, Hertfordshire, England: Evangelical Press, 1984), 113.

9. Roger Steer, ed., *The George Müller Treasury* (Westchester, IL: Crossway, 1987), 183.

10. Roger Steer, ed., *Spiritual Secrets of George Müller* (Wheaton, IL: Harold Shaw Publishers; and Robesonia, PA: OMF Books, 1985), 103.

11. June 23, 1989

Chapter 9: Fasting . . . for the Purpose of Godliness

1. For instance, 1 Corinthians 7:5 speaks of a married couple mutually deciding to temporarily abstain from sex "that you may devote yourselves to prayer."

2. D. Martyn Lloyd-Jones, *Studies in the Sermon on the Mount* (Grand Rapids, MI: Eerdmans, 1960), vol. 1, 38.

3. Those whose physical health requires balanced meals at all times can observe a partial fast by eating a balanced meal, but not as much as usual. Others may be able to eat just one simple food, such as bread or rice, so that they get what they need but without much of the pleasure of eating. In all such cases, the goal is to get the minimal nutritional intake necessary to prevent physical problems while, if possible, still experiencing at least some hunger or desire for something else. As we'll see later, the person who is fasting *wants* to sense hunger or the desire for more as this becomes a servant to the spiritual purpose of the fast.

4. Since the great lawgiver (Moses) and the great prophet (Elijah) experienced supernatural fasts, it is reasonable to assume that Jesus' fast in Matthew 4/ Luke 4 was also a supernatural fast. But the text does not make that clear.

5. R. D. Chatham, *Fasting: A Biblical-Historical Study* (South Plainfield, NJ: Bridge, 1987), 96–97, 161–181.

6. John Piper, *A Hunger for God: Desiring God Through Fasting and Prayer* (Wheaton, IL: Crossway, 1997; 2013), 17.

7. Andy Anderson, *Fasting Changed My Life* (Nashville, TN: Broadman, 1977), 47–48.

8. Or, for those who cannot engage in a normal fast, the following will explain why it is important that they still sense some non-health-threatening degree of desire for more or tastier food.

312 || SPIRITUAL DISCIPLINES FOR THE CHRISTIAN LIFE

9. Piper, 48.
10. John Calvin, *Institutes of the Christian Religion*, ed. John T. McNeil, trans. and indexed by Ford Lewis Battles (Philadelphia, PA: Westminster, 1960), vol. 2, 1242.
11. Piper, 25.
12. Arthur Wallis, *God's Chosen Fast* (Fort Washington, PA: Christian Literature Crusade, 1968), 42.
13. Wallis, 43.
14. Jonathan Edwards, *The Life and Diary of David Brainerd*, vol. 7 of *The Works of Jonathan Edwards*, ed. Norman Pettit (1749; reprint, New Haven, CT: Yale University Press, 1985), 162. Available at Edwards.yale.edu.
15. Edwards, 162.
16. Edwards, 169.
17. Edwards, 169–170.
18. Thomas Boston, *The Complete Works of the Late Rev. Thomas Boston, Ettrick*, ed. Samuel M'Millan (London: William Tegg and Company, 1853; reprint, Wheaton, IL: Richard Owen Roberts, 1980), vol. 11, 347.
19. Calvin, 1243–1244.
20. David R. Smith, *Fasting: A Neglected Discipline* (Fort Washington, PA: Christian Literature Crusade, 1954; American ed., 1969), 46–47.
21. Piper, 51–52.
22. Piper, 14.
23. Smith, 44.
24. John Piper, *A Hunger for God: Desiring God Through Fasting and Prayer* (Wheaton, IL: Crossway, 1997; 2013).
25. Matthew Henry, *A Commentary on the Whole Bible* (New York: Funk and Wagnalls, n.d.), vol. 4, 1478.
26. Piper, 48.

Chapter 10: Silence and Solitude . . . for the Purpose of Godliness

1. Anton Chekhov, "The Bet," in *Introduction to Literature* (New York: Rinehart and Company, 1948), vol. 2, 474–480.
2. As mentioned in a similar context in chapter 1, for more on the interpersonal Spiritual Disciplines see Donald S. Whitney, *Spiritual Disciplines Within the Church: Participating Fully in the Body of Christ* (Chicago: Moody, 1996).
3. Jean Fleming, *Finding Focus in a Whirlwind World* (Dallas: Roper Press, 1991), 73.
4. Jonathan Edwards, "On Sarah Pierpont," in *Letters and Personal Writings*, vol. 16 of *The Works of Jonathan Edwards*, ed. George S. Claghorn (New Haven, Conn.: Yale University Press, 1998), 789–790. Available at Edwards.yale.edu.
5. George Whitefield, *Journals* (Edinburgh, Scotland: The Banner of Truth Trust, 1738–1741; reprint, 1985), 263–264.
6. Jonathan Edwards, *The Life and Diary of David Brainerd*, vol. 7 of *The Works*

of Jonathan Edwards, ed. Norman Pettit (1749; reprint, New Haven, CT: Yale University Press, 1985), 165, emphasis added. Available at Edwards.yale.edu.

7. C. H. Spurgeon, "Solitude, Silence, Submission," in *Metropolitan Tabernacle Pulpit* (London: Passmore and Alabaster, 1896; reprint, Pasadena, TX: Pilgrim Publications, 1976), vol. 42, 266.

8. John Pollock, *Billy Graham: The Authorised Biography* (London: Hodder and Stoughton, 1966), 80–81.

9. John Owen, *The Works of John Owen* (London: Johnstone and Hunter, 1850–1853; reprint, Edinburgh, Scotland: The Banner of Truth Trust, 1965), vol. 5, 455.

10. Dr. and Mrs. Howard Taylor, *Hudson Taylor and the China Inland Mission: The Growth of a Work of God* (Singapore: China Inland Mission, 1918; special anniversary ed., Singapore: Overseas Missionary Fellowship, 1988), 31–32.

11. A friend and colleague, Rob Plummer, challenges the idea that silence and solitude are biblical Spiritual Disciplines in themselves, but instead are presented in Scripture as the context in which believers practice Spiritual Disciplines. As this is basically a semantical distinction and does not affect the actual practice of silence and solitude as I present them, I have no qualm with this approach. See Robert L. Plummer, "Are the Spiritual Disciplines of Silence and Solitude Really Biblical?" *Southern Baptist Journal of Theology* 10/4 (Winter 2006): 4–12.

12. Austin Phelps, *The Still Hour: or, Communion with God* (1859; reprint, Edinburgh, Scotland: The Banner of Truth Trust, 1974), 64.

13. From the hymn "Take My Life and Let It Be," emphasis added.

14. John Blanchard, comp., *More Gathered Gold: A Treasury of Quotations for Christians* (Welwyn, Hertfordshire, England: Evangelical Press, 1986), 295.

15. At www.biblicalspirituality.org, search for "Suggested Schedule for Four Consecutive Hours of Silence & Solitude." Without at least a general schedule to guide the time, there is a tendency for many to drift into an unproductive aimlessness.

16. A. W. Tozer, *The Best of A. W. Tozer: 52 Favorite Chapters*, comp. Warren Wiersbe (Grand Rapids, MI: Baker, 1978), 151.

17. See the chapter on "Have a Real Prayer Closet" in my *Simplify Your Spiritual Life: Spiritual Disciplines for the Overwhelmed* (Colorado Springs, CO: NavPress, 2003), 87–88.

18. Jonathan Edwards, "Personal Narrative," in *Letters and Personal Writings*, vol. 16 of *The Works of Jonathan Edwards*, ed. George S. Claghorn (New Haven, Conn.: Yale University Press, 1998), 798. Available at Edwards.yale.edu.

19. Edwards, "Personal Narrative," 801.

20. Betty Lee Skinner, *Daws: The Story of Dawson Trotman, Founder of the Navigators* (Grand Rapids, MI: Zondervan, 1974), 257.

21. Arnold Dallimore, *George Whitefield: The Life and Times of the Great Evangelist of the Eighteenth-Century Revival*, vol. 1 (Westchester, IL: Cornerstone, 1979), 239.

22. Tozer, 151–152.

23. Francis A. Schaeffer, *True Spirituality* (Wheaton, IL: Tyndale, 1971), ix.
24. Schaeffer, ix.
25. Francis Wayland, *A Memoir of the Life and Labors of the Rev. Adoniram Judson, D.D.* (London: James Nisbet and Company, 1853), vol. 1, 435.
26. Wayland, 437.
27. Jonathan Edwards, *Religious Affections*, vol. 2 of *The Works of Jonathan Edwards*, ed. John E. Smith (1754; New Haven, Conn.: Yale University Press, 1959), 374, 376. Available at Edwards.yale.edu.

Chapter 11: Journaling . . . for the Purpose of Godliness

1. Historically, there appears to be some differentiation between a journal and a diary, but not much. For instance, one of the most famous diaries in Christian history is that of David Brainerd, excerpts of which have already appeared in this book and will do so again later in this chapter. In addition to this *diary*, Brainerd also kept a *journal*. The only difference seems to be that the former was strictly for Brainerd's personal devotional use while the latter was intended for publication as a detailed missionary report from Brainerd to the missionary society in Scotland that supported him financially. As such, Brainerd excluded from the journal some of the diary entries that were strictly of a personal nature or that were irrelevant to the interests of the missionary society. Today what we call a journal, because it typically is a private document, probably corresponds more closely to what in history has been termed a diary. Though again, despite the distinct terms, in reality there has usually been a great deal of overlap between the definitions of the two and very little significant difference.
2. Some contend that the word *journaling* is grammatically incorrect, and that the proper term is *journal-keeping, journalizing*, or *keeping a journal*. But *journaling* has become widely acceptable by common usage.
3. Maurice Roberts, "Are We Becoming Reformed Men?" *The Banner of Truth*, issue 330, March 1991, 5.
4. John Calvin, *Institutes of the Christian Religion*, ed. John T. McNeil, trans. and indexed by Ford Lewis Battles (Philadelphia, PA: Westminster, 1960), vol. 2, 35.
5. Josiah H. Pratt, ed., *The Thought of the Evangelical Leaders* (James Nisbet, 1856; reprint, Edinburgh, Scotland: The Banner of Truth Trust, 1978), 305.
6. Edmund S. Morgan, *The Puritan Family* (New York: Harper & Row, 1966), 5.
7. Jonathan Edwards, *The Life and Diary of David Brainerd*, vol. 7 of *The Works of Jonathan Edwards*, ed. Norman Pettit (1749; reprint, New Haven, CT: Yale University Press, 1985), 278. Available at Edwards.yale.edu.
8. Edwards, 287–288.
9. Roberts, 6.
10. Similar to the transcription responsibility of the kings, copying—word-by-word—entire chapters or books of the Bible into your journal can be a fruitful practice and another method of slowly savoring the text of Scripture.

11. LaVonne Neff, et al., ed., *Practical Christianity* (Wheaton, IL: Tyndale, 1987), 310.

12. Ralph L. Woods, ed., *A Treasury of the Familiar* (Chicago, IL: Peoples Book Club, 1945), 14.

13. C. H. Spurgeon, *Autobiography, Volume 1: The Early Years, 1834–1859*, rev. ed. in 2 vols., comp. Susannah Spurgeon and Joseph Harrald (Edinburgh, Scotland: The Banner of Truth Trust, 1962), 122.

14. Stephen Charnock, *The Existence and Attributes of God* (Robert Carter and Brothers, 1853; reprint, Grand Rapids, MI: Baker, 1979), vol. 1, 277.

15. Roger Steer, ed., *The George Müller Treasury* (Westchester, IL: Crossway, 1987), 55–56.

16. Jonathan Edwards, "Resolutions," in *Letters and Personal Writings*, vol. 16 of *The Works of Jonathan Edwards*, ed. George S. Claghorn (New Haven, Conn.: Yale University Press, 1998), 753–759. Available at Edwards.yale.edu.

17. Edwards, "Resolutions," 760.

18. Edwards, "Resolutions," 760.

19. George M. Marsden, *Jonathan Edwards: A Life* (New Haven and London: Yale University Press, 2003), 53.

20. Arnold Dallimore, *George Whitefield: The Life and Times of the Great Evangelist of the Eighteenth-Century Revival*, vol. 1 (Westchester, IL: Cornerstone, 1979), 80.

21. Dallimore, 80–81.

22. Maurice Roberts, "Where Have the Saints Gone?" *The Banner of Truth*, October 1988, 4.

23. Elisabeth Elliot, ed., *The Journals of Jim Elliot* (Old Tappan, NJ: Fleming H. Revell, 1978), 474.

24. Ronald Klug, *How to Keep a Spiritual Journal* (Nashville, TN: Thomas Nelson, 1982), 58.

25. This is a standard 8½" x 11" sheet of paper cut in half. This means I don't have to buy any special paper for my journal.

26. See the chapter on "Journal with a Fountain Pen" in my *Simplify Your Spiritual Life: Spiritual Disciplines for the Overwhelmed* (Colorado Springs, CO: NavPress, 2003), 104–105.

27. For a revolving list of ideas for journal topics, see the chapters on "Use Journal Prompts, Part 1" and "Use Journal Prompts, Part 2" in *Simplify Your Spiritual Life*, 100–103.

28. Edward Donnelly, ed., "The Diary of Thomas Houston of Knockbracken," *The Banner of Truth*, August–September 1989, 11–12.

Chapter 12: Learning . . . for the Purpose of Godliness

1. Samuel Hopkins, "The Life and Character of the Late Reverend Mr. Jonathan Edwards," in *Jonathan Edwards: A Profile*, ed. David Levin (New York: Hill and Wang, 1969), 40.

2. R. C. Sproul, "Burning Hearts Are Not Nourished by Empty Heads," *Christianity Today*, September 3, 1982, 100.

3. John Blanchard, comp., *Gathered Gold: A Treasury of Quotations for Christians* (Welwyn, Hertfordshire, England: Evangelical Press, 1984), 203.

4. Jonathan Edwards, "The Importance and Advantage of a Thorough Knowledge of Divine Truth" in *Sermons and Discourses, 1739–1742*, vol. 22 of *The Works of Jonathan Edwards*, ed. Harry S. Stout (New Haven, Conn.: Yale University Press, 2003), 789. Available at Edwards.yale.edu.

5. Edwards, "The Importance and Advantage of a Thorough Knowledge of Divine Truth," 789.

6. Jo H. Lewis and Gordon A. Palmer, *What Every Christian Should Know* (Wheaton, IL: Victor, 1990), 80, 82.

7. For example, the publisher of this book has also made available a separate study guide that can be used by individuals or small groups.

8. For more on this, see "Collect Great Questions" in my *Simplify Your Spiritual Life: Spiritual Disciplines for the Overwhelmed* (Colorado Springs, CO: NavPress, 2003), 113–114.

9. I develop this idea a bit more in "Read One Page Per Day" in *Simplify Your Spiritual Life*, 111–112.

10. Jean's testimony of her own battle for a devotional life while she had three children in diapers is found in "Do What You Can" in *Simplify Your Spiritual Life*, 157–158.

11. Paul Thigpen, "No Royal Road to Wisdom," *Discipleship Journal*, issue 29 (1984), 7.

12. As quoted in *Discipleship Journal*, issue 23 (1984), 16.

Chapter 13: Perseverance in the Disciplines . . . for the Purpose of Godliness

1. D. A. Carson, "Spiritual Disciplines," *Themelios* 26, no. 3 (November 2011): 5. http://thegospelcoalition.org/themelios/article/spiritual_disciplines (accessed September 27, 2013).

2. Jerry Bridges, *The Discipline of Grace: God's Role and Our Role in the Pursuit of Holiness* (Colorado Springs, CO: NavPress, 2006), 135.

3. Timothy K. Jones, "What Can I Say?" *Christianity Today*, November 5, 1990, 28.

4. In the paragraphs that follow, even though I am primarily describing *conversational* fellowship, the use of the term *fellowship* in this entire section refers generally to active participation in all aspects of life in a local church, particularly congregational worship where biblical preaching, prayer, praise, and the ordinances are central. I am also referring to the aspects of healthy church life outside the worship event, such as serving, evangelism, teaching, and more. All these complement our practice of the personal spiritual disciplines and fill their own unique place in the pursuit of godliness. A more detailed presentation of the role played by these congregational spiritual disciplines is in my *Spiritual Disciplines Within the Church: Participating Fully in the Body of Christ* (Chicago: Moody, 1996).

5. The New Testament was first written in Greek, and *koinonia* is the Greek word frequently translated into English as "fellowship."

6. J. I. Packer, *God's Words: Studies of Key Bible Themes* (Downers Grove, IL: InterVarsity, 1981), 195.

7. Thomas Watson, *A Body of Divinity* (1692; reprint, Edinburgh, Scotland: The Banner of Truth Trust, 1970), 249.

8. John Geree, *The Character of an Old English Puritane or Nonconformist* (1646), as quoted in J. I. Packer, *A Quest for Godliness: The Puritan Vision of the Christian Life* (Wheaton, IL: Crossway, 1990), 23.

9. J. I. Packer, *Keep in Step with the Spirit* (Old Tappan, NJ: Fleming H. Revell, 1984), 111.

10. John Guest, "Wrong-Headed Spontaneity," *Christianity Today*, April 23, 1990, 33.

11. http://www.hoophall.com/hall-of-famers/tag/peter-p-pete-maravich (accessed October 4, 2013).

12. As quoted by Larry King in "A Brilliant Baseball Mind That Deserves Recognition; Big Bucks by the Book," *USA Today*, January 18, 1988, 2D.

About the Author

DON WHITNEY has been professor of biblical spirituality and associate dean at the Southern Baptist Theological Seminary in Louisville, Kentucky, since 2005. Before that, he held a similar position (the first such position in the six Southern Baptist seminaries) at Midwestern Baptist Theological Seminary in Kansas City, Missouri, for ten years. He is the founder and president of The Center for Biblical Spirituality. Don is a frequent speaker in churches, retreats, and conferences in the United States and abroad.

Don grew up in Osceola, Arkansas, where he came to believe in Jesus Christ as Lord and Savior. He was active in sports throughout high school and college and worked in the radio station his dad managed.

After graduating from Arkansas State University, Don planned to finish law school and pursue a career in sportscasting. While at the University of Arkansas School of Law, he sensed God's call to preach the gospel of Jesus Christ. He then enrolled at Southwestern Baptist Theological Seminary in Fort Worth, Texas, graduating with a master of divinity degree in 1979. In 1987, Don completed a doctor of ministry degree at Trinity Evangelical Divinity School in

Deerfield, Illinois. He earned a PhD in theology at the University of the Free State in South Africa in 2013.

Prior to his ministry as a seminary professor, Don was pastor of Glenfield Baptist Church in Glen Ellyn, Illinois (a suburb of Chicago), for almost fifteen years. Altogether, he has served local churches in pastoral ministry for twenty-four years.

He is the author of *Spiritual Disciplines for the Christian Life*, which has a companion study guide. He has also written *How Can I Be Sure I'm a Christian?*, *Spiritual Disciplines Within the Church*, *Ten Questions to Diagnose Your Spiritual Health*, *Simplify Your Spiritual Life*, and *Family Worship*. His hobby is restoring and using old fountain pens.

Don lives with his wife, Caffy, in their home near Louisville. She regularly teaches a class for seminary wives; works from their home as an artist, muralist, and illustrator; and enjoys gardening and beekeeping. The Whitneys are parents of Laurelen Christiana.

Don's website address is www.BiblicalSpirituality.org. You can find him on Twitter via @DonWhitney and on Facebook.

Scripture Index

Subject Index

enemies of, *186*
generous, *174–176*
God's expectation of, *196–198*
legalistic, *177–178*
love as motivation for, *177–178*
percentage, *183–185*
planned, *182–185*
receiving in return, *185–187*
reflecting faith in God's provision, *173–174*
in response to needs, *180–182*
results of, *185–187*
risk in, *174*
sacrificial, *174–176*
spiritual trustworthiness shown by, *176–177*
systematic, *182–185*
willingly, *179–180*
gladness, *144, 146–147*
glory of God, *190, 210*
gluttony, *218*
goals, monitoring, *261–264*
God. *See also* Holy Spirit; Jesus Christ
great things done for you by, *145–146*
means of revealing Himself, *104*
nature and character of, *84, 106, 107*
prayers to. *See* prayer
promises of. *See* promises of God
trusting, *40*
worthiness of, *103–104, 108*
godliness, *4, 9, 159. See also* Christlikeness
development sequence of, *19*
effects on body of believers, *295*
freedom of, *18*
growth in, *5, 114–115, 265, 277, 292*
hindrances to, *161*
knowledge of, *276–278*
opposition to, *296–300*
power of, *126–127*
purpose of, *4*
pursuit of, *139, 156, 300, 316n4(2)*
in speech, *236*
Spiritual Disciplines necessary for, *7, 10*

through Holy Spirit, *290–293*
time for developing, *163*
God's Word. *See* Scripture
good, God's working all things for, *10–11*
gospel, the, *60. See also* Scripture
communicating, *120–121, 123–124*
knowledge of, *135–136*
learning, *276–278*
living, *132–134*
passion for, *139*
power of, *125–126*
responding to, *188, 272*
Spiritual Disciplines and, *7–9*
Gould, Glenn, *232*
grace, *19, 117, 215, 247*
encountering through discipline, *28*
forgiveness and, *167*
growth in, *5*
means of, *210*
opportunities to receive, *11, 82, 214, 218, 219*
salvation and, *165. See also* salvation
Spiritual Disciplines and, *11–13, 289*
Graham, Billy, *233–234*
gratitude, *98, 102, 145–146*
Great Commission, *120–121, 128–129*
grief, *204–205*
growth, spiritual. *See* spiritual growth
grudge giving, *179*
Guest, John, *301–302*
guidance by God, *202–204*
guilt, *147–148, 231*
guitar playing, *1–2, 17–18, 19, 259, 302*

Habakkuk, *228*
habits, *4, 6, 238, 284*
Hall, Joseph, *64*
Halverson, Richard, *37*
Harris, Howell, *242*
Havner, Vance, *21*
healing, *227*

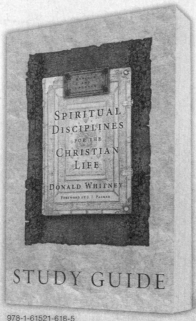